HOW TO FILE FOR DIVORCE IN MICHIGAN

with forms

Edward A. Haman
Attorney at Law

Sphinx Publishing
A Division of Sourcebooks, Inc.
Naperville, IL • Clearwater, FL

Second edition, 1998
Published by: **Sphinx® Publishing, A Division of Sourcebooks, Inc.®**

Naperville Office
P.O. Box 372
Naperville, Illinois 60566
(630) 961-3900
Fax: 630-961-2168

Clearwater Office
P.O. Box 25
Clearwater, Florida 33757
(727) 587-0999
Fax: 727-586-5088

Interior Design and Production: Edward A. Haman/Shannon E. Harrington, Sourcebooks, Inc.

This publication is designed to provide accurate and authoritative information in regard to the subject matter covered. It is sold with the understanding that the publisher is not engaged in rendering legal, accounting, or other professional service. If legal advice or other expert assistance is required, the services of a competent professional person should be sought.

From a Declaration of Principles Jointly Adopted by a Committee of the
American Bar Association and a Committee of Publishers and Associations

Library of Congress Cataloging-in-Publication Data
Haman, Edward A.
    How to file for divorce in Michigan : with forms / Edward A.
Haman. —2nd ed.
      p.   cm.
Includes bibliographical references and index.
    ISBN 1-57071-409-6 (pbk.)
    1. Divorce—Law and legislation—Michigan—Popular works.
2. Divorce suits—Michigan—Popular works.   I. Title.
KFM4300.Z9H36   1998
346.77401'66—dc21

98-39523
CIP

Printed and bound in the United States of America.

Paperback — 10 9 8 7 6 5 4 3 2 1

Contents

Using Self-Help
Law Books

Whenever you shop for a product or service, you are faced with various levels of quality and price. In deciding what product or service to buy, you make a cost/value analysis on the basis of your willingness to pay and the quality you desire.

When buying a car, you decide whether you want transportation, comfort, status, or sex appeal. Accordingly, you decide among such choices as a Neon, a Lincoln, a Rolls Royce, or a Porsche. Before making a decision, you usually weigh the merits of each option against the cost.

When you get a headache, you can take a pain reliever (such as aspirin) or visit a medical specialist for a neurological examination. Given this choice, most people, of course, take a pain reliever, since it costs only pennies, whereas a medical examination costs hundreds of dollars and takes a lot of time. This is usually a logical choice because rarely is anything more than a pain reliever needed for a headache. But in some cases, a headache may indicate a brain tumor, and failing to see a specialist right away can result in complications. Should everyone with a headache go to a specialist? Of course not, but people treating their own illnesses must realize that they are betting on the basis of their cost/value analysis of the situation, they are taking the most logical option.

The same cost/value analysis must be made in deciding to do one's own legal work. Many legal situations are very straight forward, requiring a simple form and no complicated analysis. Anyone with a little intelligence and a book of instructions can handle the matter without outside help.

But there is always the chance that complications are involved that only an attorney would notice. To simplify the law into a book like this, several legal cases often must be condensed into a single sentence or paragraph. Otherwise, the book would be several hundred pages long and too complicated for most people. However, this simplification necessarily leaves out many details and nuances that would apply to special or unusual situations. Also, there are many ways to interpret most legal questions. Your case may come before a judge who disagrees with the analysis of our authors.

Therefore, in deciding to use a self-help law book and to do your own legal work, you must realize that you are making a cost/value analysis and deciding that the chance your case will not turn out to your satisfaction is outweighed by the money you will save in doing it yourself. Most people handling their own simple legal matters never have a problem, but occasionally people find that it ended up costing them more to have an attorney straighten out the situation than it would have if they had hired an attorney in the beginning. Keep this in mind while handling your case, and be sure to consult an attorney if you feel you might need further guidance.

INTRODUCTION

Going through a divorce is probably one of the most common and most traumatic encounters with the legal system. Paying a divorce lawyer can be expensive, and it comes at a time when you are least likely to have extra funds. In a contested divorce case it is not uncommon for the parties to run up legal bills of over $10,000, and horror stories abound of lawyers charging substantial fees with little progress to show for it. This book is designed to enable you to obtain a divorce without hiring a lawyer. Even if you do hire a lawyer, this book will help you to work with him or her more effectively, which can also reduce your legal fee.

This is not a law school course, but a practical guide to get you through "the system" as easily as possible. Legal jargon has been kept to a minimum. For ease of understanding, this book uses the term *spouse* to refer to your husband or wife (whichever applies), and the terms *child* and *children* are used interchangeably.

Please keep in mind that different judges, and courts in different counties, may have their own particular (if not peculiar) procedures and ways of doing things. The court clerk's office can often tell you if they have any special forms or requirements. Court clerks cannot give legal advice, but they can tell you what their court or judges require.

The first two chapters of this book will give you an overview of the law and the legal system. Chapters 3 and 4 will help you decide if you want an attorney and if you want a divorce. The remaining chapters will show you what forms you need, how to fill out the forms, and what procedures to follow. You will also find three appendices in the back of the book. Appendix A contains selected portions of the Michigan law dealing with property division, alimony, and child support. Although these provisions are discussed in the book, it is sometimes helpful to read the law exactly as the legislature wrote it.

Appendix B contains portions of the Michigan Child Support Formula. These are the guidelines, tables, and calculations for determining the child support amount.

Finally, appendix C contains the forms you will complete. You will not need to use all of the forms. This book will tell you which forms you need, depending upon your situation.

Read this entire book before you prepare or file any papers. This will give you the information you need to decide what forms you need and how to fill them out.

Be sure to read "An Introduction to Legal Forms" in chapter 5 before you use any of the forms in this book.

MARRIAGE "INS AND OUTS" 1

Several years (or maybe only months) ago you made a decision to get married. This chapter will discuss, in a very general way, what you got yourself into, and how you can get yourself out. Throughout this book you will see references to Michigan laws. There are two sets of books containing the Michigan laws, and references will be given to both sets. Both sets contain the same laws, but they have different publishers and use different numbering systems. These two sets are *Michigan Statutes Annotated* (abbreviated "M.S.A.") and *Michigan Compiled Laws Annotated* (abbreviated "M.C.L.A."). The symbol "§" means *section*, and "§§" means *sections*. For example: "M.S.A. §§25.86 & 25.89" is a reference to sections 25.86 and 25.89 of the *Michigan Statutes Annotated*. See chapter 2 on "Legal Research" for more information.

MARRIAGE

Marriage is frequently referred to as a contract. It is a legal contract, and for many, it is also a religious contract. This book will deal only with the legal aspects. The wedding ceremony involves the bride and groom reciting certain vows, which are actually mutual promises about how they will treat each other. There are also legal papers signed, such as a marriage license and a marriage certificate. These formalities create certain rights and obligations for the husband and wife. Although the focus at the ceremony is on the emotional and romantic aspects of the relationship, the legal reality is that financial and property rights are being created. It is these financial and property rights and obligations which cannot be broken without a legal proceeding.

Marriage will give each of the parties certain rights in property, and it creates certain obligations with respect to the support of any children they have together (or adopt). Unfortunately, most people don't fully realize that these rights and obligations are being created until it comes time for a divorce.

DIVORCE

A divorce is the most common method of terminating or breaking the marriage contract. In a divorce, the court declares the marriage contract broken, divides the parties' property and debts, decides if either party should receive alimony, and determines the custody, support, and visitation with respect to any children the parties may have. Traditionally, a divorce could only be granted under certain specific circumstances, such as for adultery, or mental cruelty. Today, a divorce may be granted simply because one or both of the parties want one. The wording used in Michigan to describe the situation is: "There has been a breakdown of the marriage relationship to the extent that the objects of matrimony have been destroyed and there remains no reasonable likelihood that the marriage can be preserved."

ANNULMENT

The basic difference between a divorce and an annulment is that a divorce says, "this marriage is broken," and an annulment says, "there never was a marriage." An annulment is more difficult and often more complicated to prove, so it is not used very often. Annulments are only possible in a few circumstances, usually where one party deceived the other. If you decide that you want an annulment, you should consult an attorney. If you are seeking an annulment for religious reasons and need to go through a church procedure (rather than, or in addition to, a legal procedure), you should consult your priest or minister.

A divorce is generally easier to get than an annulment. This is because all you need to prove to get a divorce is that your marriage is broken. How do you prove this? Simply by saying it. The Complaint for Divorce (Form 8), reads: "There has been a breakdown of the marriage relationship to the extent that the objects of matrimony have been destroyed and there remains no reasonable likelihood that the marriage can be preserved." That is all you need to do. However, in order to get an annulment you'll need to prove more. This proof will usually involve introducing various documents into evidence, and having other people come to testify at the court hearing.

GROUNDS FOR
ANNULMENT

Annulments can only be granted based on one of the following grounds:

1. One of the parties was too young to get married. In Michigan, both parties must be at least sixteen years old to get married (There is an exception if a person under the age of sixteen has the consent of their living parents or legal guardian.)

2. If one of the parties is guilty of fraud, and there has been no subsequent cohabitation. For example, where one party just got married in order to have the right to inherit from the other, with no intention of ever living together as husband and wife.

3. If one party was under duress when he or she got married, and there has been no subsequent cohabitation. *Duress* means that the person was being threatened, or was under some kind of pressure, so that he or she did not get married voluntarily.

4. If one party "was insane or an idiot" or was a "lunatic" (these are the words used by the legislature), if there was no cohabitation after the person was restored to sound mind.

5. If one party was already married to another person. This might occur if one party married, mistakenly believing his divorce from his previous wife was final, or in the case of bigamy.

6. If the marriage is incestuous. Michigan law prohibits marriage between certain family members, such as brother and sister, aunt and nephew, or uncle and niece. See M.S.A. §§25.3 & 25.4; M.C.L.A. §§551.3 & 551.4 for a complete list of prohibited marriages.

7. If one party did not have the physical capacity for a marital relationship (such as being incapable of conceiving a child).

If your spouse wants to stop an annulment, there are several arguments he or she could make to further complicate the case. This area of the law is not as well defined as divorce. The Michigan laws concerning annulments are found in M.S.A. §25.83 and §§25.111 through 25.115; or M.C.L.A. §552.3 and §§552.35 through 552.39 (see the section on "Legal Research" in chapter 2 for more information about researching Michigan law). The annulment procedure is much less common than divorce, can be extremely complicated, and should not be attempted without consulting a lawyer.

LEGAL SEPARATION

A legal separation is used to divide the property and provide for child support and custody in cases where the husband and wife live separately, but remain married. This is usually used to divide the financial rights and obligations of a couple whose religion does not permit divorce. In Michigan, this is referred to as an action for *separate maintenance*. The grounds for a legal separation are the same as for divorce. See M.S.A. §25.87; M.C.L.A. §552.7 for more information about actions for separate maintenance. Legal separations are not covered in detail in this book, although it would be possible to modify some of the forms for use in a separate maintenance case.

Do You Really Want a Divorce?

Getting a divorce is one of the most emotionally stressful events in a person's life. It will also have an impact on several aspects of your life, and can change your entire lifestyle. Before you begin the process of getting a divorce, you need to take some time to think about how it will affect your life. This chapter will help you examine these things, and offer alternatives in the event you want to try to save your relationship. Even if you feel absolutely sure that you want a divorce, you should still read this chapter so that you are prepared for what may follow.

LEGAL DIVORCE   In emotional terms, the legal aspect is the easiest part of divorce. It is simply the breaking of your matrimonial bonds; the termination of your marriage contract and partnership. The stress created here is that of going through a court system procedure, and having to deal with your spouse as you go through it. However, when compared to the other aspects of divorce, the legal divorce doesn't last as long. On the other hand, the legal divorce can be the most confrontational and emotionally explosive stage.

There are generally three matters to be resolved in the legal divorce:

1. The divorce of two people: Basically, this gives each the legal right to marry someone else.

2. The division of their property (and responsibility for debts).

3. The care and custody of their children.

Although it is theoretically possible for the legal divorce to be concluded within a few months, the legalities most often continue for years. This is mostly caused by the emotional aspects leading to battles over the children.

SOCIAL AND   Divorce will have a tremendous impact on your social and emotional
EMOTIONAL   life, which will continue long after you are legally divorced. This impact
DIVORCE   includes:

Lack of companionship. Even if your relationship is quite "stormy," you are probably still accustomed to having your spouse around. You may be able to temporarily put aside your problems, and at least somewhat support each other in times of mutual adversity (such as in dealing with a death in the family, the illness of your child, or hurricane damage to your home). You may also feel a little more secure at night knowing you are not alone in the house. Even if your marriage is one of the most miserable, you may still notice at least a little emptiness, loneliness, or solitude after the divorce. It may not be that you miss your spouse in particular, but just miss another person being around.

Grief. Divorce may be viewed as the death of a marriage, or maybe the funeral ceremony for the death of a marriage. And like the death of anyone or anything you've been close to, you will feel a sense of loss. This aspect can take you through all of the normal feelings associated with grief, such as guilt, anger, denial, and acceptance. You'll get angry and frustrated over the years you've "wasted." You'll feel guilty because you "failed to make the marriage work." You'll find yourself saying, "I can't believe this is happening to me." And, for months or even years, you'll spend a lot of time thinking about your marriage. It can be extremely difficult to put it all behind you, and to get on with your life.

The single's scene: dating. If you want to avoid solitary evenings before the TV, you'll find yourself trying to get back into the "single's scene." This will probably involve a change in friends, as well as a change in lifestyle. First, you may find that your current friends, who are probably all married, no longer find that you, as a single person, fit in with their circle. Gradually, or even quickly, you may find yourself dropped from their guest list. Now, you've got to start making an effort to meet single people at work, going out on the town, and even dating! This experience can be very frightening, tiring, and frustrating after years of being away from this lifestyle. It can also be very difficult if you have custody of the kids. And the dating scene is (or at least should be) entirely changed with the ever-present threat of AIDS and other communicable diseases.

FINANCIAL
DIVORCE

In financial terms, a divorce can be a very long and drastic adjustment. Divorce has a significant financial impact in almost every case. Many married couples are just able to make ends meet. After getting divorced there are suddenly two rent payments, two electric bills, etc. For the spouse without custody, there is also child support to be paid. For at least one spouse, and often for both, money becomes even tighter than it was before the divorce. Also, once you've divided your property, each of you will need to replace the items the other person got to keep. If she got the bedroom furniture and the pots and pans, he will need to buy his own. If he got the television and the sofa, she will need to buy her own television and sofa.

CHILDREN AND
DIVORCE

The effect of a divorce upon your children, and your relationship with them, can be the most painful and long-lasting aspect of divorce. Your family life will be permanently changed, as there will no longer be the "family." Even if you remarry, step-parents rarely bring back that same family feeling. Your relationship with your children may become strained as they work through their feelings of blame, guilt, disappointment, and anger. This strain may continue for many years. Your children may even need professional counseling. Also, as long as there is child support and visitation involved, you will be forced to have at least some contact with your ex-spouse.

ALTERNATIVES
TO DIVORCE

By the time you've purchased this book, and read this far, you have probably already decided that you want a divorce. However, if what you've just read and thought about has changed your mind, or made you want to make a last effort to save your marriage, there are a few things you can try. These are only very basic suggestions. Details, and other suggestions, can be offered by professional marriage counselors.

Talk to your spouse. Choose the right time (not when your spouse is trying to unwind after a day at work or quiet a crying baby), and talk about your problems. Establish a few ground rules such as:

☞ Talk about how you feel, instead of making accusations that may start an argument.

☞ Each person listens while the other speaks (no interrupting).

☞ Each person must say something that he or she likes about the other, and about the relationship.

As you talk you may want to discuss such things as where you'd like your relationship to go, how it has changed since you got married, and what can be done to bring you closer together.

Change your thinking. Many people get divorced because they won't change something about their outlook or their lifestyle. Then, once they get divorced, they find they've made that same change they resisted for so long.

For example, George and Wendy were unhappy in their marriage. They didn't seem to share the same lifestyle. George felt overburdened with responsibility, and bored. He wanted Wendy to be more independent and outgoing, to meet new people, to handle the household budget, and to go out with him more often. But Wendy was more shy and reserved, wasn't confident in her ability to find a job and succeed in the business world, and preferred to stay at home. Wendy wanted George to give up some of his frequent nights "out with the guys," to help with the cooking and laundry, to stop leaving messes for her to clean up, and to stop bothering her about going out all the time. But neither would try change, and eventually all of the "little things" built up into a divorce.

After the divorce, Wendy was forced to get a job to support herself. Now she's made friends at work, she goes out with them two or three nights a week, she's successful and happy at her job, and she's quite competent at managing her own budget. George now has his own apartment, and has to cook his own meals (something he finds he enjoys) and do his own laundry. He's also found it necessary to clean up his own messes and keep the place neat, especially if he's going to entertain guests. George has even thought about inviting Wendy over for dinner and a quiet evening at his place. Wendy has been thinking about inviting George out for a drink after work with her friends.

Both George and Wendy have changed in exactly the way the other had wanted. It's just too bad they didn't make these changes before they got divorced! If you think some change may help, give it a try. You can always go back to a divorce if things don't work out.

Marriage counseling. Counseling is not the same as giving advice. A counselor should not be telling you what to do. A counselor's job is to assist you in figuring out what you really want to do. A counselor's job is mostly to ask questions that will get you thinking.

Actually, just talking things out with your spouse is a form of self-counseling. The only problem is that it's difficult to remain objective and non-judgmental. You both need to be able to calmly analyze what the problems are, and discuss possible solutions.

Very few couples seem to be able to do this successfully, which is why there are professional marriage counselors. As with doctors and lawyers, good marriage counselors are best discovered by word of mouth. You may have friends who can direct you to someone who helped them. You can also check with your family doctor or your clergyman for a referral, or even check the telephone yellow pages under "Marriage and Family Counselors" or some similar category. You can see a counselor either alone or with your spouse It may be a good idea to see a counselor even if you are going through with the divorce. Another form of individual counseling is talking to a close friend. Just remember the difference between counseling and advice giving! Don't let your friend tell you what you should do.

Trial separation. Before going to the time, expense, and trouble of getting a divorce, you and your spouse may want to try just getting away from each other for awhile. This can be as simple as taking separate vacations, or as complex as actually separating into separate households for an indefinite period of time.

This may give each of you a chance to think about how you'll like living alone, how important or trivial your problems are, and how you really feel about each other.

THE LEGAL SYSTEM 2

This chapter will give you a general introduction to the legal system. There are things you need to know in order to obtain a divorce (or help your lawyer get the job done), and to get through any encounter with the legal system with a minimum of stress. These are some of the realities of our system. If you don't learn to accept these realities, you will experience much stress and frustration.

THEORY VS. REALITY

Our legal system is a system of rules. There are basically three types of rules:

1. Rules of law: These are the basic substance of the law, such as a law telling a judge how to go about dividing your property.

2. Rules of procedure: These outline how matters are to be handled in the courts, such as requiring court papers to be in a certain form, or filed within a certain time.

3. Rules of evidence: These set forth the manner in which facts are to be proven.

The theory is that these rules allow each side to present evidence most favorable to that side, and an independent person or persons (the judge or jury) will be able to figure out the truth. Then certain legal principles will be applied to that "truth" which will give a fair resolution of the dispute between the parties. These legal principles are supposed to be relatively unchanging so that we can all know what will happen in any given situation and can plan our lives accordingly. This will provide order and predictability to our society. Any change in the legal principles is supposed to occur slowly, so that the expected behavior in our society is not confused from day-to-day. Unfortunately, the system does not really work this way. What follows are only some of the problems in the real legal system:

THE SYSTEM IS NOT PERFECT

Contrary to how it may seem, legal rules are not made just to complicate things and confuse everyone. They are attempts to make the system fair and just. They have been developed over several hundred years, and in most cases they do make sense. Unfortunately, our efforts to find fairness and justice have resulted in a complex set of rules. The legal system affects our lives in important ways, and it is not a game. However, it can be compared to a game in some ways. The rules are designed to apply to all people, in all cases. Sometimes the rules don't seem to give a fair result in a certain situation, but the rules are still followed. Just as a referee can make a bad call, so can a judge. There are also cases where one side wins by cheating.

JUDGES DON'T ALWAYS FOLLOW THE RULES

This is a shocking discovery for many young lawyers. After spending three years in law school learning legal theory, and after spending countless hours preparing for a hearing and having all of the law on your side, you find that the judge isn't going to pay any attention to legal theories and the law. Many judges are going to make a decision simply on what they think seems fair under the circumstances. This concept is actually being taught in some law schools now. Unfortunately, what "seems fair" to a particular judge may depend upon his personal ideas and philosophy. For example, there is nothing in the divorce laws which gives one parent priority in child custody; however, a vast majority of judges believe that a child is generally better off with its mother. All other things being equal, these judges will find a way to justify awarding custody to the mother.

THE SYSTEM IS
OFTEN SLOW

Even lawyers get frustrated at how long it can take to get a case completed (especially if they don't get paid until it's done). Whatever your situation, things will take longer than you expect. Patience is required to get through the system with a minimum of stress. Don't let your impatience or frustration show. No matter what happens, keep calm and be courteous.

NO TWO CASES
ARE ALIKE

Just because your friend's case went a certain way doesn't mean yours will have the same result. The judge can make a difference, and more often the circumstances will make a difference. Just because your co-worker makes the same income as you and has the same number of children, you can't assume you will be ordered to pay the same amount of child support. There are usually other circumstances your co-worker doesn't tell you about, and possibly doesn't understand.

HALF OF THE
PEOPLE LOSE

Remember, there are two sides to every legal issue, and there is usually only one winner. Don't expect to have every detail go your way, especially if you let the judge decide.

DIVORCE LAW AND PROCEDURE

This section will give you a general overview of the law and procedures involved in getting a divorce. To most people, including lawyers, the law appears very complicated and confusing. Fortunately, many areas of the law can be broken down into simple and logical steps. Divorce is one of those areas.

THE PLAYERS

Law and the legal system are often compared to games, and just like games, it is important to know the players:

The judge. The judge has the power to decide whether you can get divorced, how your property will be divided, which of you will get custody of the children, and how much the other will pay for child support. The judge is the last person you want to make angry with you! In general, judges have large caseloads and like it best when your case can be concluded quickly and without hassle. This means that the more you and your spouse agree upon, and the more complete your paperwork is, the better the judge will like it. Most likely, your only direct contact with the judge will be at the final hearing, which may last as little as five minutes. (See chapter 6 for more about how to deal with the judge.)

The judge's secretary. The judge's secretary sets the hearings for the judge, and can frequently answer many of your questions about the procedure and what the judge would like or require. Once again, you don't want to make an enemy of the secretary. This means that you don't call often, and don't ask too many questions. A few questions are okay, and you may want to start off saying that you just want to make sure you have everything in order for the judge. You'll get much farther by being nice.

The court clerk. Where the secretary usually only works for one judge, the court clerk handles the files for all of the judges. The clerk's office is the central place where all of the court files are kept. The clerk files your court papers and keeps the official records of your divorce. Most people who work in the clerk's office are friendly and helpful. While they can't give you legal advice (such as telling you what to say in your court papers), they can help explain the system and the procedures (such as telling you what type of papers must be filed). The clerk has the power to accept or reject your papers, so you don't want to anger the clerk either. If the clerk tells you to change something in your papers, just change it. Don't argue or complain.

The Friend of the Court. The Office of the Friend of the Court is the agency that assists the court in divorce cases. Actually, the Friend of the Court is a person who is hired by the judges, but the phrase *Friend of the Court* as used in this book means the office, not just the person. The Friend of the Court has the following main functions:

1. Conduct investigations and hold hearings on matters of property division, alimony, child custody and visitation, and child support.

2. Make recommendations to the court on these matters.

3. Collect, process, and account for child support and alimony payments.

4. Enforce court orders relating to alimony, child support, and child custody and visitation.

You will become involved with the Friend of the Court if any of the following situations exist in your case:

1. You and your spouse have a minor child.

2. You and your spouse have one or more matters in dispute and the judge refers your case to the Friend of the Court for investigation and recommendation.

Lawyers. Lawyers serve as guides through the legal system. They try to guide their own client, while trying to confuse, manipulate, or out-maneuver their opponent (and the judge). In dealing with your spouse's lawyer (if he or she has one) try to be polite. You won't get anywhere by being antagonistic. Generally the lawyer is just doing his job to get the best situation for his client. Some lawyers are truly nasty people. These lawyers simply can't be reasoned with, and you shouldn't try. If your spouse gets one of these lawyers, it is a good idea for you to get a lawyer also. Chapter 3 will provide more information to help you decide if you want a lawyer.

This book. This book will serve as your map through the legal system. In most cases, the dangers along the way are relatively small. If you start getting lost, or the dangers seem to be getting worse, you can always hire a lawyer to jump to your aid.

THE LAW   The law relating to divorce, as well as to any other area of law, comes from two sources. The first source is the laws passed by the Michigan Legislature. There are two separate sets of books which contain these laws. Each is produced by a different publisher. One is called *Michigan Statutes Annotated* (abbreviated "M.S.A."), and the other is called *Michigan Compiled Laws Annotated* (abbreviated "M.C.L.A."). Each has a different numbering system, but each has a reference table to the other. A portion of this law (giving both reference numbers), relating to property division, alimony, and child support, can be found in appendix A of this book.

The other source of law is the past decisions of the Michigan courts. These are much more difficult to locate and follow. For most situations the law is clearly spelled out in the statutes, and the past court decisions are not all that important. However, if you wish to learn more about how to find these court decision, see the section of this chapter on "Legal Research."

Residency requirement. One basic law you need to be aware of is that either you or your spouse must live in Michigan for at least 180 days, and be a resident of the county where the case is filed for at least ten days, immediately before filing a Complaint for Divorce with the court. The one exception to this is if your spouse was born in, or is a citizen of, a foreign country, and you can convince the judge that your child is at risk of being taken out of the United States and kept in another country by your spouse.

The law is really very simple in most divorce cases. You will need to show the following three things:

1. That there has been "a breakdown of the marriage relationship." (This is done simply by stating this fact, which means that your marriage relationship is broken and can't be saved.)

2. How your property should be divided between you and your spouse.

3. Who should have custody of your children and how they should be supported.

THE
PROCEDURE

The basic uncontested divorce process may be viewed as a five-step process:

1. File court papers asking the judge to grant a divorce (which includes dividing your property and deciding how the children will be taken care of).

2. Notify your spouse that you are filing for divorce.

3. File papers explaining you and your spouse's agreement.

4. Obtain a hearing date.

5. Attend a hearing with the judge, and have the judge sign a judgment granting the divorce.

Now we'll look at these steps in a little more detail, and later chapters will provide even more details and tell you how to carry out these steps.

Complaint for Divorce. This is simply a written request for the judge to grant you a divorce and divide your property. You may also see this referred to as a "Bill of Complaint for Divorce." A Complaint for Divorce form is provided in appendix C of this book, and full instructions are also provided in later chapters. Once the Complaint for Divorce is completed, it is taken to the court clerk to be filed.

Notifying your spouse. After you've prepared the Complaint for Divorce you need to officially notify your spouse. Even though your spouse may already know that you are filing for divorce, you still need to have him or her officially notified. This is done by having a copy of your Complaint for Divorce delivered to your spouse. This must be done in a certain way, which will be explained in detail later. (This step is eliminated in the consent divorce procedure.)

Obtaining a hearing date. Once all of your paperwork has been filed, you need to set a date for a hearing. A hearing is simply a meeting with the judge so that he or she can give you a divorce. This is usually done by contacting the judge's secretary and asking for a hearing date. This can often be done over the telephone.

The hearing. Finally, you go to the hearing. The judge will review the papers you have submitted, any recommendation of the Friend of the Court, and any additional information you have, and will make a decision about whether to grant the divorce, how your property should be divided, who should have custody of your children, and how the children are to be supported. If it applies to your situation, he may also decide whether alimony will be paid. If you and your spouse agree on these matters, the judge will simply approve your agreement.

LEGAL RESEARCH

This book has been designed so that you don't need to do research. However, if you need or want to find out more about the divorce law in Michigan, this section will give you some guidance. Most of the books discussed below will not be found at your local public library. To find them you will probably need to go to a specialized law library. Most counties have a law library affiliated with the circuit court. Your court clerk's office can probably tell you where to find the law library. If you are lucky enough to live near a law school, you can also find a law library there. Law school libraries are usually much more extensive than county law libraries. Just like court clerks, law librarians cannot give you legal advice. However, they can show you where to find the books you will need to help you.

MICHIGAN
STATUTES

The main source of information on Michigan divorce law is the laws passed by the Michigan Legislature. There are two sets of books which contain these laws. Each set is by a different publisher, and each has a completely different numbering system. One set is called *Michigan Statutes Annotated* (abbreviated "M.S.A." or "MSA"). The other is called *Michigan Compiled Laws Annotated* (abbreviated "M.C.L.A." or "MCLA"). The word "annotated" means that after each section you will find additional information, such as how that section has been interpreted by the courts. Each set has a cross-reference table, so if you have the section number for a particular law in one set you can look up the number for that law in the other set. In this book we list the section numbers for both set of books. One of these sets can sometimes be found at the regular public library, although you will need to check to be sure they have the most recent information. These books are updated each year, by a supplement which will be found in the back of each volume. These updates are called *pocket parts*, because they slide into a "pocket" on the inside of the back cover.

In addition to the laws passed by the legislature, law is also made by the decisions of the judges in various cases each year. You will definitely not find this case law at the regular public library, so you will need to go to a law library. In addition to the annotation portion of M.S.A. and M.C.L.A., case law may be found in the reference materials that follow.

DIGESTS — *Digests* are sets of books which give short summaries of cases, and a reference to the place where you can find the court's full written opinion. There are two digests for Michigan: *Callaghan's Michigan Digest* (look for volume 6A), and *West's Michigan Digest, 2nd* (look for volume 15). The information in the digest is arranged alphabetically by subject. Find the chapter on "divorce," then look for the subject you want.

NORTHWESTERN REPORTER — The *Northwestern Reporter* is where the Michigan appeals courts publish their written opinions on the cases they hear. There are two series of the *Northwestern Reporter*, the older cases being found in the *Northwestern Reporter* (abbreviated "N.W."), and newer cases being found in the *Northwestern Reporter 2d Series* ("N.W.2d"). For example, if the digest refers you to "*Smith v. Smith*, 149 N.W.2d 721 (1987)," this tells you that the case of *Smith v. Smith* can be found in Volume 149 of the *Northwestern Reporter 2d Series*, on page 721. The number in parentheses is the year in which the case was decided.

LEGAL ENCYCLOPEDIA — A *legal encyclopedia* is similar to a regular encyclopedia. You simply look up the subject you want ("divorce"), in alphabetical order, and it gives you a summary of the law on that subject. It will also refer to specific court cases, which can then be found in the Northwestern Reporter. There are legal encyclopedia sets which give general information for the

the entire United States, but you would get more helpful information from the two legal encyclopedia sets specifically relating to Michigan law:

☞ *Callaghan's Michigan Civil Jurisprudence*. Look for volume 8.

☞ *Callaghan's Michigan Pleading and Practice*. Look for volume 10.

MICHIGAN
RULES OF
COURT

The *Michigan Rules of Court* are the rules which are applied in the various courts in Michigan, and they also contain some approved forms. These rules mainly deal with forms and procedures. You would be primarily concerned with the "Rules of Civil Procedure." Portions of the Michigan Court Rules are included in appendix A.

MICHIGAN
FAMILY LAW
SOURCEBOOK

The *Michigan Family Law Sourcebook*, published by the Institute for Continuing Legal Education (ICLE). Volume I contains the statutes relating to Michigan family law. Volume II contains valuable information about specific requirements and practices of particular counties, and even particular judges within these counties. Counties included in Volume II are Bay, Berrien, Calhoun, Genesee, Grand Traverse (which also includes Antrim and Leelanau), Ingham, Jackson, Kalamazoo, Kent, Macomb, Marquette, Midland, Oakland, Saginaw, Washtenaw, and Wayne.

FORM BOOKS

Form books are books containing sample forms for use in a variety of situations. Two such form books are *Michigan S.C.A.O. Approved Forms*, by West Publishing Company (look for volume I and any Supplement); and *Michigan Civil Practice Forms*, by Lawyers Cooperative Publishing (look for volume 5, chapter 71).

OTHER
SOURCES

Other books you may want to ask for at the law library are:

☞ *Michigan Basic Practice Handbook*, published by the Institute for Continuing Legal Education (ICLE). Look for chapter 1.

☞ *Michigan Family Law*, by N. Robbins and L. Collins.

☞ *Gilmore on Michigan Civil Procedure Before Trial*, published by ICLE. Look for chapter 19.

☛ *Michigan Child Support Formula Manual*, these are the official child support guidelines, and are published by both West Group and Lawyers Cooperative Publishing.

☛ *Michigan Marriage and Divorce*, by Arthur E. Moore, Eugene Arthur Moore and Walter Denison, published by West Publishing.

For more help with legal research, look for *Legal Research Made Easy*, by Suzan Herskowitz, available through your local bookstore or directly from Sphinx Publishing by calling 1-800-432-7444.

LAWYERS 3

Whether or not you need an attorney will depend upon many factors, such as how comfortable you feel handling the matter yourself, whether your situation is more complicated than usual, how much opposition you get from your spouse, and whether your spouse has an attorney. It may also be advisable to hire an attorney if you encounter a judge with a hostile attitude, or if your spouse gets a lawyer who wants to fight. There are no court appointed lawyers in divorce cases, so if you want an attorney you will have to hire one.

A very general rule is that you should consider hiring an attorney whenever you reach a point where you no longer feel comfortable representing yourself. This point will vary greatly with each person, so there is no easy way to be more definite.

Rather than asking if you *need* a lawyer, a more appropriate question may be: "Do you *want* a lawyer?" The next section will discuss some of the "pros" and "cons" of hiring a lawyer, and some of the things you may want to consider in making this decision.

Do You Want a Lawyer?

One of the first questions you will want to consider, and most likely the reason you are reading this book, is: How much will an attorney cost? Attorneys come in all ages, shapes, sizes, sexes, racial and ethnic groups—and price ranges. For a very rough estimate, you can expect an attorney to charge anywhere from $150 to $1,000 for an uncontested divorce, and from $800 and up for a contested divorce. Lawyers usually charge an hourly rate for contested divorces, ranging from about $75 to $300 per hour. Most new (and therefore less expensive) attorneys would be quite capable of handling a simple divorce, but, if your situation became more complicated, you would probably prefer a more experienced lawyer.

ADVANTAGES TO HIRING A LAWYER

Some advantages to hiring a lawyer include:

☞ Judges and other attorneys may take you more seriously if you have an attorney represent you. Most judges prefer both parties to have attorneys. They feel this helps the case move in a more orderly fashion because both sides will know the procedures and relevant issues. Persons representing themselves very often waste a lot of time on matters which have absolutely no bearing on the outcome of the case.

☞ A lawyer will serve as a "buffer" between you and your spouse. This can lead to a quicker passage through the system by reducing the chance for emotions to take control and confuse the issues.

☞ Attorneys prefer to deal with other attorneys for the same reasons listed above. However, if you become familiar with this book, and conduct yourself in a calm and proper manner, you should have no trouble. (Proper courtroom manners will be discussed in a later chapter.)

☞ You can let your lawyer worry about all of the details. By having an attorney you need only become generally familiar with the contents of this book, as it will be your attorney's job to file the proper papers in the correct form, and to deal with the court clerk, the judge, the process server, your spouse, and your spouse's attorney.

☞ Lawyers provide professional assistance with problems. In the event your case is complicated, or suddenly becomes complicated, it is an advantage to have an attorney who is familiar with your case. It can also be comforting to have a lawyer to turn to for advice, and to get your questions answered.

ADVANTAGES TO
REPRESENTING
YOURSELF

Some advantages to representing yourself include:

☞ Sometimes judges feel more sympathetic toward a person not represented by an attorney. Sometimes this results in the unrepresented person being allowed a certain amount of leeway with the procedure rules.

☞ The procedure may be faster. Two of the most frequent complaints about lawyers received by the bar association involve delay in completing the case, and failure to return phone calls. Most lawyers have a heavy caseload, which sometimes results in cases being neglected for various periods of time. If you are following the progress of your own case you'll be able to push it along the system diligently.

☞ Selecting any attorney is not easy. As the next section shows, it is hard to know whether you are selecting an attorney that will make you happy.

MIDDLE
GROUND

You may want to look for an attorney who will be willing to accept an hourly fee to answer your questions and give you help as you need it. This way you will save some legal costs, but still get professional assistance.

SELECTING A LAWYER

Selecting a lawyer is a two-step process. First you need to decide which attorney to make an appointment with, then you need to decide if you want to hire that attorney.

FINDING
LAWYERS

There are several ways to go about finding a lawyer, including:

☛ Ask a friend. A common, and frequently the best, way to find a lawyer is to ask someone you know to recommend one to you. This is especially helpful if the lawyer represented your friend in a divorce or other family law matter.

☛ Lawyer referral service. You can find a referral service by looking in the yellow pages phone directory under "Attorney Referral Services" or "Attorneys." This is a service, usually operated by a bar association, which is designed to match a client with an attorney handling cases in the area of law the client needs. The referral service does not guarantee the quality of work, nor the level of experience or ability, of the attorney. Finding a lawyer this way will at least connect you with one who is interested in divorce and family law matters, and probably has some experience in this area.

☛ Yellow pages. Check under the heading for "Attorneys" in the yellow pages phone directory. Many of the lawyers and law firms will place display ads here indicating their areas of practice and educational backgrounds. Look for firms or lawyers that indicate they practice in areas such as "divorce," "family law," or "domestic relations."

☛ Ask another lawyer. If you have used the services of an attorney in the past for some other matter (for example, a real estate closing, traffic ticket, or a will), you may want to call and ask if he or she could refer you to an attorney whose ability in the area of family law is respected.

EVALUATING A
LAWYER

From your search you should select three to five lawyers worthy of further consideration. Your first step will be to call each attorney's office, explain that you are interested in seeking a divorce, and ask the following questions:

☛ Does the attorney (or firm) handle this type of matter?

☛ How much can you expect it to cost? (Don't expect to get much of an answer.)

☛ How soon can you get an appointment?

If you like the answers you get, ask if you can speak to the attorney. Some offices will permit this, but others will require you to make an appointment. Make the appointment if that is what is required. Once you get in contact with the attorney (either on the phone or at the appointment), ask the following questions:

☛ How much will it cost?

☛ How will the fee be paid?

☛ How long has the attorney been in practice?

☛ How long has the attorney been in practice in Michigan?

☛ What percentage of the attorney's cases involve divorce cases or other family law matters? (Don't expect an exact answer, but you should get a rough estimate that is at least twenty percent.)

☛ How long will it take? (Don't expect an exact answer, but the attorney should be able to give you an average range and discuss things which may make a difference.)

If you get acceptable answers to these questions, it's time to ask yourself the following questions about the lawyer:

☛ Do you feel comfortable talking to the lawyer?

☛ Is the lawyer friendly toward you?

☛ Does the lawyer seem confident in himself or herself?

☛ Does the lawyer seem to be straightforward with you, and able to explain things so that you understand?

If you get satisfactory answers to all of these questions, you probably have a lawyer that you be able to work with easily. Most clients are happiest with an attorney that make them feel comfortable.

WORKING WITH A LAWYER

In general, you will work best with your attorney if you keep an open, honest, and friendly attitude. You should also consider the following suggestions.

ASK QUESTIONS

If you want to know something, or if you don't understand something, ask your attorney. If you don't understand the answer, tell your attorney and ask him or her to explain it again. There are many points of law that many lawyers don't even fully understand, so you shouldn't be embarrassed to ask questions. Many people who say they had a bad experience with a lawyer either didn't ask enough questions, or had a lawyer who wouldn't take the time to explain things to them. If your lawyer isn't taking the time to explain what he's doing, it may be time to look for a new lawyer.

GIVE COMPLETE INFORMATION

It is important to give your lawyer complete information. Anything you tell your attorney is confidential. An attorney can lose his license to practice if he reveals information without your permission, so don't hold back. Tell your lawyer everything, even if it doesn't seem important to you. There are many things which seem unimportant to a non-attorney, but can change the outcome of a case. Also, don't hold something back because you are afraid it will hurt your case. It will definitely hurt your case if your lawyer doesn't find out about it until he hears it in court from your spouse's attorney! But if he knows in advance, he can plan to eliminate or reduce damage to your case.

ACCEPT
REALITY

Listen to what your lawyer tells you about the law and the system. It will do you no good to argue because the law or the system doesn't work the way you think it should. For example, if your lawyer tells you that the judge can't hear your case for two weeks, don't try demanding that he set a hearing tomorrow. By refusing to accept reality, you are only setting yourself up for disappointment. And remember: It's not your attorney's fault that the system isn't perfect or that the law doesn't say what you'd like it to say.

BE PATIENT

You will be much happier if you can be patient with the system (which is often slow, as we discussed earlier), as well as with your attorney. Don't expect your lawyer to return your phone call within an hour. He may not be able to return it the same day either. Most lawyers are very busy, and often overworked. It is rare that an attorney can maintain a full caseload and still make each client feel as if he or she is the only client.

TALK TO THE
SECRETARY

Your lawyer's secretary can be a valuable source of information, so be friendly and get to know him or her. Often the secretary will be able to answer your questions, and you won't get a bill for this time.

LET YOUR
ATTORNEY
DEAL WITH
YOUR SPOUSE

It is your lawyer's job to communicate with your spouse, or with your spouse's lawyer. One of the biggest advantages to hiring a lawyer is that you don't have to deal with your spouse. Let your attorney do this job. Many lawyers have had clients lose or damage their cases when the client decides to say or do something on their own.

BE ON TIME

You should always be on time, both to appointments with your lawyer and to court hearings.

KEEPING YOUR
CASE MOVING

Many lawyers operate on the old principle of the squeaking wheel gets the oil. Work on a case tends to get put off until a deadline is near, an emergency develops, or the client calls. There is a reason for this. Many lawyers take more cases than can be effectively handled in order to earn the income they desire. Your task is to become a squeaking wheel that doesn't squeak so much as to become annoying to the attorney and his or her staff. Whenever you talk to your lawyer ask the following questions:

- ☞ What is the next step?

- ☞ When do you expect it to be done?

- ☞ When should I talk to you next?

If you don't hear from the lawyer when you expect, call him the following day. Don't remind him that he didn't call; just ask how things are going.

HOW TO SAVE MONEY

Of course you don't want to spend unnecessary money for an attorney. Here are a few things you can do to avoid excess legal fees:

- ☞ Don't make unnecessary phone calls to your lawyer.

- ☞ Give information to the secretary whenever possible.

- ☞ Direct your question to the secretary first. She or he will refer your question to the attorney if necessary.

- ☞ Plan your phone calls so that you can get to the point, and take less of your attorney's time.

- ☞ Do some of the "leg work" yourself. Pick up and deliver papers yourself, for example. Ask your attorney what you can do to assist with your case.

- ☞ Be prepared for appointments. Have all related papers with you, plan your visit to get to the point, and make an outline of what you want to discuss and what questions you want to ask.

PAY YOUR ATTORNEY'S BILL WHEN IT'S DUE

No client gets prompt attention like a client who pays his lawyer on time. However, you are entitled to an itemized bill, showing what the attorney did and how much time it took. Many attorneys will have you sign an agreement which states how you will be charged, what is included in the hourly fee, and what is extra. Review your bill carefully. There are numerous stories of people paying an attorney $500 or $1,000 in advance, only to have the attorney make a few phone calls to the spouse's lawyer, then ask for more money. If your attorney asks for $500 or $1,000 in advance, you should be sure that you and the lawyer agree on what is to be done for this fee. For $500 you should at least expect to have a petition prepared, filed with the court, and served on your spouse (although the filing and service fees will probably be extra).

FIRING YOUR
LAWYER

If you find that you can no longer work with your lawyer, or don't trust your lawyer, it is time to either go it alone or get a new attorney. You will need to send your lawyer a letter stating that you no longer desire his or her services, and are discharging him or her from your case. Also state that you will be coming by his or her office the following day to pick up your file. The attorney does not have to give you his or her own notes or other work in progress, but he or she must give you the essential contents of your file (such as copies of papers already filed or prepared and billed for, and any documents you provided). If he or she refuses to give you your file, for any reason, contact the Michigan Bar Association about filing a complaint or *grievance* against the lawyer. Of course, you will need to settle any remaining fees charges.

EVALUATING YOUR SITUATION 4

YOUR SPOUSE

First, you need to evaluate your situation with respect to your spouse. Have you both already agreed to get a divorce? If not, what kind of reaction do you expect from him or her? The expected reaction can determine how you proceed. If he or she reacts in a rational manner, you can probably use the consent or uncontested procedure. If you expect an extremely emotional and possibly violent reaction, you will need to take steps to protect yourself, your children, and your property (see chapter 12 for more information about how to handle these situations); and you will have to start out expecting to use the contested procedure.

You were warned on the back cover of this book not to let your spouse find this book, and it was for a very good reason. Unless you and your spouse have already decided together to get a divorce, you may not want your spouse to know you are thinking about filing for divorce. This is a defense tactic, although it may not seem that way at first. If your spouse thinks you are planning a divorce, he or she may do things to prevent you from getting a fair result. These things include withdrawing money from bank accounts, hiding information about income, and hiding assets. Don't let on until you've collected all of the information you will need and are about to file with the court, or until you are prepared to protect yourself from violence, if necessary.

> *Caution:* Tactics such as withdrawing money from bank accounts and hiding assets are dangerous. If you try any of these things you risk looking like the "bad guy" before the judge. This can result in anything from having disputed matters resolved in your spouse's favor, to being ordered to produce the assets (or be jailed for contempt of court).

Theoretically, the "system" would prefer you to keep evidence of the assets (such as photographs, sales receipts, or bank statements), to present to the judge if your spouse hides them. Then your spouse will be the bad guy and risk being jailed. However, once your spouse has taken assets, and hidden them, or sold them and spent the money, even a contempt order may not get the money or assets back. If you determine that you need to get the assets in order to keep your spouse from hiding or disposing of them, be sure you keep them in a safe place, and disclose them on any financial statements you may be required to submit to the Friend of the Court or the judge. Do not dispose of the property either. If your spouse claims you took them, you can explain to the judge why you were afraid that your spouse would dispose of them and that you merely got them out of his or her reach.

GATHERING INFORMATION

It is very important that you collect any financial information you can get, including originals or copies of the following:

- ☞ your most recent income tax return (and your spouse's if you filed separately).

- ☞ the most recent W-2 tax forms for yourself and your spouse.

- ☞ any other income reporting papers (such as interest, stock dividends, etc.).

☛ your spouse's most recent paystub, hopefully showing year-to-date earnings (otherwise try to get copies of all paystubs since the beginning of the year).

☛ deeds to all real estate; and titles to cars, boats, or other vehicles.

☛ your and your spouse's will or wills.

☛ life insurance policies.

☛ stocks, bonds or other investment papers.

☛ pension or retirement fund papers and statements.

☛ health insurance card and papers.

☛ bank account or credit union statements.

☛ your spouse's social security number, and driver's license number.

☛ Names, addresses and phone numbers of your spouse's employer, close friends and family members.

☛ Credit card statements, mortgage documents, and other credit and debt papers.

☛ A list of vehicles, furniture, appliances, tools, etc., owned by you and your spouse. (See the next section in this chapter on "Property and Debts" for forms and a detailed discussion of what to include.)

☛ Copies of bills or receipts for recurring, regular expenses, such as rent, electric, gas or other utilities, car insurance, etc.

☛ Copies of bills, receipts, insurance forms, or medical records for any unusual medical expenses (including for recurring or continuous medical conditions) for yourself, your spouse or your children.

☛ Any other papers showing what you and your spouse earn, own, or owe.

Make copies of as many of these papers as possible, and keep them in a safe and private place (where your spouse won't be able to get them). Try to make copies of new papers as they come in, especially as you get close to filing court papers, and as you get close to a court hearing.

PROPERTY AND DEBTS

This section is designed to help you get a rough idea of where things stand regarding the division of your property, and to prepare you for completing the court papers you will need to file. The following sections will deal with the questions of your debts, and child support, custody and visitation, and alimony. If you are still not sure whether you want a divorce, these sections may help you to decide.

PROPERTY Michigan law divides property in a divorce according to the principle of *equitable distribution*. Basically, this means "a fair and equitable distribution under all of the circumstances." The judge has a great amount of discretion in dividing property.

According to various court cases, the judge should consider such things as: (1) the source of the property, (2) the length of the marriage, (3) the needs of the parties, (4) the earning ability of each party, (5) the cause of the divorce, (6) the needs of the children, (7) each party's contribution toward the acquisition of the property, and (8) any encumbrances (i.e., loans or liens) on the property. Generally, an inheritance is considered the separate property of the spouse who inherited it, but this can also be subject to distribution if the other property is not sufficient for the other party's support and maintenance. [See *Lee v. Lee*, 477 NW2d 429 (1991).] Also, a court award for pain and suffering in a personal injury lawsuit is considered separate property.

This section basically assists you in completing the Property Inventory (Form 1). This form is a list of all of your property, and key information about that property. You will notice that this form is divided into nine columns, designated as follows:

Column (1): You will check the box in this column if that piece of property that you believe should be considered as "separate" property. This might be property that you or your spouse acquired before you were married, or which was given to you or your spouse separately, or which was inherited by you or your spouse separately.

Column (2): In this column you will describe the property. A discussion regarding what information should go in this column will follow.

Column (3): In this column write the serial number, account number, or other number which will help clearly identify that piece of property.

Column (4): This is for the current market value of the property.

Column (5): This will show how much money is owed on the property, if any.

Column (6): Subtract the "Balance Owed" (column 5) from the "Value" (column 4). This will show how much the property is worth to you (your *equity*).

Column (7): This column will show the current legal owner of the property. (H) designates the husband, (W) the wife, and (J) is for jointly owned property (in both of your names).

Column (8): This column will be checked for those pieces of property you expect the husband will keep.

Column (9): This column is for the property you expect the wife will keep.

Use columns (1) through (9) to list your property, including the following:

Cash. List the name of the bank, credit union, etc., and the account number, for each account. This includes savings and checking accounts, and certificates of deposit (CDs). The balance of each account should be listed in the columns entitled "Value" and "Equity." (Leave the

"Balance Owed" column blank.) Make copies of the most recent bank statements for each account.

Stocks and bonds. All stocks, bonds or other "paper investments" should be listed. Write down the number of shares and the name of the company or other organization which issued them. Also copy any notation such as *common* or *preferred* stock or shares. This information can be obtained from the stock certificate itself, or from a statement from the stock broker. Make a copy of the certificate or the statement.

Real estate. List each piece of property you and your spouse own. The description might include a street address for the property, a subdivision name and lot number, or anything which lets you know what piece of property to which you are referring. There probably won't be an ID number, although you might use the county's tax number. Real estate (or any other property) may be in both of your names (joint), in your spouse's name alone, or in your name alone. The only way to know for sure is to look at the deed to the property. (If you can't find a copy of the deed, try to find mortgage papers or payment coupons, homeowners insurance papers, or a property tax assessment notice.) The owners of property are usually referred to on the deed as the *grantees*. In assigning a value to the property, consider the market value, which is the amount for which you could probably sell the property. This might be what similar houses in your neighborhood have sold for recently. You might also consider how much you paid for the property, or for how much the property is insured. *Do not* use the tax assessment value, as this is usually considerably lower than the market value.

Vehicles. This category includes cars, trucks, motor homes, recreational vehicles (RVs), motorcycles, boats, trailers, airplanes, and any other means of transportation for which the State requires a title and registration. Your description should include the following information (which can usually be found on the title or on the vehicle itself):

☞ year it was made.

- make: The name of the manufacturer, such as "Ford," "Honda," "Chris Craft," etc.

- model: You know it's a Ford, but is it a Mustang, an LTD, or an Aerostar. The model may be a name, a number, a series of letters, or a combination of these.

- serial number: This is most likely found on the vehicle, as well as on the title or registration.

Make a copy of the title or registration. Regarding a value, you can go to the public library and ask to look at the *blue book* for cars, trucks or whatever it is you're trying to find. A blue book (which may actually be yellow, black or any other color) gives the average values for used vehicles. Your librarian can help you find what you need. Another source is to look in the classified advertising section of a newspaper to see what the prices are for similar vehicles. You might also try calling a dealer to see if he can give you a rough idea of the value. Be sure you take into consideration the condition of the vehicle.

Furniture. List all furniture as specifically as possible. You should include the type of piece (such as sofa, coffee table, etc.), the color, and if you know it, the manufacturer, line name, or the style. Furniture usually won't have a serial number, although if you find one be sure to write it on the list. Just estimate a value, unless you just know what it's worth.

Appliances, electronic equipment, yard machines, etc. This category includes such things as refrigerators, lawn mowers, and power tools. Again, estimate a value, unless you are familiar enough with them to simply know what they are worth. There are too many different makes, models, accessories, and age factors to be able to figure out a value otherwise. These items will probably have a make, model, and serial number on them. You may have to look on the back, bottom, or other hidden place for the serial number, but try to find it.

Jewelry and other valuables. You don't need to list inexpensive, or costume jewelry. You can plan on keeping your own personal watches, rings, etc. However, if you own an expensive piece you should include it in your list, along with an estimated value. Be sure to include silverware, original art, gold, coin collections, etc. Again, be as detailed and specific as possible.

Life insurance with cash surrender value. This is any life insurance policy that you may cash in or borrow against, and therefore has value. If you can't find a cash surrender value in the papers you have, you can call the insurance company and ask.

Other "big ticket" items. This is simply a general reference to anything of significant value that doesn't fit in one of the categories already discussed. Examples might be a portable spa, an above-ground swimming pool, golf clubs, guns, pool tables, camping or fishing equipment, or farm animals or machinery.

Pensions and military benefits. The division of pensions, and military and retirement benefits, can be a complicated matter. Whenever these types of benefits are involved, you will need to consult an attorney or a CPA to determine the value of the benefits and how they should be divided. Be sure to read the section in chapter 12 on pension plans.

What not to list. You will not need to list your clothing and other personal effects. Pots, pans, dishes, and cooking utensils ordinarily do not need to be listed, unless they have an unusually high value.

Division of property. Once you have completed your list, go back through it and try to determine who should end up with each item. The ideal situation is for both you and your spouse to go through the list together, and divide things fairly. However, if this is not possible, you will need to offer a reasonable settlement to the judge. Consider each item, and make a check-mark in either column (8) or (9) to designate whether that item should go to the husband or wife.

You may make the following assumptions:

- ☞ Your separate property will go to you.

- ☞ Your spouse's separate property will go to your spouse.

- ☞ You should get the items that only you use.

- ☞ Your spouse should get the items only used by your spouse.

- ☞ The remaining items should be divided, evening out the total value of all the marital property, and taking into consideration who would really want that item.

To somewhat equally divide your property (we're only talking about marital property, not separate property), you first need to know the total value of your property. First of all, do not count the value of the separate property items. Add the remaining amounts in the "Equity" column of Form 1, which will give you an approximate value of all marital property.

When it comes time for the hearing, you and your spouse may be arguing over some or all of the items on your list. This is when you'll be glad that you made copies of the documents relating to the property on your list. Arguments over the value of property may need to be resolved by hiring appraisers to set a value; however, you'll have to pay the appraiser a fee. Dividing your property will be discussed further in later chapters.

DEBTS   This section relates to the Debt Inventory (Form 2), that will list your debts. Although there are cases where, for example, the wife gets a car but the husband is ordered to make the payments, generally whoever gets the property also gets the debt owed on that property. This seems to be a fair arrangement in most cases. On Form 2 you will list each debt owed by you or your spouse. As with separate property, there is also separate debt. This is any debt incurred before you were married, that is yours alone. Form 2 contains a column for "S" debts, which should be checked for each separate debt. Generally, you will be responsible for your separate debts, and your spouse will be responsible for his or hers.

To complete the Debt Inventory (Form 2), list each debt as follows:

Column (1): Check if this is a separate debt. (Separate debts would be those related to separate property, or those which for any other reason you believe should not be considered as your joint responsibility. Keep in mind that you may need to convince the judge why these debts should be considered separate.)

Column (2): Write in the name and address of the creditor (the bank, company, or person to which the debt is owed).

Column (3): Write in the account, loan or mortgage number.

Column (4): Write in any notes to help identify the purpose of the loan (such as "Christmas gifts," "Vacation," etc.).

Column (5): Write in the amount of the monthly payment.

Column (6): Write in the balance still owed on the loan.

Column (7): Write in the date (approximately) when the loan was made.

Column (8): Note whether the account is in the husband's name (H), the wife's name (W), or jointly in both names (J).

Columns (9) & (10): These columns note who will be responsible for the debt after the divorce. As with your property, each of you will keep your separate debts, and the remainder should be divided taking into consideration who will keep the property the loan was for and equally dividing the debt. (See chapter 9 for information on dividing debts in contested cases.)

CHILD CUSTODY AND VISITATION

As with everything else in divorce, things are ideal when both parties can agree on the question of custody of the children. Generally the judge will accept any agreement you reach, provided it doesn't appear that your agreement will cause harm to your children.

If you and your spouse cannot agree on how these matters will be handled, you will be leaving this important decision to a total stranger: the judge. The judge cannot possibly know your child as well as you and your spouse, so doesn't it make sense for you to work this out yourselves?

CUSTODY
FACTORS

If the judge must decide the question, he will consider the following factors [see M.S.A. §25.312(2); M.C.L.A. §722.23]:

1. the love, affection, and other emotional ties existing between the parties involved and the child;

2. the capacity and disposition of the parties involved to give the child love, affection, and guidance, and to continue the education and raising of the child in his or her religion or creed, if any;

3. the capacity and disposition of the parties involved to provide the child with food, clothing, medical care or other remedial care recognized and permitted under the laws of Michigan in place of medical care, and other material needs;

4. the length of time the child has lived in a stable, satisfactory environment, and the desirability of maintaining continuity.

5. the permanence, as a family unit, of the existing or proposed custodial home or homes;

6. the moral fitness of the parties involved;

7. the mental and physical health of the parties involved;

8. the home, school, and community record of the child;

9. the reasonable preferences of the child, if the court considers the child to be of sufficient age to express a preference;

10. the willingness and ability of each of the parties to facilitate and encourage a close and continuing parent-child relationship between the child and the other parent or the child and the parents;

11. any domestic violence, regardless of whether the violence was directed against or witnessed by the child; and

12. any other factor considered by the court to be relevant to a particular child custody dispute.

JOINT CUSTODY

Michigan law also provides for the possibility of joint custody, and requires that you be advised of this possibility. In Michigan, joint custody means that the child will live with each parent for specified periods of time, and that the parents "share decision-making authority as to the important decisions affecting the welfare of the child." While joint custody is a great idea in its concept, it is usually not a very practical one. Very few parents can put aside their anger at each other to agree on what is best for their child. Joint custody merely leads to more fighting. Also, joint custody does not eliminate child support. [For the full text of the joint custody statute, see MSA §25.312(6a); MCLA §722.26a, in appendix A.]

CUSTODY DISPUTES

It is difficult to predict the outcome of a custody battle. There are too many factors and individual circumstances to make such a guess. The only exception is where one parent is clearly unfit and the other can prove it. Drug abuse is probably the most common charge against a spouse, but unless there has been an arrest and conviction it is difficult to prove to a judge. Don't charge your spouse with being unfit unless you can prove it. Judges are not impressed with unfounded allegations, and they can do more harm than good.

ALLOWING YOUR CHILD TO DECIDE

If your children are older (not infants), it may be a good idea to seriously consider their preference for with whom they would like to live. Your "fairness" and respect for their wishes may benefit you in the long run. Just be sure that you keep in close contact with them and visit them often.

CHILD SUPPORT

Once again, the judge will probably go along with any agreement you and your spouse reach, as long as he or she is satisfied that the child will receive adequate care. The following information and the four Child Support Recommendation Worksheets (Forms 3 through 6), will help you get an idea of the proper amount of child support. At this point you are only trying to get a rough idea of the amount of child support to expect. The Friend of the Court will eventually complete these forms and make an official recommendation of the child support amount. For more information, see the Child Support Guidelines in appendix B of this book.

HOW CHILD SUPPORT IS DETERMINED

Generally there are two factors used to determine the proper amount of support to be paid: (1) the needs of the child, and (2) the financial ability of each parent to meet those needs. Michigan has simplified this procedure by establishing a formula to be used in calculating both the needs of the child and each parent's ability to meet those needs. In filling out Forms 3 through 6 be sure to convert everything to weekly amounts. The following steps are used in determining the proper amount of support to be paid by the noncustodial parent:

1. You and your spouse each provide proof of your gross income.

2. Taxes and other deductions are allowed to determine each of your net incomes.

4. Your net incomes and the number of children you have are used to establish the children's needs. (This is done by using a table or chart.)

5. The net income of the parent without custody is divided by the combined income. This gives that parent's percentage of the combined income.

6. That percentage is multiplied by the needs of the children, to arrive at the amount of support to be paid by the parent without custody.

This procedure can be used by most people. However, if you or your spouse's net income is less than $100 per week, support will be set as follows: If the noncustodial parent's net income is $100 per week or less, support will be set at 10% of the noncustodial parent's weekly net income (regardless of how many children there are), reduced by 1% for each $100 earned by the custodial parent. Also, the judge may depart from the guidelines by up to five percent. These guidelines will be discussed more below, and in appendix B of this book.

INCOME
DETERMINATION

Gross income. The first thing you will need to do is determine your gross income. This is basically your income before any deductions for taxes, social security, etc. The categories listed below are found in the Child Support Recommendation-Worksheet A (Form 3). The following sources are considered part of gross income:

☛ salary or wages, including shift premiums and COLA.

☛ overtime.

☛ income from a second job.

☛ commissions.

☛ bonuses and profit sharing.

☛ interest and dividends.

☛ annuity and trust fund payments.

☛ pensions and longevity pay.

☛ deferred compensation and IRA payments.

☛ unemployment compensation.

☛ strike pay and Supplemental Unemployment Benefits (SUB pay).

☞ sick pay or disability benefits.

☞ worker's compensation.

☞ social security benefits.

☞ Veterans Administration benefits.

☞ G.I. benefits (excluding education allotment).

☞ armed service pay (base pay plus allowance for quarters, rations, and specialty pay); National Guard and Reserves Drill pay.

☞ rent allowance, if provided by employer as a fringe benefit; and rental income (gross receipts, minus ordinary and necessary expenses—but not depreciation).

☞ alimony or spousal support received.

On Form 3, you will find a category for "Other." This would include such things as:

☞ Business income from self-employment, partnerships, corporations, and independent contracts (gross receipts, minus ordinary and necessary expenses).

☞ Income from royalties, trusts, or estates.

☞ Reimbursed expenses to the extent they reduce living expenses (such as a rent allowance, or the value of an apartment provided by your employer).

☞ Gains derived from dealings in property, unless the gain is non-recurring.

☞ Dividends from life insurance policies.

☞ Net gambling winnings.

☞ Tax-exempt income, such as interest and dividends on municipal bonds or other government securities.

☞ Insurance or similar payments as compensation for lost earnings (but not for medical bills or property loss or damage).

☞ Adoption subsidy (standard/basic needs portion for child in a case under consideration).

Various types of *means tested* benefits, such as aid to families with dependent children (AFDC), general assistance (GA), and Supplemental Security Income (SSI) are not included as income. Fill in the amounts for yourself and your spouse on lines 1 through 20 on Form 3. Write in the totals on line 21. If any items are not subject to tax, deduct them and fill in the taxable gross income on Line 22.

If you voluntarily reduce your income or quit your job, the judge can refuse to recognize the reduction or loss of income. This is *imputed income*. The only exception is where you are required to take such an action to stay home and care for your child. If this question comes up, the judge will decide whether you need to stay home, so be ready to explain your reasons. Where the Friend of the Court determines that there is imputed income, it will make two recommendations to the court: one with the imputed income, and one without. You can then argue to the judge which recommendation should be followed.

The court can also consider *expected income* from non-income or low-income producing assets. The basis for this is that one should not be allowed to obtain a low support amount while having substantial assets that could be used to generate more income. This will involve taking the value of the asset and figuring income at rates which would be available if the asset were sold and the money placed in a passbook savings account, treasury bills and bonds, certificates of deposit, etc.

If your children receive benefits from social security retirement, survivor's, or disability insurance programs, it is not considered income to the custodial parent if it is based on the noncustodial parent's earning record. In this case, determine child support according to the regular schedule, then reduce that amount by the amount of benefits received by the child. If benefits are not based on the noncustodial parent's earning record, it is income to the custodial parent.

Net income. Net income is determined by subtracting certain deductions from your gross income. The following deductions are allowed:

- federal, state and local income taxes (after alimony). (The amount of each deduction will be determined by the filing status and number of dependents allowable on your tax return.)

- Social Security (FICA), or self-employment taxes (before alimony).

- alimony or spousal support payments.

- mandatory withholdings (such as union dues where you must pay dues to keep your job, or where you must contribute to a retirement plan to keep your job).

- court-ordered health insurance payments, but only the portion for coverage of your minor child.

- term life insurance premiums for your minor child, or the term value of a whole life policy.

- employer contributions to private qualified pension plans, to the extent they are less than 5.5% of gross income.

Fill in the allowable deductions for yourself and your spouse on lines 23 through 29 on Form 3, then total the deductions and write the answers on line 30. Now subtract the total deductions (line 30) from the gross income (line 21), and write the answers on line 31.

Other adjustments may also be made if you have pre-existing support orders or if there are other minor children living in your household. If any of these situations apply to you or your spouse, you will need to complete the Child Support Recommendation-Worksheet B (Form 4). See the Child Support Guidelines in appendix B for more details about these adjustments, then fill in the required information on Form 4. Any adjustments as a result of completing Form 4 are filled in on Line 32 of Form 3.

Combined Income. Combined income is simply your net income added to your spouse's net income. Add your net income and your spouse's net income from Form 3, Line 31 (or Line 32 if either of you had adjustments from Form 4), and write the answer on Line 33 of Form 3. This is your combined income. For example: Your net income is $300 per week. Your spouse's net income is $450 per week. Your combined income is $750 (300 + 450).

CALCULATING
CHILD SUPPORT

Next, divide your net income from Form 3, Line 31 or 32, by the combined income from Line 33. Fill in the answer on Line 34. This is your percentage of the combined income. Then, divide your spouse's net income, by the combined income, which will give your spouse's percentage of the combined income. Fill in the answer on Line 35. If the children are receiving any Social Security benefits, fill in the amount on Line 36.

Again using our example: We've established that you and your spouse have a combined income of $750 per week. To get your share, divide your net income by the combined income ($300 divided by $750). The answer is .4 or 40%. The figure "40" would go on Line 34. Next divide your spouse's net income by the combined income ($450 divided by $750). The answer is .6 or 60%. The figure "60" would go on Line 35.

Now we will determine the needs of your children. Turn to page 187, which is part of the Child Support Guidelines in appendix B of this book. You will see the heading "Calculating Child Support Using Table III." Below this you will see "Table III." For our example, let's suppose you and your spouse have two children. You would find the table for "Two Children." Read down the left column until you come to your combined income amount. In this case, you would use $727 because your combined income is less than the next higher figure on the table. Reading across the table to the column titled "Percentage Allocated," you will see that the percentage of combined income allowed for two children at your income level is 30.2%. Reading on across to the third column, you will see that the children's needs are "$219.55 + 21.74% over $727." This means that you must take $219.55, and add 21.74% of your combined income over $727. Take the combined income ($750) and subtract $727 from it, which will give you $23. Next, multiply $23 by .2174 (21.74%), which will give you $5.00. Add the $5.00 to $219.55 to get the total needs of the children ($224.55 per week).

Your share of this support obligation would be 40% or $89.82 ($224.55 x .4). Your spouse's share would be 60% or $134.73 ($224.55 x .6). Therefore, if you have custody of the two children, your spouse would pay $134.73 per week. If your spouse had custody, you would pay $89.82 per week.

This works fine, except when parents have split custody (each parent has custody of one child), or joint physical custody (the children move back and forth between the parents). If either of these situations apply to you, read the Child Support Guidelines in appendix B, then follow the instructions and fill in the required information on the Child Support Recommendation-Worksheet C (Form 5). This will give you the adjusted child support amount.

The Child Support Recommendation-Worksheet D (Form 6) adjusts for child care expenses, by apportioning them between the parties according to the percentages of combined income from Form 3.

Remember, you are only using Forms 3 through 6 to get an idea of what amount of child support will be ordered. You will not file these forms with the court. Eventually the Friend of the Court will collect your (and your spouse's) financial information and will fill out these forms as part of its recommendation to the court. (You should be aware that there is also a Child Support Recommendation-Worksheet E, which is used for imputed or expected income, but this is not used in most cases.)

Spousal Support (Alimony)

Spousal support (the Michigan term for *alimony*) may be granted to either the husband or the wife, but there are few cases where a wife will be ordered to pay alimony. There are two types of spousal support:

- *rehabilitative*. This is for a limited period of time, and is to enable one of the spouses to get the education or training necessary to find a job. This is usually awarded where one of the parties has not been working during the marriage.

- *permanent*. This continues for a long period of time, possibly until the death of the party receiving the alimony. This is typically awarded where one of the parties is unable to work due to age, or a physical or mental illness.

The only specific statement in the Michigan statutes as to when alimony may be awarded refers to cases where "the estate and effects awarded…are insufficient for the suitable support and maintenance of either party and any children of the marriage as are committed to the care and custody of either party." The type and amount of alimony will be determined "as the court considers just and reasonable, after considering the ability of either to pay and the character and situation of the parties, and all other circumstances of the case."

As an alternative to alimony, you may want to try to negotiate to receive a greater percentage of the property instead. This may be less of a hassle in the long run, but beware, it may change the tax consequences of your divorce. (See the section on "Taxes" in chapter 12.)

Which Procedure to Use

There is technically only one divorce procedure in Michigan, however, we will discuss divorce as if there are three types of divorce procedures.

These are really divorces under different situations, with each situation calling for a different approach. These situations are:

1. Consent divorce

2. Uncontested divorce

3. Contested divorce

> ***Caution:*** Before you can use any procedure, you or your spouse must have lived in Michigan for at least 180 days, and in the county where you file for at least ten days. (The one exception to this is if your spouse was born in, or is a citizen of, a foreign country, and you can convince the judge that your child is at risk of being taken out of the United States and kept in another country by your spouse.)

Chapter 7 of this book describes the consent divorce, chapter 8 describes the uncontested divorce, and chapter 9 describes the contested divorce. You should read this entire book once before you begin filling out any court forms.

CONSENT DIVORCE

A *consent* divorce is where you and your spouse agree on everything. To be eligible for the consent procedure you and your spouse will need to be in total agreement on the following six matters:

1. That you want a divorce.

2. Whether any alimony will be paid, and if so, how much.

3. How your property and debts will be divided.

4. Who will have primary custody of your children (if any).

5. How much child support will be paid by the spouse without primary custody.

6. That you both are willing to sign an agreement about these matters, and any other papers required to get a divorce in the easiest and simplest manner.

If you are in agreement on all six of these matters, you may use the procedure outlined in chapter 6.

UNCONTESTED DIVORCE

If you can't qualify for the consent divorce procedure (because your spouse won't cooperate on one or more of the six matters listed above), you will have to use the uncontested procedure or the contested procedure. The uncontested procedure is mainly designed for the following circumstances:

1. When your spouse does not respond to your petition, but isn't really putting up a fight.

2. When your spouse cannot be located.

To use the uncontested procedure, you will need to read both chapter 6 and chapter 7.

CONTESTED DIVORCE

The contested procedure will be necessary where you and your spouse are arguing over some matter, and can't resolve it. This may be the result of disagreement over custody of the children, the payment of child support or alimony, the division of your property, or any combination of these items. The chapter of this book dealing with the contested divorce builds on the consent and uncontested procedure chapters. So, first you will need to read chapter 6 and chapter 7 to get a basic understanding of the forms and procedures, then read chapter 8 for additional instructions on handling the contested situation. Be sure to read through all three chapters before you start filling out any forms.

If your case becomes contested, it is also time to seriously consider getting a lawyer. If you don't think you can afford a lawyer, you may be able to require your spouse to pay for your lawyer. Find a lawyer who will give you a free, or inexpensive (i.e., about $20) initial consultation. He or she will explain your options regarding the lawyer's fees. (See chapter 3 for more information about lawyers.)

GENERAL PROCEDURES 5

This chapter includes general information that will be of use to you regardless of the divorce procedure you use. Some of the information presented here will not be used until you have selected the procedures you will use and are preparing your forms. This is done to avoid unnecessarily repeating information. For example, in all cases you will need to file forms with the court clerk, and use certain forms to notify your spouse. Rather than repeat this information in the following chapter, you will simply be referred back to the appropriate section of this chapter.

AN INTRODUCTION TO LEGAL FORMS

Many of the forms in this book follow forms created by the State Court Administrative Office (SCAO). An advantage to having such standard forms is that court clerks and judges will accept them. However, these "official" forms are changed frequently, with some forms being eliminated entirely. If you need additional forms, or want to be sure you have the most recent forms, look for a book entitled *SCAO Approved Forms*, which should be found at law libraries (and possibly at your public library). The librarian can help you find the most recent updates.

The forms in appendix C of this book are legally correct, however, you may encounter a clerk or judge who is very particular about how he or she wants the forms. If you have any problem with the forms being accepted, you can try one or more of the following:

☞ Ask the clerk or judge what is wrong with your form, then try to change it to suit the clerk or judge.

☞ Ask the clerk or judge if there is either a local form or an "SCAO form" available. If there is, find out where you can get it, and use it. The instructions in this book will still help you.

☞ Consult a lawyer.

Do not tear the forms out of this book to file with the court. It is best to make photocopies of the forms, and keep the originals blank to use in case you make mistakes.

Although the instructions in this book will tell you to "type in" certain information, it is not absolutely necessary to use a typewriter. If typing is not possible, you can print the information required in the forms. Just be sure your handwriting can be easily read, or the clerk may not accept your papers for filing.

Each form is referred to by both the title of the form and a form number. Be sure to check the form number because some of the forms have similar titles. The form number is found in the top outside corner of the first page of each form. Also, a list of the forms, by both number and name, is found at the beginning of appendix C. (Do not confuse our form numbers with the numbers that appear at the bottom of some of the forms, which are numbers assigned by the court, such as CC-375, MC-07, FOC-50, etc.)

You will notice that many of the forms in appendix C of this book have similar headings. The top portion of these court forms will all be completed in the same manner. This portion of a court form is sometimes referred to as the *caption* or the *case style*, and contains three basic elements: the identity of the court (by judicial circuit number and county), the names of the parties, and the case number. The very top of the form tells in which court your case is filed. You will need to type in the number of the judicial circuit and the county in which the court is located. You can either look in the phone book, or call the court clerk's office to find out your court's circuit number.

For the names of the parties, you need to type your full name, and your spouse's full name on the appropriate lines or in the appropriate boxes. Do not use nicknames or shortened versions of names. You should use the names as they appear on your marriage license, if possible. You won't be able to type in a case number until after you file your Complaint for Divorce with the court clerk. The clerk will assign a case number and will write it on your petition and any other papers you file with it. You must type in the case number on all papers you file later.

Prior to the SCAO forms, cases styles looked like the following example:

STATE OF MICHIGAN

_____SIXTEENTH_____JUDICIAL CIRCUIT,_____MACOMB_____COUNTY

RHETT BUTLER_____,
                   Plaintiff,

    vs.   Case No._____97-1868_____

SCARLETT O'HARA BUTLER_____,
                   Defendant.

The newer SCAO forms also contain the basic case style information, but it is arranged in a different format. Although most of the forms in appendix C use the newer SCAO format, a few use the traditional style. The SCAO forms may require additional information, such as the parties' addresses, telephone numbers, social security numbers, etc., but this will be indicated on the form. At the top of the following page is an example of the SCAO case style format:

	Original - Court	2nd copy - Plaintiff
	1st copy - Friend of the Court	3rd copy - Return

STATE OF MICHIGAN	JUDGMENT OF DIVORCE	CASE NO.
16TH **JUDICIAL CIRCUIT** MACOMB **COUNTY**	Page 1 of 2 pages	97-1868

Court address	Court telephone no.
40 N. Main Street, Mt. Clemens, MI 48043	(810) 555-5555

Plaintiff		Defendant
RHETT BUTLER	V	SCARLETT O'HARA BUTLER

FILING WITH THE COURT CLERK

Once you have decided which forms you need, and have them all prepared, it is time to file your case with the court clerk. The instructions for particular forms will tell you how many copies you will need. You will usually need at least the original to leave with the clerk, a copy for yourself, a copy for your spouse, and a copy for the Friend of the Court. It is probably a good idea to make an extra copy just in case the clerk asks for more copies or you decide to hire an attorney later.

Filing is actually about as simple as making a bank deposit, although the following information will help things go smoothly. Call the court clerk's office. You can find the phone number under the county government section of your phone directory. Ask the clerk the following questions (along with any other questions that come to mind, such as where the clerk's office is located and what hours they are open if you don't already know):

☛ How much is the filing fee for a divorce?

☛ Does the court have any special forms that need to be filed with the Complaint for Divorce? If there are such special forms which do not appear in this book you will need to go to the law library or clerk's office to get them.

☛ How many copies of the Complaint for Divorce and other forms do you need to file with the clerk?

Next, take your Complaint for Divorce, and any other forms you determine you need, to the clerk's office. The clerk handles many different types of cases, so be sure to look for signs telling you which office or window to go. You should be looking for signs that say such things as "Family Court," "Family Division," "Filing," etc. If it's too confusing, ask someone where you file a Complaint for Divorce.

Once you've found the right place, simply hand the papers to the clerk and say, "I'd like to file this." The clerk will examine the papers, then do one of two things: either accept it for filing (and either collect the filing fee or direct you to where to pay it), or tell you that something is not correct. If you're told something is wrong, ask the clerk to explain to you what is wrong and how to correct the problem.

Although clerks are not permitted to give legal advice, the types of problems they spot are usually minor things that they can tell you how to correct. Often it is possible to figure out how to correct it from the way they explain what is wrong.

Any papers you need to file after filing your Complaint for Divorce will be filed in the same manner, except you won't need to pay a filing fee.

Notifying Your Spouse

If you are using the consent divorce procedure you do not need to worry about the information in this section. In a consent divorce your spouse will sign either an Answer and Waiver (Form 13) or a Marital Settlement Agreement (Form 10), so it will be obvious that he or she knows about the divorce. However, in all other cases, you are required to notify your spouse that you have filed for divorce. This gives your spouse a chance to respond to your Complaint for Divorce. If you are unable to find your spouse, you will also need to read chapter 10.

SUMMONS   The usual way to notify your spouse that you filed for a divorce is called *personal service*, which is where the sheriff, or someone else designated by the judge, personally delivers the papers to your spouse.

Call the county sheriff's office in the county where your spouse lives, and ask how much it will cost to have your spouse served with divorce papers. Deliver or mail one copy of your Complaint for Divorce (Form 8) (together with any affidavits you filed), two copies of the Summons (Form 7), and a check or money order for the service fee, to the sheriff's office. To complete the Summons (Form 7), see the instructions for the Summons in chapter 7.

The Complaint for Divorce (Form 8) should be stapled to the Summons (Form 7). You will note that Form 7 is actually titled "Summons and Complaint." This follows the SCAO form, which includes a blank page for a complaint of any type to be prepared from scratch. This would be of little use to you in preparing a divorce complaint, so appendix C contains a Complaint for Divorce as a separate form which needs to be attached to the Summons (Form 7). Also, if you use the consent procedure outlined in chapter 6, you will not need the Summons and will need the Complaint for Divorce as a separate document.

A sheriff's deputy will personally deliver the papers to your spouse. Of course, you must give the sheriff accurate information about where your spouse can be found. If there are several addresses where your spouse might be found (such as home, a relative's, and work), enclose a letter to the sheriff with all of the addresses and any other information which may help the sheriff find your spouse (such as the hours your spouse works).

If you expect your spouse to attempt to avoid service, you may also want to provide the sheriff with a description or photograph. The deputy will fill out the second page of the Summons to verify that the papers were delivered (including the date and time they were delivered), and will file a copy with the court clerk.

PROOF OF
MAILING

Once your spouse has been served with the Summons and Complaint for Divorce, you may simply mail him or her copies of any papers you file later (with the exception of certain temporary orders and restraining orders which are issued without the usual hearing and advance notice to your spouse, and which will be discussed in more detail in later chapters of this book). All you need to do is sign a statement (called a *Proof of Mailing*) that you mailed copies to your spouse. Some of the forms in this book have a section titled "Certificate of Service," which has the same function as the Proof of Mailing. If any form you file does not contain a certificate of service section, you will need to complete the Proof of Mailing (Form 17). To complete Form 17:

1. Complete the top portion according to the instructions in the first section of this chapter.

2. Type your name in the box for "Plaintiff(s)" and your spouse's name in the box for "Defendant(s)."

3. Type in the name or title of the papers being sent on the lines after the phrase: "On the date below I sent by first class mail a copy of."

4. After the words "to: Names and addresses," type the name and address of your spouse or his or her attorney. If copies are being sent to anyone else, such as the Friend of the Court, also type in those names and addresses.

5. At the bottom of the forms, type in the date the papers are being sent, sign your name on the signature line, and type your name on the line below the signature line. Be sure you mail the papers on the date indicated, and file Form 17 with the court clerk.

NOTICE OF
HEARING

Once you get a hearing date set, you will need to notify your spouse of when the hearing will be. This is done by preparing a Notice of Hearing (Form 16). To complete the Notice of Hearing (Form 16):

1. Complete the top portion of the form according to the instructions in the first section of this chapter.

65

2. After the word "To," type in your spouse's name and address. If your spouse is represented in the divorce case by a lawyer, type in the lawyer's name and address instead.

3. Fill in the day of the week (e.g., Monday, Tuesday, etc.), the date, and time of the hearing on the lines provided. Also type in the judge's name, and the address of where the hearing will be held, including where in the building (this will typically be a room number, courtroom number, or a phrase such as "in his courtroom," or "in his chambers").

4. Fill in the date, sign your name, and type in your name, address, and telephone number on the lines provided. Then, mail this form to your spouse (or his or her lawyer) about one or two weeks before the hearing. Also, file a copy of the Notice of Hearing with the clerk, along with a Proof of Mailing (Form 17).

THE FRIEND OF THE COURT

If you have children, or you and your spouse have disputes over property division or alimony, you will have contact with the Friend of the Court. This will consist of meeting with an employee of the Friend of the Court, providing him or her with the information requested, and filling out forms. It may also involve a hearing before a Friend of the Court referee, which will be similar to a hearing before a judge. After the information is reviewed, the Friend of the Court will issue a written recommendation to the judge, and a copy will be sent to you.

FRIEND OF THE COURT CASE QUESTIONNAIRE

One form you will need to fill out is the Friend of the Court Case Questionnaire (Form 9). This is a four-page form that provides basic information about you, your spouse, and your children. The information required by the form is self-explanatory. The office of the Friend of the Court may require you to use their form, in which case you can use Form 9 in appendix C as a worksheet so that you have all of the necessary information when you visit the Friend of the Court.

OBJECTION TO
REFEREE'S
RECOMMENDED
ORDER

If you disagree with the referee's recommendation, you may file an Objection to Referee's Recommended Order (Form 39). To complete Form 39:

1. Fill in the top portion according to the instructions in the first part of this chapter.

2. Type in "Plaintiff" or "Defendant," whichever applies to you, on the first line in the first paragraph, and type in the date of the recommendation on the second line.

3. After the first paragraph, type in a brief explanation of why you think the recommendation is wrong.

4. After the word "Wherefore," type in "Plaintiff" or "Defendant," whichever applies to you.

5. Fill in the date and your name, address, and phone number on the lines indicated, and sign your name on the signature line.

File this form with the clerk. Also send or deliver a copy to the Friend of the Court, and to your spouse. The judge will decide whether to follow the recommendation or conduct an independent hearing.

SETTING A COURT HEARING

You will need to schedule a hearing for the final judgment, or for any preliminary matters which require a hearing (these will be discussed later in this book). The court clerk may be able to give you a date, but you will probably have to get a date from the Friend of the Court, or the judge's secretary. (If you don't know which judge, call the court clerk, give the clerk your case number, and ask for the name and phone number of the judge assigned to your case.) You can then call or go see that judge's secretary to set a date for the final hearing (or for whatever other matter needs a hearing). Usually the judge's phone number can be found in the government section of your phone book.

The secretary may ask you how long the hearing will take. If you and your spouse have agreed on everything, tell the secretary it is an uncontested divorce and ask for ten minutes (unless she advises you differently). If you have a contested divorce, it could take anywhere from thirty minutes to several days, depending upon such things as what matters you disagree about and how many witnesses will testify. One general rule of thumb is that the more time you need for a hearing, the longer it will take to get the hearing. Also, it is better to over-estimate the time required, rather than not schedule enough time and have to continue the hearing for several weeks. Judges do not go over the time scheduled. The secretary will then give you a date and time for the hearing, but you will also need to know where the hearing will be. Ask the secretary for the location. You'll need the street address of the courthouse, as well as the room number, floor, or other location within the building.

Courtroom Manners

There are certain rules of procedure that are used in a court. These are really rules of good conduct, or good manners, and are designed to keep things orderly. Many of the rules are written down, although some are unwritten customs that have just developed over many years. They aren't difficult, and most of them do make sense. Following these suggestions will make the judge respect you for your maturity and professional manner, and possibly even make him forget for a moment that you are not a lawyer. It will also increase the likelihood that you will get the things you request.

SHOW RESPECT FOR THE JUDGE | Showing respect for the judge basically means, don't do anything to make the judge angry at you, such as arguing with him. Be polite, and call the judge "Your Honor" when you speak to him, such as "Yes, Your Honor," or "Your Honor, I brought proof of my income." Although many lawyers address judges as "Judge," this is not proper. Many of the following rules also relate to showing respect for the court. This also means wearing appropriate clothing, such as a coat and tie for men and a dress for women. This especially means no T-shirts, blue jeans, shorts, or "revealing" clothing.

WHEN THE JUDGE TALKS; YOU LISTEN

Whenever the judge talks, you listen. Even if the judge interrupts you, stop talking immediately and listen. And don't ever interrupt the judge when he or she is talking. If you have something to say, wait until the judge is finished, then ask "Your honor, may I respond?" This is all part of showing respect for the judge.

ONLY ONE PERSON CAN TALK AT A TIME

Each person is allotted his or her own time to talk in court. The judge can only listen to one person at a time, so don't interrupt your spouse when it's his or her turn. As difficult as it may be, stop talking if your spouse interrupts you. (Let the judge tell your spouse to keep quiet and let you have your say.)

TALK TO THE JUDGE; NOT TO YOUR SPOUSE

Many people get in front of a judge and begin arguing with each other. They actually turn away from the judge, face each other, and begin arguing as if they are in the room alone. This generally has several negative results: The judge can't understand what either one is saying since they both start talking at once, they both look like fools for losing control, and the judge gets angry with both of them. So whenever you speak in a courtroom, look only at the judge. Try to pretend that your spouse isn't there. Remember, you are there to convince the judge that you should have certain things. You don't need to convince your spouse.

TALK ONLY WHEN IT'S YOUR TURN

The usual procedure is for you to present your case first. When you are done saying all you came to say, your spouse will have a chance to say whatever he or she came to say. Let your spouse have his or her say. When he or she is finished you will get another chance to respond to what has been said.

STICK TO THE SUBJECT

Many people can't resist the temptation to get off the track and start telling the judge all the problems with their marriage over the past twenty years. This just wastes time, and aggravates the judge. So stick to the subject, and answer the judge's questions simply and to the point.

KEEP CALM

Judges like things to go smoothly in their courtrooms. They don't like shouting, name calling, crying, or other displays of emotion. Generally, judges don't like family law cases because they get too emotionally charged. So give your judge a pleasant surprise by keeping calm and focusing on the issues.

SHOW RESPECT
FOR YOUR
SPOUSE

Even if you don't respect your spouse, act like you do. All you have to do is refer to your spouse as "Mr. Smith" or "Ms. Smith" (using his or her correct name, of course).

NEGOTIATING

It is beyond the scope of this book to present a comprehensive course in negotiation techniques, however, a few basic rules may be of help.

ASK FOR MORE
THAN YOU
WANT

Asking for more than you want always gives you some room to compromise by giving up a few things, and end up with close to what you really want. With property division, this means you will review your Property Inventory (Form 1), and decide which items you really want, would like to have, and don't care much about. Also try to figure out which items your spouse really wants, would like to have, and doesn't care much about. At the beginning you will say that you want certain things. Your list will include: (1) Everything you really want, (2) everything you'd like to have, (3) some of the things you don't care about, and (4) some of the things you think your spouse really wants or would like to have. Once you find out what is on your spouse's list, you begin trading items. Generally you try to give your spouse things that he really wants and that you don't care about, in return for your spouse giving you the items you really care about and would like to have.

Child custody tends to be an issue that can't be negotiated. It is often used as a threat by one of the parties in order to get something else, such as more of the property, or lower child support. If the real issue is one of these other matters, don't be concerned by a threat of a custody fight. In these cases the other party probably doesn't really want custody, and won't fight for it. If the real issue is custody, you won't be able to negotiate for it and will end up letting the judge decide anyway.

If you will be receiving child support, first figure out what you think the judge will order based on the child support guidelines discussed in chapter 4. Then, ask for more and negotiate down to the guidelines. If your spouse won't settle for something very close to the guidelines, give up trying to work it out and let the judge decide.

LET YOUR
SPOUSE START
THE BIDDING

A general rule of negotiating is: the first person to mention a dollar figure loses. Whether it's a child support figure or the value of a piece of property, try to get your spouse to name the amount he or she thinks it should be first. If your spouse starts with a figure almost to what you had in mind, it will be much easier to get to your figure. If your spouse begins with a figure far from yours, you know how far in the other direction to begin your bid.

GIVE YOUR
SPOUSE TIME TO
THINK AND
WORRY

Your spouse is probably just as afraid as you about the possibility of losing to the judge's decision, and would like to settle. Don't be afraid to state your "final offer," then walk away. Give your spouse a day or two to think it over. Maybe he or she will call back and make a better offer. If not, you can always "reconsider" and make a different offer in a few days, but don't be too willing to do this or your spouse may think you will give in even more.

KNOW YOUR
BOTTOM LINE

Before you begin negotiating, set a point that you will not go beyond. If you have decided that there are four items of property that you absolutely must have, and your spouse is only willing to agree to let you have three, it's time to end the bargaining session and go home.

REMEMBER
WHAT YOU'VE
LEARNED

By the time you've read this far you should be aware of two things:

1. The judge will roughly divide your property equally.

2. The judge will use the child support guidelines.

This awareness should give you an approximate idea of how things will turn out if the judge is asked to decide these issues, which should help you to set your bottom line on them.

CONSENT DIVORCE 6

IN GENERAL

The procedures described in this chapter may be used in the most simple cases. The following chapters build on this chapter, so be sure to read this chapter entirely even if you need to use one of the other procedures. In order to have a consent divorce, you must meet the following basic requirements:

1. You or your spouse have resided in Michigan for at least the past 180 days, and in the county where the case will be filed for at least ten days.

2. You and your spouse agree that you want a divorce, and are both willing to sign any papers and attend any court hearings necessary to obtain a divorce.

3. You and your spouse agree as to how your property will be divided.

4. You and your spouse agree on the subject of alimony (either that neither of you will pay alimony, or who will pay and how much).

5. If you have a child, you and your spouse agree on who will have custody and how much child support the other will pay.

If you don't meet all five of these conditions, you do not have a consent divorce. However, you should still read this chapter, as it will help you understand divorce procedures better. If your disagreements are not major, you may want to try to work out a compromise. Read this chapter, and have your spouse read it. Then compare the consent divorce procedure to the procedures in chapter 7 and chapter 8 of this book. Once you see how much easier a consent divorce is, you may want to try harder to resolve your differences.

Basically, the procedure is as follows:

1. You and your spouse complete the necessary forms.

2. You file those forms with the court clerk.

3. If you have any children, you and your spouse appear for any necessary meetings with the Friend of the Court, and provide them with any additional required papers and information.

4. You (and your spouse if he or she wants) appear for a brief hearing with the judge.

The forms listed below are discussed in this chapter. There may be other forms needed, but they will be prepared and provided by the Friend of the Court. The following can serve as a checklist of the basic forms you may need for your consent divorce:

❏ Complaint for Divorce (Form 8).

❏ Verified Statement (Form 21).

❏ Marital Settlement Agreement (Form 10).

❏ Uniform Child Custody Jurisdiction Act Affidavit (Form 20).

❏ Answer and Waiver (Form 13).

❏ Judgment of Divorce (Form 11)

❏ Record of Divorce or Annulment (Form 18).

COMPLAINT FOR DIVORCE

The Complaint for Divorce (Form 8) is the paper needed to open your case. The Complaint for Divorce asks the judge to give you a divorce. Currently, there is no SCAO Complaint for Divorce form. To complete the Complaint for Divorce (Form 8):

1. Complete the top portion according to the instructions in chapter 5 for the case style. Leave the file number blank, as the clerk will fill this in when you file.

2. In paragraph 1, check one box for how residency is satisfied, and type in the county where you will file.

3. In paragraphs 2 and 3, type in the information called for about you and your spouse.

4. In paragraph 4, fill in the date and city and state where you were married (or the country if you were not married in the U.S.).

5. In paragraph 6, check the appropriate box or boxes. If you have children, fill in the information for each child.

6. In paragraph 7, check one box.

7. In paragraph 8, check one box. If spousal support (alimony) is to be paid, type in: "Pursuant to the agreement of the parties as set forth in the Marital Settlement Agreement to be filed in this action."

8. In paragraph 9, check the box for "Marital Settlement Agreement."

9. After "Wherefore," check the boxes that apply. If split custody, or anything other than reasonable visitation, is agreed to, type in: "As set forth in the Marital Settlement Agreement to be filed in this action." If you or your spouse's maiden name is to be restored, type in the full name to be restored.

10. Type in the date, and your name, address and telephone number on the lines indicated. Sign your name on the signature line.

VERIFIED STATEMENT

The Verified Statement (Form 21) provides the Friend of the Court with basic information about you and your family. This will be used for obtaining information, and later, to enforce your divorce judgment if necessary. This form will probably be given to you at your first meeting with the Friend of the Court. The form in this book can be used as a worksheet, so that you can have the information ready when you meet with the Friend of the Court.

MARITAL SETTLEMENT AGREEMENT

The Marital Settlement Agreement (Form 10) is the paper in which you and your spouse spell out the details of your agreement. Currently, there is no SCAO form for a Marital Settlement Agreement. In order to have a true consent divorce, you and your spouse should be in agreement about all of the matters covered in this form. For each section there is a box to check, if needed, to indicate that an additional sheet has been attached which spells out the details of your agreement. If you attach any additional sheets, be sure that you clearly indicate on the additional sheet which subject you are covering.

To complete the Marital Settlement Agreement (Form 10):

1. Complete the top portion according to the instructions in chapter 6.

2. In the first, unnumbered paragraph, type in the date, your name, and your spouse's name on the lines provided.

3.   Under the heading "I. Child Custody," you will need to check one of the three boxes. If you check the third box, you will need to fill in the table listing each child's name, date of birth, who will have legal custody, and who will have physical custody. Just above the table you will see a code for the custody columns. If a third party is to have custody, type in that person's name.

4.   Under the heading "II. Child Support," check one of the first two boxes. If you check the second box, you will also need to check a box to show whether the husband or wife will pay support, and fill in the weekly support amount and the date the first payment will be made.

5.   Under the heading "III. Health Care Insurance and Expenses," check the appropriate boxes for your agreement. Be sure to read the definitions of "health care expenses," "health insurance," "health care," and "reasonable and necessary expenses" found in the Judgment of Divorce (Form 11).

6.   Under the heading "IV. Child Visitation," check the appropriate boxes for your agreement. If you check the box for specific visitation, you will type in the details of your visitation agreement.

7.   Under the heading "V. Division of Property and Debts," you will see boxes before the first three paragraphs. Check the box or boxes which applies to your situation. If you check the third box, fill in paragraphs 1 and 2 with descriptions of the items of property that each of you will keep. Refer back to Form 1 to help you make a complete list. Use additional sheets if necessary. Remember to be fairly specific in describing the property so that it is clear as to exactly what property each of you will get. Under the subheading "B. Debts," check one of the boxes. If you check the second box, fill in paragraphs 3 and 4 with descriptions of which debts each of you will be responsible. Use Form 2 to help you. Use additional sheets if needed.

8. Under the heading "VI. Alimony," check the appropriate boxes for your situation, and fill in any necessary dates or amounts on the line provided.

9. Under the heading "VII. Other Provisions," check one of the boxes. Attach the additional sheets with other provisions if you check the second box.

10. You and your spouse each need to date and sign on the lines indicated. Also, type in the name, address, and telephone number for each of you on the lines provided. This form will be filed either with your Complaint for Divorce, or some time before your final hearing.

UNIFORM CHILD CUSTODY JURISDICTION ACT AFFIDAVIT

The Uniform Child Custody Jurisdiction Act Affidavit (Form 20) must be completed if you have minor children. To complete the Uniform Child Custody Jurisdiction Act Affidavit (Form 20):

1. Complete the top portion according to the instructions in chapter 6. "Case name" refers to the names of the parties, such as "John Smith v. Jane Smith."

2. In paragraph 1, type in the name and present address of each of your children.

3. In paragraph 2, type in the addresses where each child has lived during the past five years. If a child is not yet five years old, type in the places the child has lived since birth.

4. In paragraph 3, type in the names and current addresses of persons with whom each child has lived during the past five years. If the child has only lived with you and your spouse, type in: "With the Husband and Wife for past five years at," then type in

the addresses where you have lived during this period. If you have lived in Michigan during this entire time, you can just type in: "With the Husband and Wife for the past five years in the State of Michigan."

5. Paragraph 4 requires you to tell whether you have been involved in any other court cases involving the custody of, or visitation with, your children. Similarly, paragraph 5 requires you to tell if you know of any court case involving custody of, or visitation with, the children (even if you weren't involved in the case). If there are no such cases, you don't need to do anything with paragraphs 4 or 5. If there are such cases, you need to check the appropriate boxes to indicate whether the other case is continuing or has been "stayed" (temporarily stopped) by the other court; and whether you want the judge in your divorce case to take some action to protect the children from abuse or neglect (usually this will not be necessary in a consent or uncontested divorce).

6. You will only complete paragraph 6 if there is any person other than you or your spouse who has custody of a child, or who claims custody or visitation rights.

7. Type in the child's or children's "home state" on the line in paragraph 7. Usually this will be Michigan, but read the definition on the back of the form.

8. Type in your name and address on the appropriate lines at the bottom of the form.

9. Take the form to a notary, and sign it on the "Signature of affiant" line before the notary. This form should then be filed along with your Complaint for Divorce.

ANSWER AND WAIVER

By signing the Answer and Waiver (Form 13), your spouse will let the judge know that he or she has received a copy of the Complaint for Divorce, is in agreement with the case proceeding to judgment, and waives notice of the final hearing and his or her right to be present at the final hearing. If your spouse will sign this form, even in an uncontested case, it may be used instead of having your spouse served with a Summons by the sheriff. If your spouse wants to actively contest the divorce he or she will also file an Answer, but it will be greatly different from Form 13. Currently, there is no SCAO form for an Answer. This form is not absolutely necessary. If your spouse doesn't sign it, then just send him or her a Notice of Hearing (Form 16) once you get a final hearing date set. To complete the Answer and Waiver (Form 13):

1. Complete the top portion according to the instructions in chapter 5.

2. Type in the your spouse's name on the line in the first, unnumbered paragraph.

3. In paragraph 5, type in any additional provisions particular to your situation. It is not necessary to put anything here in a consent divorce.

4. Have your spouse fill in the date on the designated line, and sign on the line marked "Signature of Defendant." Then, either you or your spouse need to type or print your spouse's name, address and telephone number on the lines indicated. This will then be filed with the court clerk.

JUDGMENT OF DIVORCE

The Judgment of Divorce (Form 11) is the paper the judge will sign at the final hearing to formally grant a divorce. Currently, there is no

SCAO form for a Judgment of Divorce, however, Form 11 is based on a former SCAO form.

If you and your spouse have agreed to everything, you can prepare the Judgment of Divorce before the hearing and give it to the judge to sign at the end of the hearing. In a consent divorce you should give your spouse a copy of the completed Judgment of Divorce before the hearing, so that he or she can tell the judge that he or she is aware of what it says, and agrees with it. Form 11 consists of several pages. To help in the explanation, each page will be noted below. To complete the Judgment of Divorce (Form 11) you will need to:

On page 1:

1. Complete the top portion of the form according to the instructions in chapter 5. Notice that just below the heading "Judgment of Divorce" it reads: "Page 1 of   pages." After your judgment is completed and ready for the judge to sign, count up the total number of pages in the Judgment of Divorce. The number of pages should be filled in here. Most will be three pages, so you would complete this to read: "Page 1 of 3 pages." In some cases there may be more pages.

2. Type in the court's address on the next line.

3. Next you will see two large boxes. Type in your name, address, and social security number in the box for the plaintiff, and your spouse's information in the box for the defendant. There is also room for attorneys to be listed in the event either of you have an attorney.

4. Just below these boxes is a line with three small boxes. Check the box for "Consent," to indicate that this is a consent divorce. Just below that, fill in the date of your final hearing and the name of the judge. Don't worry about the judge's "Bar no."

5. In paragraph 2, check the box that applies to your situation. If you have property which has not yet been divided, but is

provided for in your settlement agreement, check the box for "Property is divided elsewhere in this judgment."

6. In paragraph 3, check the box to indicate whether you and your spouse have any minor children.

7. In paragraph 4, if the wife wants her former name restored, type in that full name on the line.

8. In paragraph 5 you will see three columns of boxes. Check the appropriate boxes to indicate what is decided about alimony for each party. For example, if the wife is to receive alimony, you would check the boxes as follows:

☒ not granted ❑ wife ☒ husband

❑ reserved for ❑ wife ❑ husband

☒ granted elsewhere in this judgment for ☒ wife ❑ husband

9. Paragraphs 7 and 8 concern your rights in each other's life insurance, annuities, and pension plans. For each paragraph check a box to indicate whether these rights are extinguished or provided for elsewhere in the judgment. If they are provided for elsewhere they will be discussed later. By checking the box for "extinguished," you are giving up any right to any part of each other's benefits.

10. Paragraph 9 concerns real estate that is still in both of your names as either "joint tenants" or "tenants by the entireties." You need to check one of the two boxes. If title is held in either of these manners and one of you dies, the other would get all of the property. If you check "converted to a tenancy in common," your share of the property would go to your heirs and your spouse's share would go to his or her heirs. If you have any other agreements regarding your real estate you must check the other box. Such other arrangements might be to sell the property and divide the proceeds; one of you buy the other out, either for cash or by giving up some other item or property; or to divide up the

real estate if you have more than one piece of property. Just be sure that property is not left as joint tenancy or tenancy by the entireties, even for a short period of time.

On page 2: (*Note:* If you and your spouse do not have any minor children, you do not need to complete page 2. You can simply eliminate it and go right on to the "Final Page.")

11. On page 2 of Form 10, complete the top portion with the judicial circuit number, name of the county, and case number. Also, you will see that just below the heading "Judgment of Divorce" it reads: "Page 2 of   pages." Fill in the same total number of pages as you did on the first page, such as "Page 2 of 3 pages."

12. Fill in your name and your spouse's name in the two boxes marked "Plaintiff" and "Defendant."

13. In paragraph 12, type in the information required for each minor child.

14. In paragraph 13, check the box for your situation. Be sure to read the definitions regarding custody and visitation on the back of page 2.

15. In paragraph 15, check the first box for payments to begin on a certain date and fill in the date. Check the second box if payments won't begin until the judgment is served on the payer.

16. Paragraph 16 relates to any past due support and service fees pursuant to any temporary orders prior to the judgment. Fill in the information and check the box or boxes as agreed upon or as directed by the judge. If there are no past due amounts, fill in zeros in the blanks.

17. In paragraph 18, check one box for either payment through the Friend of the Court, or directly to the payee. Payment through the Friend of the Court involves service fees of $24.00 per year (paid by the person paying support) and dealing with a

government bureaucracy, but it also offers good accounting for payments. If you are the one to receive support payments, the Friend of the Court also offers good enforcement services if payments are not made.

18. In paragraph 20, check the appropriate box for when income withholding will begin. The box marked "continue" will only be used if there is currently income withholding under a temporary support order.

On the continuation page: You will note that on the back of the "Final page" is a page of definitions. After the definitions page you will find another page, also titled "Judgment of Divorce." This will only be used if there is not enough room on any of the other pages to fit in all of the additional provisions. If you don't need this page, simply leave it out. If you do need to use this page, note that just below the heading "Judgment of Divorce" it reads: "Page   of   pages." Fill in the number of the continuation page and same total number of pages as you did on the first page, such as "Page 3 of 4 pages." Fill in the judicial circuit, county and case number. After the phrase "It Is Further Ordered," type in the additional provisions.

On the final page:

19. Complete the top portion in the same manner as page 2.

20. After the phrase "It Is Further Ordered," check the box if you have a Marital Settlement Agreement. In the space below that you can type in any provisions not covered in other parts of the judgment or in your Marital Settlement Agreement.

21. Just above the signature lines you will see a line of items with three boxes. Check one of the boxes. If you and your spouse are in agreement on everything and have filed a Marital Settlement Agreement, check the box marked "I stipulate to entry." If the judge made a decision at a hearing because your spouse contested the divorce, you will need to check the box marked

"Approved as to form," and have a copy of the judgment sent to your spouse with a request that your spouse sign it (by signing it with this box checked, your spouse is simply agreeing that the judgment accurately states what the judge ordered; it does not mean that he or she agrees with the judge's decision). If your spouse signed an Answer in which he or she waived notice and hearing, check the middle box.

22. Below this are spaces for signature by you, your spouse, and attorneys if either of you have one. There is also the space for the judge to sign and fill in the date of the judgment.

23. The Certificate of Mailing section of this form is to be completed if a copy of the judgment is to be mailed to any of the parties. This would be done either because the judge didn't sign the judgment at the hearing, or because the defendant did not attend the hearing.

Record of Divorce or Annulment

The Record of Divorce or Annulment (Form 18) is an administrative form that the court and state government use to keep track of divorces. You will need to fill one out for the court clerk. The form in this book can be used as a worksheet so that you have the information ready.

Income Withholding

If there is child support or alimony involved, the matter of income withholding will arise. This is where the child support or alimony payments are taken out of your (or your spouse's) paycheck by the employer, and sent to the Friend of the Court. The Friend of the Court then forwards the funds to the party entitled to receive them. The advantage to income withholding is that the person obligated to pay support or alimony has the convenience of the payment being made automatically, and is less likely to be tempted to skip payments and end up before a judge or referee for non-payment. The disadvantages are that it may displease your employer to deal with the administrative hassles of income withholding, and occasionally an employer will deduct the money from the paycheck but fail to send it to the Friend of the Court. This will ultimately get the employer in trouble, but it can also result in you or your spouse being called back to court to explain why payments are not being made.

AGREEMENT
SUSPENDING
IMMEDIATE
INCOME
WITHHOLDING

Michigan law currently requires immediate income withholding, unless the parties agree that it will not take effect immediately. (However, income withholding will be required if the children are receiving AFDC benefits.) If you and your spouse agree to suspend immediate income withholding, you will need to complete an Agreement Suspending Immediate Income Withholding (Form 34). To complete Form 34:

1. Complete the top portion of the form according to the instructions in the first section of chapter 5.

2. Fill in your name, address, and social security number, and your spouse's name, address, and social security number in the plaintiff and defendant boxes.

3. In paragraph 2, type in an explanation as to how support will be paid. For example: "Support shall be paid by the defendant directly to the Friend of the Court;" or "Support shall be paid by the defendant directly to the plaintiff by mailing said payments, in the form of personal checks, to the plaintiff's address as stated above." Although many complaints are heard about the Friend of the Court, it can be an advantage to have the Friend of the Court's payment records in the event of a dispute over what has been paid.

4. You and your spouse fill in the date and sign your names on the lines indicated at the bottom of the form.

ORDER
SUSPENDING
IMMEDIATE
INCOME
WITHHOLDING

In order for the judge to approve your alternate payment arrangement, you will need to submit an order for the judge to sign. To prepare the Order Suspending Immediate Income Withholding (Form 35):

1. Complete the top portion of the form according to the instructions in the first section of chapter 5.

2. Fill in your name, address, and social security number, and your spouse's name, address, and social security number in the plaintiff and defendant boxes.

3. In paragraph 1, fill in the date of the hearing and the judge's name.

4. In paragraph 2, check the box for "The parties have entered into a written agreement that has been reviewed and entered in the record as follows:"

The judge will sign and date this form if he or she agrees to suspend income withholding. Even if you and your spouse agree to suspend income withholding, if the person who is to pay support misses some payments the income withholding will begin.

UNCONTESTED DIVORCE 7

This chapter will provide a general overview of the uncontested divorce procedure.

Most lawyers have had the following experience: A new client comes in, saying she wants to file for divorce. She has discussed it with her husband, and it will be a "simple, uncontested" divorce. Once the papers are filed the husband and wife begin arguing over a few items of property. The lawyer then spends a lot of time negotiating with the husband. After much arguing, an agreement is finally reached. The case will proceed in the court as "uncontested," but only after a lot of "contesting" out of court.

For purposes of this book, a *contested* case is one where you and your spouse will be doing your arguing in court, and leaving the decision up to the judge. An *uncontested* case is one where you will do your arguing and deciding before court, and the judge will only be approving your decision.

You probably won't know if you are going to have a contested case until you try the uncontested route and fail. Therefore, the following sections are presented mostly to assist you in attempting the uncontested case. Chapter 8 specifically discusses the contested case, but builds on information in this chapter.

There are actually two ways that a case can be considered uncontested. One is where your spouse simply ignores the fact that you have filed for divorce. If you have your spouse served by the sheriff (as described in chapter 5), and he or she does not respond, you will need to file certain forms. The other uncontested situation is where you can't locate your spouse. In this situation you will need to file other forms which are discussed more in chapter 11.

The forms listed below are discussed in this chapter. There may be other forms needed, but they will be prepared and provided by the Friend of the Court. The following can serve as a checklist of the basic forms you may need for your uncontested divorce:

❑   Summons (Form 7).

❑   Complaint for Divorce (Form 8).

❑   Verified Statement (Form 21).

❑   Uniform Child Custody Jurisdiction Act Affidavit (Form 20).

❑   Default, Application, Entry, Affidavit (Form 11).

❑   Request for Certificate of Military Service Status (Form 24).

❑   Notice of Hearing (Form 16).

❑   Judgment of Divorce (Form 11).

❑   Record of Divorce or Annulment (Form 18).

Once all of the necessary forms have been filed, you will need to call the judge's secretary to arrange for a hearing date for the final judgment (see chapter 5 regarding setting a hearing). You should tell the secretary that you need to schedule a "final hearing for an uncontested divorce." Such a hearing should not usually take more than ten minutes. See chapter 9 for information on how to handle the final hearing.

The following sections give instructions for when you need each form, and how to complete it.

SUMMONS

The Summons (Form 7) notifies your spouse of his or her rights and obligations in responding to the Complaint for Divorce. In some of the previous SCAO forms the Summons and Complaint for Divorce were combined into one form, and sometimes they were separate forms. Currently, there is an SCAO Summons which is titled "Summons and Complaint," but no Complaint form for divorce is included. There is not currently a separate SCAO Complaint form for divorce cases. Therefore, they will be discussed as separate forms here.

To complete the Summons (Form 7):

1. Type in the number of the judicial circuit where indicated in the top (case style) portion of the form.

2. Type in your name, address, and telephone number in the box for "Plaintiff," and your spouse's name, address, and telephone number in the box for "defendant."

3. Place an "X" in the box before the sentence: "There is no other pending or resolved civil action arising out of the same transaction or occurrence as alleged in the complaint."

4. In the box marked "Venue," type in your name, and the county where you reside, in the box for the "Plaintiff(s) residence." This must be the county in which you meet the ten-day residency requirement.

5. Fill in the date on the "Date" line, and sign your name on the line marked "Signature of attorney/plaintiff."

6. Staple your completed Complaint for Divorce to the Summons.

7. The clerk will fill in the other spaces on the first page when you file your Summons and Complaint for Divorce. The sheriff deputy or other process server will fill in the second page after your spouse is served.

COMPLAINT FOR DIVORCE

The Complaint for Divorce (Form 8) is the paper needed to open your case. The Complaint for Divorce asks the judge to give you a divorce. Currently, there is no SCAO Complaint for Divorce form. To complete the Complaint for Divorce (Form 8):

1. Complete the top portion according to the instructions in chapter 5 for the case style. Leave the file number blank, as the clerk will fill this in when you file your papers.

2. In paragraph 1, check one box for how residency is satisfied, and type in the name of the county where you will file.

3. In paragraphs 2 and 3, type in the information called for about you and your spouse. You are the plaintiff and your spouse is the defendant. In item "3C," check one of the boxes to indicate if the address being given is your spouse's current address (that is, you know he or she is now living there) or is a last known address (that is, he or she is probably not now living there and you don't know where your spouse is currently living).

4. In paragraph 4, fill in the date and city and state where you were married (or the country if you were not married in the U.S.).

5. In paragraph 6, check the appropriate box or boxes. If you have children, fill in the information for each child. The last part of paragraph 6 has a line to list any prior court cases with continuing jurisdiction of any of your children. If there is a prior case, fill in the information from the case style (the names of the parties; the name of the county and type of court, such as "Washenaw County Probate Court" or "Kent County Circuit Court;" and the case number. If there are no such cases, type in the words "none."

6. In paragraph 7, check one box as appropriate. You would only check the box indicating there is no property to be divided if you and your spouse have signed a Marital Settlement Agreement

(Form 10) which divides all of your property, or if you and your spouse have already divided your property (so that every item of property with documents showing title have only one of your names on the title documents, and every item without a title document is in the possession of the person who will keep it).

7. In paragraph 8, check one box to indicate whether you are requesting spousal support (alimony). If you are requesting spousal support, type in a statement of the facts that you believe entitle you to spousal support. As stated in the section on spousal support in chapter 4, Michigan law provides that you are only entitled to spousal support if the property you receive in the divorce will be insufficient for the "suitable support and maintenance" of you or any children of the marriage who are in your custody. If you need more room, type in "See attached sheet," then on an extra sheet of paper type in "8. Spousal Support" and the needed information and attach it to the Complaint for Divorce.

8. Do not check the box in paragraph 9.

9. After "Wherefore," check the boxes that apply. If split custody is requested, type in the details of the split custody you desire in paragraph 4. If anything other than reasonable visitation is requested, type in the details of the desired visitation schedule in paragraph 5. If you need more room for any of these items, type in "See attached sheet," then type in the paragraph number and the needed information on an extra sheet of paper and attach it to the Complaint for Divorce. If you or your spouse's maiden name is to be restored, type in the full name to be restored in paragraph 7.

10. Paragraph 8 is to fill in any other requests not covered in the other paragraphs. Again, attach additional sheets if needed.

11. Type in the date, and your name, address, and telephone number on the lines indicated. Sign your name on the signature line.

Once you have completed the Summons and the Complaint for Divorce, you need to file them with the court clerk (see chapter 5) and arrange for service by the sheriff or other process server (see chapter 5). To save you a trip to the clerk, you may also want to prepare and file the Uniform Child Custody Jurisdiction Act Affidavit (Form 20) and Verified Statement (Form 21).

VERIFIED STATEMENT

The Verified Statement (Form 21) provides the Friend of the Court with basic information about you and your family. This will be used for obtaining information, and later, to enforce your divorce judgment if necessary. This form will probably be given to you at your first meeting with the Friend of the Court. The form in this book can be used as a worksheet, so that you can have the information ready when you meet with the Friend of the Court.

UNIFORM CHILD CUSTODY JURISDICTION ACT AFFIDAVIT

The Uniform Child Custody Jurisdiction Act Affidavit (Form20) must be completed if you and your spouse have any minor children. See the instructions for the Uniform Child Custody Jurisdiction Act Affidavit in chapter 6.

DEFAULT, APPLICATION, ENTRY, AFFIDAVIT

If your spouse fails to respond to the Complaint for Divorce within twenty-one days after being served with the Summons and Complaint for Divorce (twenty-eight days if he or she was served in another state), and is *not* in the military service, you will need to complete the Default, Application, Entry, Affidavit (Form 12).

If your spouse *is* in the military service, you do not need to complete this form and should consult a lawyer. Federal laws designed to protect service personnel while overseas can create special problems in these situations. However, if your spouse is in the military and will cooperate by signing an Answer and Waiver (Form 13) or a Marital Settlement Agreement (Form 10), you can proceed without a lawyer.

If you don't know whether your spouse is in the military service, you will need to complete the Request for Certificate of Military Service Status (Form 25), which is discussed in the next section of this chapter.

To complete the Default, Application, Entry, Affidavit (Form 12):

1. Complete the top portion of the form according to the instructions in chapter 5.

2. Type the date your spouse was served with a copy of the Complaint on the line in paragraph 1, and check one of the boxes to indicate whether the proof of service is attached to Form 12 or is already on file with the court. This refers to the proof of service of the Summons and Complaint for Divorce. In most cases the sheriff will file the proof of service with the court.

3. Sign before a notary public on the line above the words "Signature of Affiant."

4. Take this form to the court clerk, who will date and sign it under the heading "Entry."

5. Mail a copy to your spouse at his or her last known address and sign and date the form under the heading "Certificate of Mailing."

Request for Certificate of Military Service Status

If you don't know whether your spouse is in the military service, you will need to complete the Request for Certificate of Military Service Status (Form 25). This is really just a letter asking each branch of the service to verify whether your spouse is in that branch.

To complete Form 25:

1. Complete the top portion of the form according to the instructions in chapter 5.

2. Type your spouse's name on the line marked "[Party]" and social security number on the line marked "[Soc. Sec. #]."

3. Type in the date on the line indicated, and your name, address, and telephone number under the signature line.

4. Sign the form on the line marked "Signature."

You will then need to make seven copies of this form, and mail one to each of the seven addresses listed on the form (one to each branch of the U.S. Government considered "military" service). Be sure to enclose a stamped envelope, addressed to yourself, with each one. A fee may be charged by the military service branch. Try checking on fees with your closest military base, the court clerk, or the Friend of the Court. Otherwise, the branch of the military will let you know if a fee is required when it receives the form.

Each service branch will then check its records and mail you a notice as to whether your spouse is in that branch (keep these notices in case the court clerk or the judge asks for evidence that your spouse is not in military service). If your spouse is in one of the service branches, his or her address will be provided. You can then send your spouse notice of the divorce, and see if some agreement can be reached so you can use the

Marital Settlement Agreement (Form 10) or the Answer and Waiver (Form 13).

If your spouse is in the military service, but cannot be contacted, or will not cooperate (by signing one of the forms listed above or filing his or her own Answer), you should contact an attorney. If all responses show that your spouse is not in the military, you can complete the Default, Application, Entry, Affidavit (Form 12).

Obtaining Information

If you have any children, your spouse will be required to provide the Friend of the Court with financial information. However, there may be times when you will want to obtain information yourself, such as if you suspect your spouse has not provided the Friend of the Court with complete or accurate information. Before you do this, tell the Friend of the Court your concerns about the information your spouse provided, and give them any information you may have. If this doesn't allow the Friend of the Court to get accurate information, you may need to subpoena records. See chapter 8 and chapter 9 for more about obtaining information.

Withdrawing an Answer

If your spouse has filed an answer which contests at least some portion of your Complaint for Divorce, but is now willing to let the case proceed as an uncontested divorce, your spouse should file a Stipulation to Withdraw Answer and Order (Form 26). This is a simple form which just needs to have the case style completed, be signed by your spouse and dated where indicated, and filed with the court clerk.

If You Reach a Settlement

In the event you and your spouse manage to reach an agreement, you can always prepare and file a Marital Settlement Agreement (Form 10). Your case will then be handled more like a consent divorce. However, it will probably be more simple to proceed with the default case.

Notice of Hearing

After you have filed your Complaint for Divorce and other papers, had your spouse served and allowed enough time for him or her to respond, met with the Friend of the Court, and obtained any information you may need, you will need to schedule a final hearing. See chapter 6 for information about arranging for a hearing with the judge. Once the hearing is set you need to officially notify your spouse, using Form 16. To complete the Notice of Hearing (Form 16), see the instructions in the section on "Notifying Your Spouse" in chapter 5.

Judgment of Divorce

In an uncontested case, your Judgment of Divorce will be completed at the end of your hearing. See chapters 8 and 9 for information about the court hearing, and see chapter 6 for information about how to complete the Judgment of Divorce (Form 11).

You should complete as much of the Judgment of Divorce as possible before the hearing, which may only mean having the case style filled in. The Judgment of Divorce form is designed so that you can complete it at the hearing according to what the judge decides on each issue. You can complete ahead of time any items which you and your spouse have agreed upon.

If the judge tells you to change something major in the Judgment of Divorce form, you will need to make a note of exactly what changes the judge ordered, then go home and prepare the Judgment of Divorce the way the judge instructed. You will then need to take the revised Judgment of Divorce back to the judge for signature. You will also complete a Proof of Mailing (Form 17), attach it to the Judgment of Divorce, and deliver it to the judge's secretary. Also give her two extra copies, along with a stamped envelope addressed to yourself and a stamped envelope addressed to your spouse. Ask the secretary whether you should sign and date the certificate of service. Sometimes the secretary will handle mailing the Judgment of Divorce after the judge signs it, in which case she may sign the Proof of Mailing.

RECORD OF DIVORCE OR ANNULMENT

See the information on the Record of Divorce or Annulment in chapter 6.

CONTESTED DIVORCE 8

PROCEDURAL DIFFERENCES FROM UNCONTESTED CASES

This book cannot turn you into a trial lawyer. It can be very risky to try to handle a contested case yourself, but it has been done. There are several differences from an uncontested case. In a consent case, the judge will usually go along with whatever you and your spouse have worked out. In an uncontested case, the judge will usually go along with whatever you want (as long as it appears reasonable), because your spouse isn't there to object or offer other options. However, in a contested case you need to prove that you are entitled to what it is you are asking. This means you will need a longer time for the hearing, you will need to prepare more for the hearing, you will need to present documents as evidence, and you may need to have witnesses testify for you.

You may also have to do extra work to get the evidence you need, such as by sending out subpoenas (which are discussed in the next section of this chapter), or even hiring a private investigator. Also, you will need to pay extra attention to assure that your spouse is properly notified of any court hearings, and that he or she is sent copies of any papers you file with the court clerk. If the Friend of the Court is involved in your case, they may have obtained some of the information you need.

FORMS

Some of the forms discussed in chapter 7 will also be used in a contested case. In fact, a contested case will begin the same way as an uncontested case. You will begin by filing the following four papers:

❏ Summons (Form 7). See chapter 7 for information about how to complete Form 7.

❏ Complaint for Divorce (Form 8). See chapter 7 for information about how to complete Form 8.

❏ Uniform Child Custody Jurisdiction Act Affidavit (Form 20), if you have any minor children. See chapter 6 for information about how to complete Form 20.

❏ Verified Statement (Form 21), if you have any minor children. See chapter 6 for more information about Form 21.

You will also need to prepare the Judgment of Divorce (Form 11), but you will not be able to prepare Form 11, except for the case style, until during or after the hearing with the judge. This is because you won't know what to put in the Judgment of Divorce until the judge decides the various matters in dispute. Other forms which will, or may, be necessary in a contested case will be discussed later in this chapter.

The case will become contested within about twenty-one days, when your spouse files an Answer that shows he or she is contesting at least one issue. Once a case becomes contested you may need to use some or all of the forms discussed in this chapter, as well as the Notice of Hearing (Form 16) explained in chapter 7.

When it becomes apparent that you have a contested divorce, it is probably time to consider hiring an attorney, especially if the issue of child custody is involved. If you are truly ready to go to war over custody, it shows that this is an extremely important matter for you, and you may want to get professional assistance. You can expect a contested case when your spouse is seriously threatening to fight you every inch of the way, or when he or she hires an attorney.

On the other hand, you shouldn't assume that you need an attorney just because your spouse has hired one. It may be easier to deal with the attorney than with your spouse. The attorney is not as emotionally involved and may see your settlement proposal as reasonable. You may first want to try to work things out with the lawyer. You can always hire your own lawyer if your spouse's isn't reasonable. Just be very cautious about signing any papers until you are certain you understand what they mean. You may want to have an attorney review any papers prepared by your spouse's lawyer before you sign them.

You will need to be more prepared for the hearing. Second, you will not prepare the Judgment of Divorce (Form 11) until during or after the hearing with the judge. This is because you won't know what to put in the Judgment until the judge decides the various matters in dispute.

The remainder of this chapter and the next chapter will discuss how to prepare for the hearing, and how to prepare the Judgment of Divorce.

OBTAINING INFORMATION

If you have minor children, or the judge orders it, the Friend of the Court will be involved in your case. If child custody and visitation are also in dispute, the Friend of the Court or a court-appointed counselor or psychologist may conduct an investigation of your family and make a recommendation regarding custody. The Friend of the Court will seek financial information about you and your spouse in order to make a recommendation to the judge about child support. This will involve having you and your spouse provide evidence of your incomes. You will be given an appointment to meet with a representative of the Friend of the Court and provide such documents as your recent income tax returns, W-2 forms, and paystubs.

SUBPOENA   If your spouse won't give information or gives inaccurate information, or if you disagree with the Friend of the Court recommendation, you may need to try to collect information yourself. This may require the use of the subpoena. A *subpoena* is simply an order for a person to appear at a specific place and time to either give testimony or to produce documents or other items. Form 14 is an example of the current SCAO subpoena form. Check with the court clerk in your county to find out if they have a subpoena form you can use.

You will most likely use this form to obtain documents. If the clerk does not have a form, you can use Form 14. To complete the Subpoena (Form 14):

1. Complete the top portion according to the instructions in chapter 5.

2. In the box for the "Plaintiff(s)/Petitioner(s)," check the second box and type your name in on the line next to that box. Also check the box for "Civil." In the box for the "Defendant(s)/Respondent(s)," type in your spouse's name. Ignore the box marked "Charge," and the box for "Probate."

3. In the space after the phrase "In the Name of the People of the State of Michigan. To," type in the name and address of the person you want to appear or produce documents or other items. This can be your spouse or any other third party who has information you need, such as your spouse's employer or bank, or your child's doctor or school. It can be a live person, a government agency, a corporation, or similar entity. If you are seeking records of a company, agency, etc., you can type in "Keeper of Records," and the name and address of the company, agency, etc.

4. In the next box, fill in the place, day, date, and time where the person is to appear. If the subpoena is to appear for a court hearing, you will check the box for "The court address above." If the subpoena is to appear for a deposition, check the box for "Other" and type in the address.

5. If the subpoena is for the person to testify at trial or a hearing, check the box for paragraph 3.

6. If you want the person to bring any documents or other items, type in a description of those documents or items in paragraph 4.

7. If the subpoena is for the person to testify at a deposition, check the box for paragraph 6.

8. Ignore paragraphs 5 and 7 through 8.

9. Check the box for paragraph 9, and type in the information called for in the box.

10. Take the subpoena to the court clerk, who will fill in the date and sign it at the bottom. You will then need to arrange for the sheriff to serve the subpoena on the person, company, agency, etc. The sheriff will complete the second page of the subpoena and file a copy with the clerk. The sheriff will need at least one extra copy of the subpoena, and a check for the service fee.

NOTICE OF TAKING RECORDS DEPOSITION

You also need to let your spouse know that you are issuing a subpoena for a deposition. Your spouse, or spouse's lawyer, has a right to attend the deposition or object to the subpoena. To provide this notice use the Notice of Taking Records Deposition (Form 15). To complete Form 15:

1. Complete the top portion according to the instructions in the section at the beginning of chapter 5.

2. Type your spouse's name and address (or his or her lawyer's name and address) after the word "To."

3. In the first paragraph, type in the date, time, name of the person being subpoenaed, and place of the deposition.

4. In the second paragraph, type in the same description of the documents or other items that you listed on the subpoena.

5. Sign your name on the "Signature" line, and fill in the date.

6. Mail a copy of Form 15, along with a copy of the Subpoena (Form 14) to your spouse or to his or her lawyer, then complete the certificate of service section. Make sure that you actually mail it on the date stated in the certificate of service. Also file a copy of Form 15 with the clerk.

This should get you the requested information. If the employer, bank, etc., calls you and says you must pay for copies, ask how much they will cost and send a check or money order (if the amount isn't too high and you don't already have some fairly recent income information). If the employer, bank, etc., doesn't provide the information, you can try sending a letter to the employer, bank, etc., saying: "unless you provide the information requested in the subpoena in 7 days, a motion for contempt will be filed with the circuit court." This may scare the employer, bank, etc., into sending you the information. The sheriff will have also filed an affidavit verifying when the subpoena was served.

There are more procedures you could go through to force the employer, bank, etc., to give the information, but it probably isn't worth the hassle and you would probably need an attorney to help you with it. At the final hearing you can tell the judge that your spouse refused to provide income information, and that the subpoena was not honored by the employer. The judge may do something to help you out, or he may advise you to see a lawyer.

There is also a procedure where you send written questions to your spouse, which he or she must answer in writing and under oath. These written questions are called *interrogatories*. If your spouse isn't cooperating about anything else, he or she probably won't answer interrogatories either, which would leave you no better off.

PROPERTY AND DEBTS

Generally, the judge will look at your property and debts, and will try to divide them "fairly." This does not necessarily mean they will be divided fifty-fifty. What you want to do is offer the judge a reasonable solution that looks "fair." Adultery or other misconduct on the part of one party may be used by the other party to justify an unequal division of property and debts.

It's time to review the Property Inventory (Form 1) and the Debt Inventory (Form 2) you prepared earlier. For each item or property, note one of the following categories (it may fit into more than one):

1.   You really want.

2.   You'd like to have.

3.   You don't care either way.

4.   Your spouse really wants.

5.   Your spouse would like to have.

6.   Your spouse doesn't care either way.

Now start a list of what each of you should end up with, using the categories listed above. You will eventually end up with a list of things you can probably get with little difficulty (you really want and your spouse doesn't care), those which you'll fight over (you both really want), and those which need to be divided but can probably be easily divided equally (you both don't really care).

At the hearing the judge will probably try to get you to work out your disagreements, but he won't put up with arguing for long. In the end he will arbitrarily divide the items you can't agree upon, or he may order you to sell those items and divide the money you get equally.

On the few items that are really important to you, it may be necessary for you to try to prove why you should get them. It will help if you can convince the judge of one or more of the following:

1.   You paid for the item out of your own earnings or funds.

2.   You owned the item before getting married.

3. You are the one who primarily uses that item.

4. You use the item in your employment, business, or hobby.

5. You are willing to give up something else you really want in exchange for that item. (Of course you will try to give up something from your "don't care" or your "like to have" list.)

6. The item is needed for your children (assuming you will have custody).

7. The item should be considered your separate property because it was a gift or inheritance to you alone (such as from one of your relatives), or was a court award for pain and suffering.

8. You got the property by exchanging it for property you had before you got married, for property you received as a gift or through an inheritance, or purchased it with a court award for pain and suffering.

The best thing you can do is make up a list of how you think the property should be divided. Make it a reasonably fair and equal list, regardless of how angry you are at your spouse. Even if the judge changes some of it to appear fair to your spouse, you will most likely get more of what you want than if you don't offer a suggestion. (No, this is not an exception to the negotiating rule of letting your spouse make the first offer, because at this point you are no longer just negotiating with your spouse. You are now negotiating with the judge. At this point you are trying to impress the judge with your fairness; not trying to convince your spouse.)

It is also a good idea to have any papers which can support your position of why you should get the item, and the value of all property. These would be papers such as dated sales receipts, cancelled checks, loan documents, bank statements, credit card statements, income tax returns, and certified copies of wills and probate court papers or court judgments.

During the hearing, the judge will announce who gets which items. Make a list of this as the judge tells you, then complete the Judgment of Divorce (Form 11) according to what the judge says.

Once you have completed the Judgment of Divorce, make a copy and send it to your spouse. Send the original to the judge (not the court clerk), along with a completed Proof of Mailing (Form 17) stapled to it showing the date you sent a copy to your spouse. If your spouse doesn't object to how you've prepared the Judgment of Divorce, the judge will sign the Judgment of Divorce and return a copy to you. You should send the judge the original and two copies of the Judgment of Divorce, along with two stamped envelopes (one addressed to yourself, and the other addressed to your spouse).

Child Custody and Visitation

Generally, if you are the wife, the odds start out in favor of you getting custody; but don't depend upon the odds. Start out by reviewing the guidelines the judge will use to decide the custody question. These can be found in chapter 5. For each item listed in that section, write down an explanation of how that item applies to you. This will be your argument when you have your hearing with the judge.

Many custody battles revolve around the moral fitness of one or both of the parents. If you become involved in this type of a custody fight, you should consult a lawyer. Charges of moral unfitness (such as illegal drug use, child abuse, "immoral" sexual conduct) can require long court hearings involving the testimony of many witnesses, as well as possibly the employment of private investigators. For such a hearing you will require the help of an attorney who knows the law, what questions to ask witnesses, and the rules of evidence.

However, if the only question is whether you or your spouse have been the main caretaker of the child, you can always have friends, neighbors and relatives come into the hearing (if they are willing to help you out) to testify on your behalf. It may not be necessary for you to hire an attorney, but if you need to subpoena unwilling witnesses to testify, you should have one.

The judge's decision regarding custody will have to be put into the Judgment of Divorce (Form 11).

CHILD SUPPORT

In Michigan, as in most states, the question of child support is mostly a matter of a mathematical calculation. Getting a fair child support amount depends upon the accuracy of the income information presented to the judge. If you feel fairly sure that the information your spouse presented to the Friend of the Court is accurate, there isn't much to argue about. The judge will simply take the income information provided, use the formula to calculate the amount to be paid, and order that amount to be paid.

There usually won't be much room to argue about the amount of child support, so there usually isn't a need to get an attorney. If you claim your spouse has not provided accurate income information, it will be up to you to prove this to the judge by showing the income information you obtained from your spouse's employer or other income source.

The only area open for argument is where special needs are claimed by the party asking for child support. Once again, it will be necessary for that party to provide proof of the cost of these special needs by producing billing statements, receipts, or other papers to show the amount of these needs.

The judge's decision regarding child support will have to be put into the Judgment of Divorce (Form 11).

Spousal Support (Alimony)

A dispute over alimony may require a lawyer, especially if there is a request for permanent alimony because of a disability. Such a claim may require the testimony of expert witnesses (such as doctors, accountants, and actuaries), which requires the special skills of an attorney. A charge of adultery may also require a lawyer and possibly a private investigator as well.

If alimony has been requested, look at the section of the Complaint for Divorce or Answer asking for alimony, and review the reasons alimony was requested. These reasons will be the subject of the court hearing on this question. You should determine what information (including papers and the testimony of witnesses) you will need to present to the judge to either support or refute the reasons alimony was requested.

For temporary (also called *rehabilitative*) alimony, the most common reason is that the person needs help until he or she can get training to enter the work force. The questions that will need to be answered are:

1. What has the person been trained for in the past?

2. What type of training is needed before the person can again be employable in that field?

3. How long will this training take?

4. What amount of income can be expected upon employment?

5. How much money is required for the training?

Questions which may be asked in either a temporary or a permanent alimony situation include an examination of the situation of the parties during their marriage that led to the person not working, what contribution to the marriage that person made, and what improper conduct on the part of the other party makes an award of alimony appropriate. You should be prepared to present evidence regarding these questions.

IF YOU REACH A SETTLEMENT

In the event that you and your spouse manage to reach an agreement before your hearing, on any or all issues, you may prepare and file a Marital Settlement Agreement (Form 10). It is to your advantage to agree on any matters possible, as it will reduce the amount of time you need to spend preparing for and attending the hearing, and the amount of money you will need to spend on an attorney if you've hired one.

You and your spouse do not need to be in agreement about everything to use the Marital Settlement Agreement (Form 10). You may use it even in a partially contested case, as long as you are in agreement about something. You will note that at the beginning of each section of this form there is a box to check to indicate that the matter needs to be determined by the court. Just check this box for any items you are not in agreement about. For example, if you are in agreement about property division and alimony, but can't agree on child custody; fill in the property and alimony sections, and check the box for the matter to be determined by the court in the custody, child support, and child visitation sections.

THE COURT 9
HEARING

PREPARATION

SETTING A
HEARING DATE

One of your first steps in preparing for a court hearing is to get a hearing date scheduled. See chapter 5 for instructions on setting a hearing date.

NOTIFYING
YOUR SPOUSE

You will need to notify your spouse of when the hearing will be. Even if you can call your spouse on the phone, you still need a to send a formal notice. For the final hearing you will use the Notice of Hearing (Form 16). Fill in the Notice of Hearing according to the instructions in the section on "Notifying Your Spouse" in chapter 5. Then make three copies of the Notice of Hearing. Mail one copy to your spouse, file the original with the court clerk, and keep two copies for yourself.

For hearings on any of the motions discussed in chapter 11 or elsewhere in this book, you will fill in the "Notice of Hearing" portion of the motion form, or any other notice of hearing form you may be instructed to use. Again, you will mail a copy to your spouse. If the hearing relates to your children, and they have a legal custodian or guardian, you will also need to send a notice of hearing to the custodian or guardian. More information about notifying others of hearing may be discussed in the instructions for particular forms.

WHAT PAPERS
TO BRING

You should have copies of all pertinent court papers with you at the hearing. Bring your copies (if available) of the following papers to the hearing:

For the final hearing:

☛ Your Complaint for Divorce (or motion form if your hearing is on a motion) and any other papers you filed or have received from your spouse or the court. In essence, this is your copy of your entire divorce file.

☛ For an uncontested or contested case, any papers you may have showing that your spouse was properly notified of the divorce (although the Sheriff's affidavit of serving papers will be in the court file, and you may not have a copy).

☛ Any papers you may have to support your financial situation. This should include copies of your most recent paystub, Federal income tax return, and W-2 forms.

☛ Any paper's showing your spouse's income or property.

☛ Your Marital Settlement Agreement (Form 10), if you have one that hasn't yet been filed with the court.

☛ Your proposed Judgment of Divorce (Form 11).

☛ Notes that you have made of the important information you want the judge to know. The idea here is to have a written outline to guide you in presenting your case in a logical and concise manner. Refer to chapter 8 for the type of information you may want to present on various matters.

For a motion hearing:

☛ Your motion and any other papers you filed or have received from your spouse relating to the motion.

☛ Any papers you may have to support what you are seeking in your motion. If you are seeking child support or spousal support, this should include proof of your financial situation, such as copies of your most recent paystub, Federal income tax return, and W-2 forms; as well as any paper's showing your spouse's financial situation.

☞ Your proposed order.

☞ Notes that you have made of the important information you want the judge to know. The idea here is to have a written outline to guide you in presenting your case in a logical and concise manner. Refer to chapter 8 for the type of information you may want to present on various matters.

THE HEARING

Your hearing may take place in a large courtroom like you see on TV or in the movies, in a small hearing room, or in what looks more like a conference room. The hearing may be before a circuit judge, or before a Friend of the Court hearing referee. If it is before a referee, it will be for the purpose of the referee making a recommendation to the judge. If either party disagrees with the referee's recommendation, a second hearing may be held before the judge. If you disagree with the referee's recommendation, you will need to quickly prepare and file an Objection to Referee's Recommended Order (Form 39). See the section on "The Friend of the Court" in chapter 5 for information about Form 39. For purposes of discussion we will refer to the "judge," although it should be understood that this may also be a referee.

THE FINAL HEARING

The judge may start the final hearing by stating what you are there for and summarizing the Friend of the Court recommendation if there is one, then ask you and your spouse if you have any additional evidence to present, and then ask each of you any questions he or she may have. The judge will review the Marital Settlement Agreement (if you filed one), and will probably ask you whether you understand and agree with what is in it. The judge may also ask you to explain why your marriage is "irretrievably broken." Just tell him or her why you're getting divorced.

Example 1: "We just don't have any interests in common anymore, and we have drifted apart."

Example 2: "My husband has had several affairs."

If you have any information which is different and more current than what is in the Friend of the Court Recommendation, you should mention to the judge that you have more current information. You will then give a copy of whatever papers you have to show the changed situation (such as current paystub showing an increase in pay, or a current bank statement showing a new balance). Your basic job at the hearing is to answer the judge's questions, and give him the information he needs to give you a divorce.

If there are any items that you and your spouse have not yet agreed upon, tell the judge what these items are. You may need to present more evidence, in the way of documents or the testimony of witnesses. Refer to chapter 8, relating to the contested divorce, for more information about how to handle these unresolved issues. Be prepared to make a suggestion as to how these matters should be settled, and to explain to the judge why your suggestion is the best solution.

If the judge asks for any information that you haven't brought with you, tell the judge that you don't have it with you but you will be happy to provide him with the information by the end of the following day. Just be sure you get the papers to the judge as promised!

At the end of the hearing the judge will tell you if he is going to grant you a divorce and accept your Marital Settlement Agreement. It would be very unusual for him not to grant the divorce and accept your agreement. You will then tell the judge that you've prepared a proposed Judgment of Divorce, and hand him the original. Refer back to chapter 6 and chapter 7 regarding how to prepare the Judgment of Divorce form. You should have three extra copies of the Judgment of Divorce with you: one for yourself, one for your spouse, and one for the Friend of the Court. You should also bring two envelopes, one addressed to yourself and one addressed to your spouse, and two stamps. This is in case the judge wants to review the Judgment of Divorce and mail it to you later, instead of signing it at the hearing.

MOTION
HEARINGS

The basic differences between the final hearing and a motion hearing are that at a motion hearing:

1. You will only be dealing with the matter raised by the motion, and

2. You will be presenting the judge with an order relating to the motion instead of a Judgment of Divorce.

GENERAL
HEARING
PROCEDURES

In addition to the information provided here, be sure to read the section in chapter 5 on "Courtroom Manners."

Plan to arrive at the hearing room at least ten minutes before the scheduled hearing time. Have your witnesses (if any) with you and be ready to present your case. Cases may be taken in the order they were scheduled, or in the order that the parties check-in on the hearing date. If the check-in method is used by your judge, it may be an advantage for you to get there early to get near the top of the list. Of course this may not help if your spouse doesn't also get there early, because usually cases won't be called unless both parties have checked in.

Usually there will be someone for you to check-in with in the hearing room. This may be the judge's clerk, the referee, the referee's secretary, or some other court officer. Being careful not to interrupt or disturb any hearing that may be in progress, you will need to give your name and then take a seat in or outside of the hearing room to wait for your case to be called.

When it is your turn to present your case, begin by stating your name, that you are representing yourself, and what you are asking the judge to do. For example, "I am here to request the entry of a Judgment of Divorce," or "I am here to request a temporary custody order." You will then be given an opportunity to present any evidence you may have to support your request. See the earlier subsection of this chapter on "The Final Hearing," as well as chapter 8, for more information to help you present your case.

It is impossible for this book to turn you into a lawyer. However, the following will give you some general guidance in properly presenting your case to the judge or referee.

Testimony of witnesses. You are entitled to have witnesses testify. Regarding such testimony, you need to be aware of a rule of evidence known as the *hearsay rule*. To put it very simply, the hearsay rule is that a witness cannot testify to what another person told the witness. For example, it would violate the hearsay rule for your friend Jane to testify that, "John Doe told me he saw Mr. Smith hit little Billy with a leather belt." Instead, you should have John Doe testify to what he saw. Law students spend many hours in the classroom studying the hearsay rule and its many exceptions, so there is no way it can be fully explained here. Just try to use witnesses who have first-hand knowledge of what they testify about.

You may be a witness on your own behalf. You may even be your only witness. When you testify, simply tell the judge what you want him or her to know. After you are finished, your spouse (or his or her attorney) may ask you questions. Also, the judge may ask you questions.

When you have another person testify on your behalf, you need to ask the witness questions. You should begin by having the witness identify himself, and telling how he knows you or your family. For example:

Question: Please state your name.
Answer: John Smith.
Question: How do you know my family?
Answer: I have worked with you for six years, and have been with you and your family on numerous social activities.

After this type of introduction, you need to ask questions that will allow your witness to tell the judge what happened. Your questions should be fairly simple. Do not ask more than one question at a time. Ask one question and wait for the witness to answer it before you ask another. Do not tell your story. Do not put words in the witness' mouth. For example:

Correct:	Question:	Where were you on July 4th of this year?
	Answer:	At your house for a Fourth of July barbeque.
	Question:	Did you observe anything unusual that day?
	Answer:	Yes. I observed Mrs. Smith spanking your son.
	Question:	Please describe exactly what you saw.
Incorrect:	Question:	You saw my wife spank my son last Fourth of July, didn't you?
Incorrect:	Question:	This past Fourth of July my wife spanked my son with a ruler because he spilled mustard on his shirt, and you were over at my house for a barbecue...

In the correct example, the witness is being allowed to tell the story. In the first incorrect example, the person asking the question is the one telling what happened; not the witness. In the second incorrect example, the person asking the questions is not only telling what happened, but is never even asking a question.

After you have finished, your spouse (or your spouse's attorney) will have an opportunity to ask questions. The judge may also ask questions. If the questioning by these people raises any matters that you believe need clarification, you may ask more questions. Once everyone is finished with your witness, he or she will be excused, and you can then call your next witness. If you don't have any more witnesses, and have presented all of your documents, you can simply say "That is all I have." If you want to be fancy, you can say "I rest."

Expert witnesses. An *expert witness* is a witness who is being called to testify because he or she has some type of special training, education, or expertise. In divorce cases, the most common expert witnesses are psychologists, psychiatrists, and counselors, who testify in custody disputes. If there are charges of physical abuse, you may also have a physician testify as an expert witness. Whereas a regular witness usually only testifies about what he or she observed, an expert witness also gives opinions and interprets what was observed. For example, a regular witness will usually not be allowed to give an opinion as to whether a person he observed was in a state of shock. This is because the witness does not have the proper expertise to determine whether a person is in a state of shock. However, a physician would be able to give such an opinion because a physician does have the proper expertise to make such a determination.

The main difference between questioning an expert witness and a regular witness, is that you must first have the judge determine that the witness qualifies as an expert. The way you do this is to ask the witness questions about his or her education and training, any licenses held, and experience working in the field for which he or she is to be qualified as an expert. Once the witness has given this testimony, you say to the judge: "I move that this witness be qualified as an expert witness."

Your spouse (or your spouse's attorney), and the judge, may ask the witness questions. Your spouse (or your spouse's attorney) may object to the witness being qualified as an expert, but will have to state the reason for the objection. Further questioning, by you or the judge, may resolve whatever objection is raised. If the judge agrees the witness is not qualified, then the witness will not be allowed to testify as an expert, but may still testify as a regular witness. Once the witness is qualified as an expert, you may ask questions so that the witness may give the judge the information you want presented.

Documents as evidence. Introducing a document into evidence is a three-step procedure:

1. Have the document marked as an exhibit. For example, the plaintiff would do this with his or her first document by saying: "Your honor, may I have this marked as Plaintiff's Exhibit A?" If you are the defendant, it will be marked as a defendant's exhibit. To help avoid any confusion, it is common to have one party's documents identified by a number (i.e., 1, 2, 3, etc.), and the other party's documents identified by a letter (i.e., A, B, C, etc.). There are several ways in which a document may be marked. The identification number or letter may be written on the document, or a sticker with the designation may be affixed to the document. Marking may be done by you, by the judge's clerk, or by the court reporter.

2. Have the document identified by a witness. Using our example above, the plaintiff would wait until the document is marked, then would hand it to the witness and say: "I am showing you what has been marked as Plaintiff's Exhibit A. Can you identify this?" The witness should then tell what the document is, and how he or she knows what it is. *Example 1*: "Yes. This is a letter I received from Mr. Smith, and it is dated August 27, 1998." *Example 2*: "Yes. This is a copy of the police report I filed after being called to a reported disturbance at the plaintiff's home on May 3, 1998." The purpose at this point is only to determine what the document is; not to discuss what information it contains or what it means.

   If you are the one introducing the document, then you will need to state what the document is. For example, "Your honor, this is a copy of the W-2 form I received from my employer last week."

3. Ask the judge to admit the document into evidence. Using our example, the plaintiff would say to the judge: "Your honor, I move that Plaintiff's Exhibit A be admitted into evidence." At this point your spouse (or your spouse's attorney) will have an opportunity to object. If there is no objection, or if the objection is overruled by the judge, the judge will admit the document into

evidence by saying something like "So admitted," or "Plaintiff's Exhibit A is admitted."

If there is an objection, you may need to ask the witness more questions to overcome the objection. For example, if the witness stated that the document is "a letter I received from Mr. Smith, and it is dated August 27, 1998," your spouse's attorney may say, "I object. How do we know it's really from Mr. Smith?" The plaintiff might then ask the witness: "How do you know the letter is from Mr. Smith?" And the witness might respond: "The envelope it came in had Mr. Smith's correct return address, and I have known Mr. Smith for twelve years and recognize the signature as Mr. Smith's."

Once the document is admitted into evidence, you may then ask the witness any questions you may have about the content, or significance of the document.

QUESTIONING YOUR SPOUSE'S WITNESSES

If you are the plaintiff at the final hearing, or are the one to file the motion, you will present your case first. After you finish, your spouse will present his or her case. If your spouse presented his or her case first, you will present your case after your spouse has finished. Either way, you will have the opportunity to question (or *cross-examine*) the witnesses who testify for your spouse. In cross-examining a witness, keep in mind one of the most basic rules followed by most lawyers: never ask a witness a question unless you know what the answer will be. If you do not obey this rule, the chances are great that asking the question will only allow the witness to give an answer that further strengthens your spouse's case. Many people feel that if they have an opportunity to question a witness, then they must do so. There is nothing wrong with saying "I have no questions," and let the witness go before he or she can do any more damage.

PREPARING THE JUDGMENT OF DIVORCE OR ORDER

Once the hearing is finished and the judge announces his or her decision, a Judgment of Divorce or order must be prepared for the judge to sign. The responsibility falls on the plaintiff to prepare the

Judgment of Divorce, and upon the person who filed the motion to prepare the order resulting from the motion. (Refer to the appropriate chapter and section of this book for specific instructions about how to prepare the Judgment of Divorce for the type of divorce procedure you are using, or the order for the type of motion filed.)

If the judge wants you to make any changes in the Judgment of Divorce or order you have submitted, make a careful note of exactly what the judge wants. Ask the judge to explain it again if you didn't understand the first time. Tell the judge that you will make the correction and deliver the revised Judgment of Divorce or order the following day. If the change requested is a small one, you might even be able to write in the change by hand at the hearing.

When the hearing is over, thank the judge and leave. The judge will sign the original Judgment of Divorce or order, and send it to the court clerk's office to be entered in the court's file. Take the copies of the Judgment of Divorce or order to the judge's secretary, who will write in the date and use a stamp with the judge's name on each copy to authenticate them.

GETTING HELP

If any serious problems develop at the hearing (such as your spouse's attorney starts making a lot of technical objections, or the judge gives you a hard time), just tell the judge you'd like to continue the hearing so you can retain an attorney. Then go get one!

WHEN YOU CAN'T FIND YOUR SPOUSE 10

Your spouse has run off, and you have no idea of where he or she might be. So how do you have the sheriff deliver a copy of your Summons (Form 7) and Complaint for Divorce (Form 8) to your spouse? The answer is, you can't use the sheriff. Instead of personal service you will use a method of giving notice called *service by publication*. This is one of the more complicated procedures in the legal system. You will need to follow the steps listed below carefully.

THE DILIGENT SEARCH

The court will only permit publication if you can't locate your spouse. This also includes the situation where the sheriff has tried several times to personally serve your spouse, but it appears that your spouse is hiding to avoid being served. First, you'll have to show that you can't locate your spouse by letting the court know what you've done to try to find him or her. In making this search you should try the following:

☛ Check the phone book and directory assistance in the area where you live.

☛ Check directory assistance in the area where you last knew your spouse to be, or in the any area where you have reason to think your spouse may be living.

☛ Ask friends and relatives who might know where your spouse may be.

☛ Check with the post office where he or she last lived to see if there is a forwarding address. (You can write to the post office and request this information by mail if it is too far away.)

☛ Check property tax records in the county where your spouse last lived to see if your spouse owns property. You can also check other counties if you have reason to think he or she may own property there.

☛ Check with the Michigan Secretary of State to see if your spouse has a current driver's license or any car registrations.

☛ Check with any other sources you know that may lead you to a current address (such as landlords, prior employers, etc.).

If you do come up with a current address, go back to personal service by the sheriff, but if not, continue with this procedure.

Preparing and Filing Court Papers

Motion and Verification for Alternative Service

Once you have made your search you need to notify the court. This is done by filing the Motion and Verification for Alternative Service (Form 22). All this form does is tell the court what you've done to try to locate your spouse, and ask for permission to publish your notice. To complete the Motion and Verification for Alternative Service (Form 22):

1. Complete the top portion of the form according to the instructions in chapter 5.

2. In paragraph 1, type your spouse's name in the space.

3. In paragraph 2, type in your spouse's last known home and business addresses on the lines indicated.

4. In paragraph "1.a.," check one, both, or neither boxes as appropriate for your situation.

5. In paragraph "1.b.," check one or both boxes only if you do not know either or both of your spouse's current addresses. Type in a summary of what you have done to try to find a current address. An example would be: "Inquired of postal authorities, checked telephone directories, inquired of relatives, friends and acquaintances, and inquired of the Secretary of State as to driver's license records."

6. Type in the date, your address, and your telephone number on the lines indicated. Sign your name on the line marked "Attorney signature," and cross out the word "Attorney." Type your name on the line marked "Attorney name (type or print)," then cross out the words "Attorney" and "Bar no." This form was designed with the assumption that it would be filed by an attorney, so you will need to make these modifications as you do not have an attorney.

7. Take this form to the sheriff (or other process server, if you did not use the sheriff), and have him or her complete the bottom portion of the form, under the heading "Verification of Process Server." Once this is done, file the form with the clerk. You should also check with the clerk or the judge's secretary to find out if the judge will require a hearing on this motion. If so, you will need to get a hearing date set. (See chapter 6 for more information about setting court hearings.)

Depending upon how you want to serve your spouse, you will either prepare an Order for Alternate Service (Form 23), or an Order for Service by Publication/Posting and Notice of Action (Form 24). Use Form 23 if you want to serve your spouse by first class mail, by tacking it to his or her door, or by delivering the Complaint for Divorce to a responsible member of the household where you know he or she lives. Generally, you will only seek this type of service if you know where your spouse lives, but he or she is trying to avoid being served. If you don't know where your spouse is, you should seek service by publication by using Form 24.

ORDER FOR
ALTERNATIVE
SERVICE

To complete the Order for Alternate Service (Form 23):

1. Complete the top portion of the form according to the instructions in chapter 5.

2. Type your name, address and telephone number in the box marked "Plaintiff name(s), address(es), and telephone no.(s)."

3. Type your spouse's name and last known address and telephone number in the box marked "Defendant name(s), address(es), and telephone no.(s)."

4. In paragraph 1, type in your spouse's name.

5. In paragraph 2, check the box, or boxes, for the manner in which you would like to serve your spouse. Also fill in the address on the line for any of the boxes that you check.

6. Deliver this form to the clerk along with your motion (Form 22). (If a hearing is required, you will give it to the judge at the hearing.) The judge will sign and date the order and return a copy to you. Once you receive the signed order, you must serve your spouse as stated in the order, and file a proof of service (on the second page of Form 23) with the clerk for each method of service used.

After you serve your spouse as required in Form 23, your spouse has twenty-one days to respond (twenty-eight days if service was by mail or outside of Michigan). If your spouse responds within this period, proceed with either the uncontested or contested procedure as necessary. If your spouse does not respond within this period, proceed with the default procedure as discussed in chapter 8.

ORDER FOR
SERVICE BY
PUBLICATION

To complete the Order for Service by Publication/Posting and Notice of Action (Form 24):

1. Complete the top portion of the form according to the instructions in chapter 5, and instructions 2 and 3 for the previous form.

2. After the word "To," type in your spouse's name.

3. On the first line in paragraph 1, type in the phrase: "obtain a judgment of divorce." The court clerk or judge will fill in the date in this paragraph.

4. In paragraph 2, type in the name of the newspaper where you intend to publish the notice. Also check the box for "three consecutive weeks." Generally, you should not use your regular daily newspaper, because they will charge you an exorbitant fee. Most, if not all, counties have a specialized newspaper which specializes in publishing legal notices for a reasonable fee. To find the legal newspaper in your county, check for a newsstand at the courthouse, or check the yellow pages and call the newspapers listed to ask about rates and whether the paper meets the legal requirements for publication of legal notices.

5. Leave paragraph 3 blank.

6. In paragraph 4, type in your spouse's name and check the box for "date of the last publication."

7. Deliver this form to the clerk along with your motion (Form 22). (If a hearing is required, you will give it to the judge at the hearing.)

The judge will sign and date the order and return a copy to you. Once you receive the signed order, you must arrange to have the notice published in the newspaper as stated in the order. After publication, the newspaper will file the "Affidavit of Publishing" (on the second page of Form 24) with the clerk for each method of service used. You will also need to mail a copy of the signed order to your spouse's last known address, and fill in the "Affidavit of Mailing" (also on the second page of Form 24).

As indicated in paragraph 1 of Form 24, your spouse has until a certain date to respond. If your spouse responds to the notice published in the newspaper, proceed with either the uncontested or contested procedure as necessary. If your spouse does not respond by the date indicated in paragraph 1, proceed with the default procedure as discussed in chapter 7.

Temporary Support, Custody, and Visitation

11

Temporary Orders in General

In many divorce cases it becomes necessary to have temporary orders issued by a judge on the matters of child support, child custody, visitation, and spousal support. Such temporary orders may be desirable for any number of reasons. It may also be necessary to change such orders from time to time.

Example 1: Your spouse has left you with the children, the mortgage, and monthly bills, and is not helping you out financially. You may want to ask the court to order your spouse to pay support for you and the children during the divorce process. Of course, if you were the only person bringing in income and have been paying all the bills, don't expect to get any temporary support.

Example 2: You and your spouse have separated, but have gotten into arguments over where the children will live until the divorce is final. Every time you allow the children to visit the other parent, you have a difficult time getting them back. You may want to ask the judge to give you temporary custody.

Example 3: You and your spouse have separated, and your spouse refuses to let the children visit you for as long as you'd like, or refuses to let you see them altogether. You may want to ask the judge to issue a detailed order as to when your children must be allowed to be with you.

Example 4: You already have a temporary order, but things are not working out, or the circumstances have changed. You may want to ask the judge to change the temporary order.

Example 5: Your spouse was able to obtain an emergency (called an *ex parte*) child support order without notifying you in advance, so you never had an opportunity to present any information. The order requires you to pay $250 per week, and you only make $300 per week. You need to get the judge to reduce the support to a more reasonable amount.

TYPES OF FORMS   The following types if forms are discussed in this chapter:

Motions. A *motion* is the basic form used to request the judge to either issue an initial order on a particular matter, or to change an existing order. These include:

- ☛ Motion Regarding Custody (Form 41).

- ☛ Motion Regarding Support (Form 27). This form deals only with child support.

- ☛ Motion Regarding Parenting Time (Form 36).

- ☛ Motion Regarding Spousal Support (Form 48).

- ☛ Objection to Ex Parte Order and Motion to Rescind or Modify (Form 32). This form is used in a situation such as Example 5 above, to seek a cancellation or change of an order entered in an emergency when one of the parties was not given an opportunity to present any information or argument.

Responses. A *response* is the basic form used by the other party to answer a motion. If your spouse has filed a motion, you will need to file a response to that motion. These include:

☞ Response to Motion Regarding Custody (Form 42).

☞ Response to Motion Regarding Support (Form 28, which deals with child support).

☞ Response to Motion Regarding Parenting Time (Form 37).

☞ Response to Motion Regarding Spousal Support (Form 48).

Orders. An *order* is the form the judge signs to resolve the issues brought up in the motion and response. These include:

☞ Order Regarding Custody, Parenting Time, and Support (Form 43).

☞ Order Regarding Support (Form 29). This deals only with child support.

☞ Order Regarding Parenting Time (Form 38).

☞ Order Regarding Spousal Support (Form 49).

☞ Order Modifying Ex Parte Order (Form 33).

Notices. A *notice* is a form used by one party to notify the other party that something is about to take place. This enables the other party to take appropriate action to protect his or her rights. The most common notice is a "notice of hearing," which informs the other party of the date, time, and place of a court hearing so that the other party may submit forms and documents, and attend the hearing. Most of the motion forms include a notice of hearing section for this purpose. Notices which are separate forms include:

☞ Notice to Enter Order Without Hearing (Form 31). After there has been a hearing, an order must be presented to the judge for signing. Normally, an order is either submitted to the judge at the hearing, or shortly after the hearing. If you are submitting an order to the judge after the hearing, your spouse has a right to see the order form to be sure it correctly states what the judge ordered. The Notice to Enter Order Without Hearing (Form 31) is sent to your spouse along with the order you have prepared, and your spouse then has a certain number of days to object to the order if it is not correct. For example, if the judge said at the hearing that child support will be $125 per week, and you prepare an order that reads "$175 per week," your spouse will probably object.

☛ Notice of Hearing to Enter Order (Form 30). Where a dispute arises regarding the accuracy of the proposed order, it may be necessary to have another hearing at which the judge will decide exactly how the order will read. Form 30 is used to notify your spouse of such a hearing.

There are separate SCAO-approved forms for creating or changing temporary orders concerning child support, child custody, and child visitation. If you are seeking a custody order, you can also include the issues of child support and visitation. However, if you are not seeking a custody order, child support and visitation will have to be requested using separate sets of forms. Spousal support (alimony) will always have to be requested separately. Forms to request temporary spousal support are included in appendix B, however, there are no SCAO-approved forms for spousal support. As these matters may have to be dealt with separately, we will discuss each type of request separately.

GENERAL
MOTION
PROCEDURES

The general procedure regarding motions for temporary custody, child support, visitation, and spousal support is as follows:

Prepare and file the motion. The person seeking the temporary order prepares and files the motion. There is a $20.00 motion filing fee. (If you can't afford the filing fee, see the section on "When You Can't Afford Court Costs" in chapter 12.)

Notify other parties. The person seeking the temporary order notifies the other party. This is done by mailing the other party a copy of the motion, which must be done at least nine days before the hearing, not including holidays. If the child has a legal custodian or guardian, that person must also be notified nine days in advance.

Other party files a response. The spouse not seeking the order may file a response.

Attend hearing. The person seeking the temporary order must attend the hearing with the judge or referee. The other party may, but is not required to, attend the hearing. The judge will then enter an order, which is prepared by the person seeking the order.

Temporary Custody

MOTION REGARDING CUSTODY

If you and your spouse agree there is a need for a temporary custody order, and can agree to what the custody order should be, you can prepare the Order Regarding Custody, Parenting Time, and Support (Form 43), and submit it to the judge for his or her approval and signature. With such an agreement it is not necessary to prepare the Motion Regarding Custody (Form 41) or the Response to Motion Regarding Custody (Form 42).

To request custody without an agreement, you will need to prepare a Motion Regarding Custody (Form 41). Form 41 also allows you to include a request for child support and visitation. (If you wish to request support or visitation without asking for custody, do not use this form. Instead, use the forms discussed under the sections below on "Temporary Child Support" and "Temporary Visitation.") To complete the Motion Regarding Custody (Form 41):

1. Complete the top portion of the form according to the instructions in chapter 5.

2. In item Ⓑ fill in the plaintiff's name, address, and telephone number, and the defendant's name, address, and phone number in the appropriate boxes. Check the box for "moving party" in the box containing your name.

3. In item Ⓒ check the first box if there is already some kind of judgment or court order regarding custody, and fill in the date of

that judgment or order. Check the second box if there is not already a judgment or order regarding custody.

4. Check item Ⓓ only if you checked box "a" in item Ⓒ, indicating that there is an existing custody order. If there is a custody order, check the appropriate box in item Ⓓ to indicate who currently has custody under that order.

5. In item Ⓔ fill in the name of the person (or persons) with whom the children are currently living, the address, and the date the children began living there. This should be for where the children are living now, regardless of what the custody order says.

6. In item Ⓕ state what circumstances have changed that make it necessary to establish a custody order, or to change the existing custody order. If there is not currently a custody order, there will usually have been an incident (or more than one incident) that caused you to file for a custody order. For example: "The defendant moved out of the family home approximately six months ago, leaving the plaintiff and children in the family home. On September 14, 1998, the defendant failed to return the children to the family home after weekend visitation, resulting in the children missing a week of school." If there is already a custody order, you will need to make some statement to show that circumstances have changed which require a change in custody. Give as much detail as possible, because this will be the basis of convincing the judge that a new custody order is needed. Use extra sheets of paper if necessary, and staple them to this form.

7. Item Ⓖ asks you to state how "proper cause exists" to require the establishment of a custody order, or to change the existing custody order. This is confusing as it sounds like it is asking the same thing as item Ⓕ, however, the fine print tells you to relate your answer to the factors in the Child Custody Act. Basically, item Ⓕ calls for a general statement of what facts have occurred to justify what you are asking, and item Ⓖ calls for a legal analysis of

why you should get custody based upon the factors the judge or referee will consider. See the section on "Custody" in chapter 4 for more information on these factors. Give as much detail as possible, because this will be the basis of convincing the judge that it is in the best interests of the children for you to have custody. Use extra sheets of paper if necessary, and staple them to this form.

8. If you and your spouse have reached an agreement, check the box for item Ⓗ and fill in your spouse's name on the line. Then, type in the details of your agreement, including child support and parenting time. Attach extra sheets if needed.

9. If you and your spouse have not reached an agreement on these matters, in item Ⓘ type in what you want the court to order, including the details regarding child support and parenting time. Attach extra sheets if needed. If you have reached an agreement, type in: "Same as 4 above."

10. In item Ⓙ write in the date and sign your name.

11. If your spouse will agree to sign the Order Regarding Custody, Parenting Time, and Support (Form 43), you will not need to set a hearing or fill in the "Notice of Hearing" portion of Form 41. If your spouse will not sign Form 43, contact the Friend of the Court and ask how to set a hearing on a Motion Regarding Custody and follow the instructions given. When you get the hearing date, fill in the "Notice of Hearing" portion of the form. On the line marked "Time," be sure to indicate "a.m." or "p.m."

12. Make five copies of Form 41, four copies of each extra sheet, and take them (along with the originals) to the court clerk, and pay the $20.00 motion filing fee. (If you can't afford the filing fee, see the section on "When You Can't Afford Court Costs" in chapter 12.) The clerk will attach the extra sheets, and will return four copies to you.

13. Mail one copy to your spouse (and any other appropriate parties) at least nine days before the hearing, then fill in the "Certificate of Mailing" portion of the form on all four copies. For more information, see the subsection on "Notifying other parties" on page 135. Keep one copy for yourself and return two copies to the clerk. The clerk will send one copy to the Friend of the Court.

RESPONSE TO MOTION REGARDING CUSTODY

If your spouse has filed a Motion Regarding Custody, you need to *immediately* prepare and file a Response to Motion Regarding Custody (Form 42). This form must be filed and mailed to your spouse at least five weekdays before the hearing. To complete Form 42:

1. Complete the top portion of the form according to the instructions in chapter 5.

2. In item Ⓑ fill in the plaintiff's name, address, and telephone number, and the defendant's name, address, and phone number in the appropriate boxes. Check the box for "moving party" in the box containing your spouse's name.

3. In item Ⓒ check the first box if there is already some kind of judgment or court order regarding custody, and fill in the date of that judgment or order. Check the second box if there is not already a judgment or order regarding custody.

4. Check item Ⓓ only if you checked box "a" in item Ⓒ, indicating that there is an existing custody order. If there is a custody order, check the appropriate box in item Ⓓ to indicate who currently has custody under that order.

5. In item Ⓔ fill in the name of the person (or persons) with whom the children are currently living, the address, and the date the children began living there. This should be for where the children are living now, regardless of what the custody order says.

6. In item Ⓕ check one of the boxes to indicate if you agree or do not agree with what is stated in item Ⓕ of the Motion Regarding

Custody filed by your spouse. If you check the box for "do not agree," type in a statement of what you do not agree with and why, giving as much detail as possible. Use extra sheets if needed.

7. In item Ⓖ check one of the boxes to indicate if you agree or do not agree with what is stated in item Ⓖ of the Motion Regarding Custody filed by your spouse. If you check the box for "do not agree," type in a statement of what you do not agree with and why, giving as much detail as possible. In item Ⓖ your spouse was asked to state how "proper cause exists" to require the establishment of a custody order, or to change the existing custody order. This is confusing as it sounds like it is asking the same thing as item Ⓕ, however, the fine print on the Motion Regarding Custody told your spouse to relate the answer to the factors in the Child Custody Act. Item Ⓕ on the Motion Regarding Custody required a general statement of what facts have occurred to justify what your spouse is asking for, and item Ⓖ calls for a legal analysis of why your spouse should get custody based upon the factors the judge or referee will consider. See the section on "Custody" in chapter 4 for more information on these factors. Give as much detail as possible, because this will be the basis of convincing the judge that it is in the best interests of the children for you to keep custody. Use extra sheets of paper if necessary, and staple them to this form.

8. Check the box for item Ⓗ only if the box for item Ⓗ is checked on your spouse's Motion Regarding Custody. If you agree to everything stated in item Ⓗ on your spouse's Motion Regarding Custody, check box "a." If there are any portions of what is stated in item Ⓗ on your spouse's Motion Regarding Custody, check box "b," then type in a detailed explanation of what portions you *do* agree upon.

9. If you agree to everything stated in item Ⓘ on your spouse's Motion Regarding Custody, check box "a" in item Ⓘ. If there are any portions of what is stated in item Ⓘ on your spouse's Motion

Regarding Custody, with which you do not agree, check box "b," then type in a detailed explanation of what you want the judge to order.

Example 1: "That the defendant be awarded custody, the plaintiff be entitled to visitation on alternate weekends from 6:00 p.m. Friday to 4:00 p.m. Sunday, and the plaintiff be ordered to pay child support according to the support guidelines."

Example 2: "That the current orders regarding custody, support, and parenting time remain in effect."

10. In item ③ write in the date and sign your name.

11. Make five copies of Form 42, four copies of each extra sheet, and take them (along with the originals) to the court clerk. The clerk will attach the extra sheets, and will return four copies to you.

12. Mail one copy to your spouse, then fill in the "Certificate of Mailing" portion of Form 42 on all four copies. Return two copies of Form 42 to the clerk.

ORDER REGARDING CUSTODY, PARENTING TIME, AND SUPPORT

If your spouse agrees to sign the Order Regarding Custody, Parenting Time, and Support (Form 43), you will not need a hearing (unless the judge requests one). In this situation, you can prepare Form 43 according to what you have agreed upon, have your spouse sign it, and submit it to the judge. If your spouse will not agree, you will need to appear for the hearing. See chapter 9 for more information about hearings.

At the hearing the judge will decide any matters that are not agreed upon, and you will prepare Form 43 according to what the judge orders. To complete the Order Regarding Custody, Parenting Time, and Support (Form 43):

1. Complete the top portion of the form according to the instructions in chapter 5. You will also fill in this information at the top of the second and third pages of this form

2. In item Ⓑ fill in the plaintiff's name, address, and telephone number, and the defendant's name, address, and phone number in the appropriate boxes.

3. If there was a hearing, fill in item Ⓒ with the date and judge's name.

4. In item Ⓓ check the appropriate box to describe the situation that resulted in the order. If there was a hearing, check the box for "after hearing." If you filed a Motion Regarding Custody and your spouse agreed to sign Form 43, check the box for "on consent of the parties." If you did not file a Motion Regarding Custody, and you and your spouse both signed Form 43, check the box for "on stipulation of the parties."

5. Check item Ⓔ only if you (or your spouse) filed a Motion Regarding Custody.

6. Check item Ⓕ only if your spouse (or you) filed a Response to Motion Regarding Custody.

7. For items Ⓖ through Ⓣ, fill in the information either to reflect your agreement with your spouse, or according to what the judge or referee orders. If you are preparing the order based on your agreement, be sure to include everything agreed upon in as much detail as possible. Anything not included in Form 43 will not be part of the order, even if it was part of your agreement. For an agreement, the following will help you complete these items:

   • Check the box for item Ⓖ and for "does."

   • Check the box for item Ⓗ and for "does."

   • Check the box for item Ⓘ and for "is." Also check the box for "establish" if this is the first custody order, or for "change" if you are changing an existing custody order.

   • If you are changing an existing custody order, check the box for item Ⓙ.

- Do not check items Ⓚ or Ⓛ. These items will only be checked if the judge orders the Motion Regarding Support to be dismissed, or if you and your spouse agree to dismiss the Motion Regarding Support (meaning that you have changed your mind and are satisfied with the way things are). In either case, the result will be that the current situation regarding custody will continue unchanged.

- In item Ⓜ, describe your agreement regarding custody by checking the appropriate boxes.

- In item Ⓝ, check one of the boxes to indicate whether this is the first parenting time order ("established") or is changing an existing parenting time order ("changed"). Then type in the details of the parenting time agreement.

- In item Ⓞ, fill in the starting date for child support, check one of the boxes to indicate whether the plaintiff or the defendant will pay support, and fill in the word "weekly," "monthly," etc., to indicate how often support payments are to be made. Also, check one of the boxes to indicate whether the child support amount "follows" or "does not follow" the child support formula, and check one of the boxes to indicate the number of children being supported under this support order.

- Items Ⓟ through Ⓣ are self-explanatory. Fill in these items according to your agreement, if they apply.

8. If you and your spouse agree, both of you must sign in item Ⓤ.

9. Make five copies of your completed Form 43.

10. Item Ⓥ is for the signature of a Friend of the Court representative in counties requiring Friend of the Court approval of the order. Contact the Friend of the Court in your county and ask if a signature is required. If required, ask how to go about getting the necessary signature of the Friend of the Court and follow the instructions. You will probably need to deliver the original and all

five copies to the Friend of the Court, and you will be notified when to come back to pick them up.

11. Deliver the original and all five copies to the judge. After the judge has signed them and returned copies to you, mail a copy of the signed order to your spouse, and complete the "Proof of Service" section at the bottom of the third page of Form 43.

TEMPORARY CHILD SUPPORT

Before preparing your own motion to establish or change child support, call or visit the Friend of the Court. It is quite possible that the Friend of the Court will be able to handle this for you, especially if you are seeking to change an existing child support order (either for an increase or a decrease) due to a change in income of either you or your spouse.

The Friend of the Court routinely deals with requests for changes in child support, and can get the process moving faster than you can. You should file your own request only after determining the Friend of the Court cannot help. If you must do this on your own, the following instructions will help you with the forms and procedures you will need.

MOTION
REGARDING
SUPPORT

To request temporary child support, or to change an existing child support order, you will need to prepare a Motion Regarding Support (Form 27). To complete Form 27:

1. Complete the top portion of the form according to the instructions in chapter 5.

2. In item ⑧ fill in the plaintiff's name, address, and telephone number, and the defendant's name, address, and phone number in the appropriate boxes. Check the box for "moving party" in the box containing your name.

3. In item © check the box "a" if there is already some kind of judgment or court order regarding child support, and fill in the date

143

of that judgment or order. Check the box "b" if there is not already a judgment or order regarding child support.

4. Check items Ⓓ, Ⓔ, and Ⓕ only if you checked box "a" in item Ⓒ (indicating an existing support order) and that order includes the relevant provision. For each item that is included in the existing child support order, check the appropriate box to indicate whether the plaintiff or the defendant is ordered to pay, and fill in the amount of the payment ordered and the frequency with which it is be paid (e.g., "week" or "month").

5. Check item Ⓖ only if you checked box "a" in item Ⓒ (indicating that there is an existing child support order). If you check this item, type in an explanation of what conditions have changed that would justify a change in the existing child support order. *Example 1:* "There has been a significant increase in child care costs." *Example 2:* "There has been a significant decrease in my income due to a layoff. My weekly income at the time the current order was entered was $500, and I am now receiving only $250 in unemployment benefits."

6. Check item Ⓗ if you and your spouse have agreed to begin child support, or change an existing child support order, and type in what you have agreed upon. Attach extra sheets if needed.

7. In item Ⓘ if you and your spouse have an agreement, check the box for "See 6. above for details." If there is not an agreement, type in what you are asking the court to order in the way of child support. *Example:* "The defendant should be ordered to pay child support in the amount of $175 per week for the two minor children." Attach extra sheets if needed.

8. In item Ⓙ, type in the date and sign your name.

9. Contact the Friend of the Court and find out how to schedule a hearing. Once you obtain the hearing date, fill in the "Notice of Hearing" portion of Form 27.

10. Make five copies of Form 27, and four copies of any extra sheets, and take them to the court clerk's office. The clerk will return four copies to you.

11. Mail a copy to your spouse at least nine days before the hearing date, then complete the "Certificate of Mailing" portion of Form 27 on the other three copies. For more information, see the subsection on "Notify other parties" on page 134. Return two copies to the court clerk.

RESPONSE TO
MOTION
REGARDING
SUPPORT

If your spouse has filed a Motion Regarding Support, you should *immediately* prepare and file a Response to Motion Regarding Support (Form 28). This form must be filed and mailed to your spouse at least five weekdays before the hearing. To complete Form 28:

1. Complete the top portion of the form according to the instructions in chapter 5.

2. In item Ⓑ fill in the plaintiff's name, address, and telephone number, and the defendant's name, address, and phone number in the appropriate boxes. Check the box for "moving party" in the box containing your spouse's name.

3. In item Ⓒ check box "a" if there is already some kind of judgment or court order regarding child support, and fill in the date of that judgment or order. Check the box "b" if there is not already a judgment or order regarding child support.

4. Check items Ⓓ, Ⓔ, and Ⓕ only if you checked box "a" in item Ⓒ (indicating that there is an existing child support order) and that order includes the relevant provision. For each item that is included in the existing child support order, check the appropriate box to indicate whether the plaintiff or the defendant is ordered to pay, and fill in the amount of the payment ordered and the payment frequency (e.g., "week" or "month").

5. Check the box for item Ⓖ only if item Ⓖ was checked on your spouse's Motion Regarding Support. If so, check one of the boxes

to indicate if you "agree" or "do not agree" with what is stated in item Ⓖ of the Motion Regarding Support filed by your spouse. If you check the box for "do not agree," type in a statement of what you do not agree with and why, giving as much detail as possible. Use extra sheets of paper if necessary.

6. Check the box for item Ⓗ only if the box for item Ⓗ is checked on your spouse's Motion Regarding Support. If you agree to everything stated in item Ⓗ on your spouse's Motion Regarding Support, check box "a." If there are any portions of what is stated in item Ⓗ on your spouse's Motion Regarding Support that you do not agree with, check box "b," then type in a detailed explanation of what you did agree upon. Use extra sheets of paper if necessary.

7. If you agree to everything stated in item Ⓘ on your spouse's Motion Regarding Support, check box "a" in item Ⓘ. If you do not agree with what is stated in item Ⓘ on your spouse's Motion Regarding Support, check box "b," then type in a detailed explanation of what you want the judge to order regarding child support. Use extra sheets of paper if necessary.

8. In item Ⓙ write in the date and sign your name.

9. Make five copies of Form 28, four copies of each extra sheet, and take them (along with the originals) to the court clerk. The clerk will attach the extra sheets, and will return four copies to you.

10. Mail one copy to your spouse, then fill in the "Certificate of Mailing" portion of Form 28 on all four copies. Return two copies of Form 28 to the clerk.

ORDER REGARDING SUPPORT

To complete the Order Regarding Support (Form 29):

1. Complete the top portion of the form according to the instructions in chapter 5. You will also fill in this information at the top of the second page of this form.

2. In item Ⓑ fill in the plaintiff's name, address, and telephone number, and the defendant's name, address, and phone number in the appropriate boxes.

3. If there was a hearing, fill in item Ⓒ with the date and judge's name.

4. In item Ⓓ check the appropriate box to describe the situation that resulted in the order. If there was a hearing, check the box for "after hearing." If you filed a Motion Regarding Support and your spouse agreed to sign Form 29, check the box for "on consent of the parties." If you did not file a Motion Regarding Support, and you and your spouse both signed Form 29, check the box for "on stipulation of the parties."

5. Check item Ⓔ only if you (or your spouse) filed a Motion Regarding Support.

6. Check item Ⓕ only if your spouse (or you) filed a Response to Motion Regarding Support.

7. Check item Ⓖ only if there is an existing child support order.

8. Check item Ⓗ if you and your spouse are agreeing to child support in an amount which is not based on the Child Support Formula. If you check this item you must type in an explanation of why the Child Support Formula would be unjust or inappropriate.

9. Do not check item Ⓘ. This item will only be checked if the judge orders the Motion Regarding Support to be dismissed, or if you and your spouse agree to dismiss the Motion Regarding Support (meaning that you have changed your mind and are satisfied with the way things are). In either case, the result will be that the current situation regarding child support won't change.

10. In item Ⓙ, fill in the starting date for child support, check one of the boxes to indicate whether the plaintiff or the defendant will

pay support, and fill in the word "weekly," "monthly," etc., to indicate how often support payments are to be made. Also, check one of the boxes to indicate whether the child support amount "follows" or "does not follow" the child support formula, and check one of the boxes to indicate the number of children being supported under this support order.

11. Check item Ⓚ if child care expenses are to be paid in addition to child support. If so, check one of the boxes to indicate whether the plaintiff or the defendant will pay child care expenses, and type in details of what will be paid, or the amount to be paid.

12. Check item Ⓛ if there is overdue child support from a previous child support order that is to be paid. If so, type in the amount due and how it is to be paid.

13. Check item Ⓜ if any credit is to be given for time the children spend with the parent who will be paying child support. If so, fill in the percentage of credit to be given.

14. Check item Ⓝ if it applies.

15. Check item Ⓞ if it applies, check the appropriate box or boxes, and fill in the percentage, to indicate how these medical expenses are to be paid. If there are any overdue health care expenses, fill in the amount and indicate how they will be paid.

16. If you and your spouse agree, both of you must sign in item Ⓟ.

17. Make five copies of your completed Form 29.

18. Item Ⓠ is for the signature of a representative of the Friend of the Court. Some counties require the Friend of the Court to approve the order before the judge will sign it. Contact the Friend of the Court in your county and ask if a signature is required. If required, ask how to go about getting the necessary signature of the Friend of the Court and follow the instructions.

You will probably need to deliver the original and all five copies to the Friend of the Court, and you will be notified when to come back to pick them up.

19. Deliver the original and all five copies to the judge. After the judge has signed them and returned copies to you, mail a copy of the signed order to your spouse, and complete the "Proof of Service" section at the bottom of the third page of Form 29.

TEMPORARY PARENTING TIME (VISITATION)

As stated earlier, Michigan has changed the term *visitation* to *parenting time*, apparently believing this sounds better to the non-custodial parent. If you and your spouse agree to a visitation order, you can prepare the Order Regarding Parenting Time (Form 38), and submit it to the judge for his or her approval and signature. With such an agreement it is not necessary to prepare the Motion Regarding Parenting Time (Form 36) or the Response to Motion Regarding Parenting Time (Form 37).

MOTION
REGARDING
PARENTING TIME

To request visitation without an agreement, you will need to prepare a Motion Regarding Parenting Time (Form 36). To complete the Motion Regarding Parenting Time (Form 36):

1. Complete the top portion of the form according to the instructions in chapter 5.

2. In item ⑧ fill in the plaintiff's name, address, and telephone number, and the defendant's name, address, and phone number in the appropriate boxes. Check the box for "moving party" in the box containing your name.

3. In item © check box "a" if there is already some kind of judgment or court order regarding parenting time, and fill in the date of that judgment or order. Check box "b" if there is not already a judgment or order regarding parenting time.

4. Check item Ⓓ only if you checked box "a" in item Ⓒ, indicating that there is an existing parenting time order, and that parenting order has been violated by your spouse. If so, fill in your spouse's name on the line, and check the appropriate box or boxes in item Ⓓ to indicate how that order was violated. Use extra sheets to explain in detail how the order was violated.

5. Check item Ⓔ only if you and your spouse have reached an agreement regarding parenting time. If so, fill in your spouse's name on the line, and type in the details of your parenting time agreement. Use extra sheets if needed.

6. In item Ⓕ check the box for "establish parenting time" if there is not a current parenting time order, or the box for "change parenting time" if there is already a parenting time order. Type in an explanation of why it is necessary to establish a parenting time order, or to change the existing custody order. Use extra sheets of paper if necessary, and staple them to this form.

7. In item Ⓖ check the box for "established" if there is not a current parenting time order, the box for "changed" if there is already a parenting time order and you want it changed, or "made up" if there is a parenting time order and you are asking that missed time be made up. Type in the details of what you want the court to order. Use extra sheets of paper if necessary.

8. In item Ⓗ write in the date and sign your name.

9. If your spouse will agree to sign the Order Regarding Parenting Time (Form 38), you will not need to set a hearing or fill in the "Notice of Hearing" portion of Form 38. If your spouse will not sign Form 38, contact the Friend of the Court and ask how to set a hearing on a Motion Regarding Parenting Time, and follow the instructions given. When you get the hearing date, fill in the "Notice of Hearing" portion of the form. On the line marked "Time," be sure to indicate "a.m." or "p.m."

10. Make five copies of Form 36, four copies of each extra sheet, and take them (along with the originals) to the court clerk. The clerk will attach the extra sheets, and will return four copies to you.

11. Mail one copy to your spouse at least nine days before the hearing, then fill in the "Certificate of Mailing" portion of Form 36 on all four copies. Return two copies of Form 36 to the clerk.

RESPONSE TO
MOTION
REGARDING
PARENTING TIME

If your spouse has filed a Motion Regarding Parenting Time, you should *immediately* prepare and file a Response to Motion Regarding Parenting Time (Form 37). This form must be filed and mailed to your spouse at least five weekdays before the hearing. To complete Form 37:

1. Complete the top portion of the form according to the instructions in chapter 5.

2. In item Ⓑ fill in the plaintiff's name, address, and telephone number, and the defendant's name, address, and phone number in the appropriate boxes. Check the box for "moving party" in the box containing your spouse's name.

3. In item Ⓒ check box "a" if there is already some kind of judgment or court order regarding parenting time, and fill in the date of that judgment or order. Check box "b" if there is not already a judgment or order regarding parenting time.

4. Check item Ⓓ only if you checked box "a" in item Ⓒ, indicating that there is an existing parenting time order. If so, check the appropriate box in item Ⓓ to indicate whether you "have" or "have not" violated that order. If you check "have not," type in a detailed explanation of how you disagree with what your spouse said in item Ⓓ of the Motion Regarding Parenting Time.

5. Check item Ⓔ only if your spouse checked item Ⓔ on the Motion Regarding Parenting Time. If so, check one of the boxes to reflect whether, and to what extent, you agree with your spouse about parenting time. If you check box "b," type in a

statement of what you do agree with, giving as much detail as possible. Use extra sheets if needed.

6. In item Ⓕ check one of the boxes to indicate if you "agree" or "do not agree" that it is in the best interests of the children to establish or change parenting time as indicated in your spouse's Motion Regarding Parenting Time. Also check one of the boxes to indicate whether parenting time is being established or changed. If you check the box for "do not agree," type in a statement of what you do not agree with and why, giving as much detail as possible. Use extra sheets of paper if necessary.

7. In item Ⓖ, check the appropriate boxes to express your desires. Check the box for "be" if you want a new parenting time order, or check the box for "not be" if you do not want a new parenting time order. Also check one of the boxes to indicate whether the change being considered is to establish, change, or make up parenting time. If you do not agree with what your spouse is requesting, type in a detailed explanation of why you disagree. Use extra sheets of paper if necessary.

8. In item Ⓗ write in the date and sign your name.

9. Make five copies of Form 37, four copies of each extra sheet, and take them (along with the originals) to the court clerk. The clerk will attach the extra sheets, and will return four copies to you.

10. Mail one copy to your spouse, then fill in the "Certificate of Mailing" portion of Form 37 on all four copies. Return two copies of Form 37 to the clerk.

ORDER
REGARDING
PARENTING TIME

How you proceed from this point depends upon whether you and your spouse agree. If your spouse agrees to sign the Order Regarding Parenting Time (Form 38), you will not need a hearing (unless the judge requests a hearing). In this situation, prepare Form 38 according to what you have agreed upon, have your spouse sign it, and submit it to the judge. If your spouse will not agree, you will need to appear for the hearing. At the hearing the judge will decide any matters that are not agreed upon, and you will prepare Form 38 according to what the judge orders. To complete the Order Regarding Parenting Time (Form 38):

1. Complete the top portion of the form according to the instructions in chapter 5.

2. In item Ⓑ fill in the plaintiff's name, address, and telephone number, and the defendant's name, address, and phone number in the appropriate boxes.

3. If there was a hearing, fill in item Ⓒ with the date and judge's name.

4. In item Ⓓ check the appropriate box to describe the situation that resulted in the order. If there was a hearing, check the box for "after hearing." If you filed a Motion Regarding Parenting Time and your spouse agreed to sign Form 38, check the box for "on consent of the parties." If you did not file a Motion Regarding Parenting Time, and you and your spouse both signed Form 38, check the box for "on stipulation of the parties."

5. Check item Ⓔ only if you (or your spouse) filed a Motion Regarding Parenting Time.

6. Check item Ⓕ only if your spouse (or you) filed a Response to Motion Regarding Parenting Time.

7. For items Ⓖ through Ⓙ, you will either fill in the information to reflect your agreement with your spouse, or according to what the judge or referee orders at the hearing. If you are preparing the order based on your agreement with your spouse, be sure to include everything you agreed upon, in as much detail as possible. Anything that is not included in Form 38 will not be part of the order, even if it was part of your agreement. Item Ⓙ is where you should type in the details of your parenting time agreement or order. Use extra sheets if needed.

8. If you and your spouse agree, both of you must sign in item Ⓚ.

9. Make five copies of your completed Form 38.

10. Item Ⓛ is for the signature of a Friend of the Court representative, which some counties require to approve the order before the judge will sign it. Contact the Friend of the Court in your county and ask if a signature is required. If required, ask how to go about getting the necessary signature of the Friend of the Court and follow the instructions. You will probably need to deliver the original and all five copies to the Friend of the Court, and you will be notified when to come back to pick them up.

11. Deliver the original and all five copies to the judge. After the judge has signed them and returned copies to you, mail a copy of the signed order to your spouse, and complete the "Proof of Service" section at the bottom of the third page of Form 38.

TEMPORARY SPOUSAL SUPPORT (ALIMONY)

MOTION
REGARDING
SPOUSAL
SUPPORT

There are no current SCAO-approved forms relating to temporary spousal support. Forms 47, 48, and 49 in appendix C have been designed to fill in this gap in the SCAO forms. To complete the Motion Regarding Spousal Support (Form 47):

1. Complete the top portion according to the instructions at the beginning of chapter 5.

2. In the plaintiff's and defendant's boxes, fill in the plaintiff's name, address, and telephone number, and the defendant's name, address, and phone number. Check the box for "moving party" in the box containing your name.

3. In item 1, check box "a" if there is already some kind of judgment or court order regarding spousal support, and fill in the date of

that judgment or order. Check box "b" if there is not already a judgment or order regarding spousal support.

4. Check items 2 and 3 only if you checked box "a" in item 1 (indicating that there is an existing spousal support order) and that existing order includes the relevant provision. For each item that is included in the existing spousal support order, check the appropriate box to indicate whether the plaintiff or the defendant is ordered to pay, and fill in the type and amount of the payment ordered, and the frequency with which it is be paid (e.g., "week" or "month").

5. Check item 4 only if you checked box "a" in item 1 (indicating that there is an existing spousal support order). If you check this item, type in an explanation of what conditions have changed that would justify a change in the existing spousal support order. *Example 1:* "There has been a significant increase in medical expenses." *Example 2:* "There has been a significant decrease in my income due to a layoff, therefore I no longer have the ability to pay the ordered amount. My weekly income at the time the current order was entered was $500, and I am now receiving only $250 in unemployment benefits."

6. Check item 5 if you and your spouse have agreed to begin spousal support, or change an existing spousal support order, and type in your spouse's name on the line, and type the details of what you have agreed upon. Attach extra sheets if needed.

7. In item 6, if you and your spouse have an agreement, check the box for "See 5. above for details." If there is not an agreement, type in what you are asking the court to order in the way of spousal support. *Example:* "The defendant should be ordered to pay spousal support in the amount of $175 per week." Attach extra sheets if needed.

8. Type in the date and sign your name on the lines indicated.

9.   Contact the Friend of the Court, court clerk, or judge's secretary and find out how to schedule a hearing. Once you obtain the hearing date, fill in the "Notice of Hearing" portion of the form.

10. Make five copies of Form 27, four copies of any extra sheets, and take them to the court clerk's office. The clerk will return four copies to you.

11. Mail a copy to your spouse at least nine days before the hearing date, then complete the "Certificate of Mailing" portion of Form 27 on the other three copies. Return two copies to the court clerk.

RESPONSE TO MOTION REGARDING SPOUSAL SUPPORT

If your spouse filed a Motion Regarding Spousal Support, you need to *immediately* file a Response to Motion Regarding Spousal Support (Form 48). This form must be filed and mailed to your spouse at least five weekdays before the hearing. To complete the Response to Motion Regarding Spousal Support (Form 48):

1.   Complete the top portion according to the instructions in chapter 5.

2.   In the plaintiff's and defendant's boxes, fill in the plaintiff's name, address, and telephone number, and the defendant's name, address, and telephone number. Check the box for "moving party" in the box containing your spouse's name.

3.   In item 1, check box "a" if there is already some kind of judgment or court order regarding spousal support, and fill in the date of that judgment or order. Check box "b" if there is not already a judgment or order regarding spousal support.

4.   Check items 2 and 3 only if you checked box "a" in item 1 (indicating that there is an existing spousal support order) and that order includes the relevant provision. For each item that is included in the existing spousal support order, check the appropriate box to indicate whether the plaintiff or the defendant is

ordered to pay, and fill in the type and amount of the payment ordered and the payment frequency (e.g., "week" or "month").

5. Check the box for item 4 only if your spouse's Motion Regarding Spousal Support included a statement that circumstances have changed. If so, check one of the boxes to indicate if you "agree" or "do not agree" with what is stated about changed circumstances in your spouse's Motion Regarding Spousal Support. If you check the box for "do not agree," type in a statement of what you do not agree with and why, giving as much detail as possible. Use extra sheets of paper if necessary.

6. Check the box for item 5 only if your spouse's Motion Regarding Spousal Support includes a statement that you agree with what is being requested. If you agree to everything as stated in your spouse's Motion Regarding Spousal Support, check box "a." If there are any portions of what is stated about your agreement in your spouse's Motion Regarding Spousal Support that you do not agree with, check box "b," then type in a detailed explanation of what you did agree upon. Use extra sheets of paper if necessary.

7. If you agree to everything being asked for in your spouse's Motion Regarding Spousal Support, check box "a" in item 6. If you do not agree with everything being asked for in your spouse's Motion Regarding Spousal Support, check box "b," then type in a detailed explanation of what you want the judge to order regarding spousal support. Use extra sheets of paper if necessary.

8. Write in the date and sign your name on the lines indicated.

9. Make five copies of Form 28, four copies of each extra sheet, and take them (along with the originals) to the court clerk. The clerk will attach the extra sheets, and will return four copies to you.

10. Mail one copy to your spouse, then fill in the "Certificate of Mailing" portion of Form 28 on all four copies. Return two copies of Form 28 to the clerk.

ORDER REGARDING SPOUSAL SUPPORT

To complete the Order Regarding Spousal Support (Form 49):

1. Complete the top portion according to the instructions in chapter 5. You will also fill in this information at the top of the second page of this form.

2. In the plaintiff's and defendant's boxes, fill in the plaintiff's name, address, and telephone number, and the defendant's name, address, and phone number. You will also fill in the parties' names on the second page of this form.

3. If there was a hearing, fill in the date of the hearing and judge's name on the lines below the Defendant's box.

4. In item 1, check the appropriate box to describe the situation that resulted in the order. If there was a hearing, check the box for "after hearing." If you filed a Motion Regarding Spousal Support and your spouse agreed to sign the order (Form 49), check the box for "on consent of the parties." If you did not file a Motion Regarding Spousal Support, and you and your spouse both signed Form 49, check the box for "on stipulation of the parties."

5. Check item 2 only if you (or your spouse) filed a Motion Regarding Spousal Support.

6. Check item 3 only if your spouse (or you) filed a Response to Motion Regarding Spousal Support.

7. Check item 5 only if there is an existing spousal support order.

8. Item 5 will only be checked if the judge orders the Motion Regarding Spousal Support to be dismissed, or if you and your spouse agree to dismiss the Motion Regarding Spousal Support (meaning that you have changed your mind and are satisfied

with the way things are). In either case, the result will be that the current situation regarding spousal support will continue unchanged.

9. In item 6, fill in the starting date for spousal support, check one of the boxes to indicate whether the plaintiff or the defendant will pay spousal support, and fill in the the amount of spousal support and the word "weekly," "monthly," etc., to indicate how often support payments are to be made.

10. Check item 7 if there is overdue spousal support from a previous spousal support order that is to be paid. If so, type in the amount due and how it is to be paid.

11. Check the appropriate box in item 8 to indicate whether spousal support will be paid to the plaintiff, the defendant, or through the Friend of the Court.

12. If you and your spouse agree, both of you must sign where indicated on the second page.

13. Just below the signature spaces for you and your spouse there is a space for the signature of a representative of the Friend of the Court. Some counties require the Friend of the Court to approve the order before the judge will sign it. Contact the Friend of the Court in your county and ask if a signature is required. If required, ask how to go about getting the necessary signature of the Friend of the Court and follow the instructions. You will probably need to deliver the original and all five copies to the Friend of the Court, and you will be notified when to come back to pick them up.

14. Make five copies of your completed Form 49.

15. Deliver the original and all five copies to the judge. After the judge has signed them and returned copies to you, mail a copy of the signed order to your spouse, and complete the "Proof of Service" section at the bottom of the second page of Form 49.

Ex Parte Orders

An *ex parte* order is one entered with only one party being involved in the process, usually only in an emergency situation where there is a good reason for not waiting until the other party is notified of the motion and given an opportunity to respond before an order is entered.

If your spouse obtained an ex parte order, you will probably first know about it when you receive a copy of the order. You may receive it in the mail, or be served by a sheriff deputy or other process server. If the order is not to your liking, you may need to file a motion to change it. You must act quickly, as the law only gives you fourteen days after you are served with the ex parte order in which to file an objection. If you file an objection, the Friend of the Court will try to resolve the dispute. If this is not successful, a Friend of the Court hearing will be held.

The following are a few examples of situation that cause people to go back to court to change an ex parte order:

- ☛ The ex parte child support order is based on your spouse's inaccurately high estimate of your income.

- ☛ The ex parte order grants your spouse custody of your child, and your spouse is an unfit parent.

- ☛ The ex parte order gives you visitation on alternate weekends, and you work weekends.

OBJECTION TO EX PARTE ORDER AND MOTION TO RESCIND OR MODIFY

The way to begin challenging an ex parte order is to prepare and file an Objection to Ex Parte Order and Motion to Rescind or Modify (Form 32). To complete Form 32:

1. Complete the top portion of the form according to the instructions in chapter 5.

2. In the plaintiff's and defendant's boxes, fill in the plaintiff's name, address, and telephone number, and the defendant's name, address, and phone number.

3. On the line marked "Name of party filing motion," type in your name.

4. On the line in paragraph 1, type in the date of the ex parte order to which you are objecting.

5. In item 2, check the appropriate box or boxes to indicate whether you are objecting to custody, visitation, or support provisions of the ex parte order. Then type in an explanation of why you object. Use extra sheets if needed.

6. Write in the date and sign your name on the lines indicated.

7. If your spouse will agree to the change you desire, and will sign an Order Modifying Ex Parte Order (Form 33), you will not need to set a hearing or fill in the "Notice of Hearing" portion of Form 32. If your spouse will not sign Form 33, contact the Friend of the Court or judge's secretary and ask how to set a hearing on an Objection to Ex Parte Order and Motion to Rescind or Modify, and follow the instructions given. When you get the hearing date, fill in the "Notice of Hearing" portion of the form. On the line marked "Time," be sure to indicate "a.m." or "p.m."

8. Make five copies of Form 32, four copies of each extra sheet, and take them (along with the originals) to the court clerk. The clerk will attach the extra sheets, and will return four copies to you.

9. Mail one copy to your spouse, then fill in the "Certificate of Mailing" portion of Form 32 on all four copies. *Warning:* You must mail a copy to your spouse at least nine days before the date of the hearing. Return two copies to the clerk, and one copy goes to the Friend of the Court.

Order Modifying Ex Parte Order

To complete the Order Modifying Ex Parte Order (Form 33):

1. Complete the top portion of the form according to the instructions in chapter 5.

2. In the plaintiff's and defendant's boxes, fill in the plaintiff's name, address, and telephone number, and the defendant's name, address, and telephone number.

3. If there was a hearing, fill in the date of the hearing and judge's name on the lines beside the Defendant's box.

4. In item 1, check the box or boxes to indicate the type of order being changed: custody, visitation, or support. Then type in the details of the new order. Use extra sheets if needed.

5. Check the box in item 2 if there are extra sheets attached.

6. On the line in item 3, type in the date the new order becomes effective.

7. You will note there are signature lines for both the plaintiff and the defendant. You will be directed to sign if it is appropriate.

8. Submit the form to the judge, who will fill in the date and judge's signature spaces at the bottom of the form.

ENTERING ORDERS

Basically, a court order is *entered* when it is signed by the judge. If you and your spouse agree, and both of you sign the order, the order can simply be mailed or delivered to the judge. The judge will see both of your signatures and will know there is no argument. No hearing is required, and the judge will sign the order and mail copies back to you.

If there has been a hearing on the motion, there are three ways to get the order signed by the judge. First, if the order can be quickly prepared at the hearing, it can be handed to the judge for his or her signature at that time. Second, the order can be prepared shortly after the hearing, and then mailed or delivered to the judge. Third, the order can be presented to the judge at a subsequent hearing.

Usually, a subsequent hearing is not necessary unless there is a dispute over what was ordered at the hearing on the motion, and whether what was ordered is accurately reflected in the proposed order. The accuracy of the proposed order can be questioned either by the judge or by your spouse (or by you if your spouse has prepared the order and you don't think it is accurate).

NOTICE TO
ENTER ORDER
WITHOUT
HEARING

If you did not get your order prepared and signed by the judge at the hearing, you will need to prepare a Notice to Enter Order Without Hearing (Form 31). To complete Form 31:

1. Complete the top portion of the form according to the instructions in chapter 5.

2. In the plaintiff's and defendant's boxes, fill in the plaintiff's name and the defendant's name. Check the box for "moving party" in the box containing your name.

3. On the lines in item Ⓒ, fill in the date of the hearing on the motion, and the subject of the motion (i.e., custody, visitation, support, or spousal support).

4. On the lines in item Ⓓ, fill in the date and sign your name.

5. Make five copies of your filled-in Form 31. Make four extra copies of the order you have prepared for the judge to sign, and type the words "Proposed Order" on the top of them. Staple the copies of the proposed order to the copies of Form 31. Take the original and all copies to the court clerk for filing. The clerk will return four copies to you.

6. Mail a copy of Form 31 (with the attached copy of the proposed order) to your spouse. This must be done within seven days of the date of the hearing.

7. Sign and date the "Certificate of Mailing" portion of Form 31, and file two copies of Form 31 with the court clerk.

8. If no objection is filed by your spouse within seven days after you mailed him or her a copy, you will take the original order to the court clerk, who will submit it to the judge for signing. You will then be notified that you may pick up the signed order. Pick up the signed order, make five copies of it and return them to the clerk. The clerk will keep the original and one copy, and return the others to you. Mail a copy of the signed order to your spouse.

If the judge wants the order changed, you will be notified of a hearing date. If your spouse files an objection, you will need to schedule a hearing (see the section below on the "Notice of Hearing to Enter Order").

OBJECTION TO
PROPOSED
ORDER

If your spouse is the one submitting a proposed order, and you agree that the proposed order accurately and completely reflects what the judge ordered, you do not need to do anything. After at least seven days, the judge will sign the order. Your spouse will then mail you a copy of the order containing the judge's signature.

If you do not agree that the proposed order accurately and completely reflects what the judge ordered, you need to *immediately* file an Objection to Proposed Order (Form 40). This must be done within seven weekdays (not including holidays) of the date the proposed order was *mailed* to you (not the date it was received by you). For example, if your spouse mailed it on Monday, you must file Form 40 no later than Wednesday of the following week, even if you didn't receive it in the mail until Thursday. So check the date your spouse filled in on the "Certificate of Mailing" section to see when the seven-day time period began. To complete Form 40:

1. Complete the top portion of the form according to the instructions in chapter 5.

2. In the plaintiff's and defendant's boxes, fill in the plaintiff's name, address, and phone number, and the defendant's name, address, and phone number. Check the box for "moving party" in the box containing your spouse's name.

3. In item Ⓒ, type in the date you received the proposed order from your spouse.

4. In item Ⓓ, type in an explanation of why you object to the proposed order. This should tell the judge how the order is inaccurate or incomplete, in relation to what the judge ordered at the hearing on the motion.

    Example 1: "The plaintiff's proposed order states that child support is to be paid every two weeks (i.e., twenty-six payments per year), but the court ordered payments twice a month (i.e., twenty-four payments per year) to coincide with the defendant's pay periods."

    Example 2: "The plaintiff's proposed order does not include the provisions for holiday visitation which were ordered in addition to alternate weekend visitation. The court ordered holiday visitation as follows: *(insert details of holiday visitation)*."

5. In item Ⓔ, fill in the date, sign your name, and print or type your name on the lines indicated.

6. Make five copies of your filled-in Form 40, and take them (along with the originals) to the court clerk. The clerk will return four copies to you.

7. Mail one copy to your spouse *immediately*, then fill in the "Certificate of Mailing" portion of Form 32 on all four copies. Return two copies to the clerk, who will keep one copy and send one copy to the Friend of the Court.

Your spouse will then need to schedule a hearing in order to have an order entered. You will need to attend the hearing and explain to the judge why you object to the order. You may need to have witnesses testify or present documents as evidence. After the judge hears any evidence presented by you and your spouse, the judge will make a decision. The judge may decide to sign the original order presented by

165

your spouse, or may order that a new order be prepared. It is up to your spouse to prepare a new order which follows the judge's decision.

NOTICE OF HEARING TO ENTER ORDER

If your spouse files an Objection to Proposed Order, or if the judge notifies you that he or she will not sign the proposed order you submitted, it will be necessary to schedule a hearing. (Note: If you filed an Objection to Proposed Order, your spouse will schedule a hearing.) Contact the judge's secretary and obtain a hearing date. You will then need to prepare a Notice of Hearing to Enter Order (Form 30). To complete Form 30:

1. Complete the top portion of the form according to the instructions in chapter 5.

2. In the plaintiff's and defendant's boxes, fill in the plaintiff's name and the defendant's name. Check the box for "moving party" in the box containing your name.

3. On the lines in item ©, fill in the date of the hearing on the motion, and the subject of the motion (i.e., custody, visitation, support, or spousal support).

4. On the lines in item ⓓ, type in the name of the judge or referee who will preside over the hearing, and the date, time, and place of the hearing.

5. On the lines in item ⓔ, fill in the date and sign your name.

6. Make five copies of your filled-in Form 30, and take them to the court clerk along with the original. The clerk will keep the original and one copy, and will return the other four copies to you.

7. Mail a copy to your spouse at least nine days before the hearing date, then date and sign the "Certificate of Mailing" section of the form on the other copies. The date entered here must be the same date that you mail the copy to your spouse.

8. Return two copies to the clerk, who will send one of them to the Friend of the Court.

You will then need to attend the hearing, and explain why you think the order you submitted is correct and should be signed. Bring the original and five copies of the order you originally submitted (as these are ready for the judge to sign, they should *not* have the words "proposed order" on them). If this hearing is because your spouse filed an Objection to Proposed Order, your spouse will be arguing why your proposed order should not be signed. By reading your spouse's Objection to Proposed Order you should have at least a basic idea of what he or she will be arguing.

If this hearing is the result of the judge notifying you the he or she will not sign your proposed order, you will first need to have the judge explain his or her objection to the proposed order. You will then have a chance to explain why you think the order should be signed, or to find out how the judge wants the order changed.

In any event, one of two things will happen. Either the judge will end up signing your original proposed order, or the judge will give you instructions about how he or she wants a new order prepared. If a new order is required, you will need to prepare the new order and submit it to the judge as soon as possible (no later than the following day).

Be sure to read chapter 9 regarding preparing for, and presenting your case at, the hearing.

SPECIAL CIRCUMSTANCES 12

WHEN YOU CAN'T AFFORD COURT COSTS

If you can't afford to pay the filing fee and other costs associated with the divorce, you can file an Affidavit and Order Suspension of Fees/Costs (Form 19). In order to qualify for a waiver of the filing fee, you must be "indigent." If you are indigent, your income is probably low enough for you to qualify for public assistance (welfare).

> **Caution.** If you decide to use this form, you will probably be asked for more information to prove that you meet the requirements for being declared indigent, and therefore, eligible to have the filing and service fees waived. Before you file this form, you may want to see if the court clerk will give you any information on what is required to be declared indigent. You should also be aware that you can be held in contempt of court for giving false information on this form.

To complete the Affidavit and Order Suspension of Fees/Costs (Form 19):

1. Complete the top portion according to the instructions in chapter 5.

2. Type your name, address and telephone number in the box marked "Plaintiff/Petitioner name, address, and telephone no."

3. Type your spouse's name, address, and telephone number in the box marked "Defendant/Respondent name, address, and telephone no." Also, if your spouse has an attorney, type in his or her name, address, and telephone number where indicated.

4. In paragraph 1, type in your name, and check the box for "plaintiff/petitioner."

5. In paragraph 2, check the box for subparagraph "a" if you are receiving public assistance, and fill in the amount of your grant and your AFDC or other public assistance case number. If you are not receiving public assistance, check the box for subparagraph "b," and fill in the income, asset and obligations (debts) information. Attach an extra sheet of paper if necessary.

6. Take this form to the court clerk and sign it before the clerk. This form will then be submitted by the clerk to the judge, who will complete the "Order" section on the second page.

PROTECTING YOURSELF AND YOUR CHILDREN

Some people have special concerns when getting prepared to file for a divorce. Two such concerns can be fear of physical attack by their spouse, and fear that their spouse will take the children, run away and go into hiding (or even take them out of the country). There are additional actions you can take if you feel you are in any of these situations.

If your spouse is determined and resourceful, there is no guaranteed way to prevent the things discussed in this section from happening. All you can do is put as many obstacles as possible in your spouse's way, and prepare for him or her to suffer consequences for acting improperly.

PETITION FOR PERSONAL PROTECTION ORDER

To protect yourself from harm, or to prevent your spouse from taking the children, you can seek a *personal protection order*. However, just being afraid that your spouse might take such action will not be enough. Your spouse must either have actually done something, or must have threatened to do something. A personal protection order will subject your spouse to arrest for violating the requirements of the order. If you think you need a personal protection order, get a copy of the booklet "Instructions for Personal Protection Orders" from the clerk and read it.

Although the forms for a personal protection order are included in appendix B, you should obtain these forms from the clerk. The clerk's Petition for Personal Protection Order has five copies, and the Personal Protection Order has six copies. You can use the forms in appendix B as worksheets, so that you have all of the necessary information to fill out and file the forms when you go to the clerk's office.

When you go to the clerk's office, you will need five copies of the Petition for Personal Protection Order. To complete the Petition for Personal Protection Order (Form 44):

1. Complete the top portion according to the instructions in chapter 5.

2. Type your name in the box marked "Plaintiff's name," and check the box if you are under age eighteen. There is also a space to fill in your address and phone number. If you don't want your spouse to know your address and phone number, write in the address of a friend or relative, so that the court can contact you.

3. Type your spouse's name, address, and phone number in the "Respondent" box. If your spouse is under age eighteen, check the box.

4. In item 1, check the box for "are husband and wife."

5. If your spouse is required to carry a firearm in the course of his or her employment, or if you do not know if he or she is required to carry a firearm, check the appropriate box in item 2. If you know that your spouse is not required to carry a firearm, do not check either box.

6. In item 3, check the appropriate boxes to indicate whether there are any pending court cases, or any court orders or judgments, regarding you and your spouse (such as a case for paternity, child support, a previously filed divorce case, previous personal protection orders). If there is another case, fill in the case number, name of the court and county, and name of the judge in the appropriate spaces.

7. In item 4, type in an explanation of what has occurred that made you decide you needed a personal protection order. This should be a fairly detailed and specific explanation of what has taken place, or what has been threatened, so that the judge has enough facts to determine that you need an personal protection order. Include dates, times, places, etc. There is not enough room on the form, so you will need to use an extra sheet of paper and staple it to the form. Use as many sheets as necessary, but try not to go over two pages or the judge may not want to read it all.

8. In item 5, check the boxes to indicate the type of protection you want. Checking some of these boxes will also require you to fill in certain information. You will need to convince the judge that you need each type of protection you ask for, so don't check boxes that aren't really necessary. Item "b" only applies to keeping your spouse away from property other than your home (such as your school or workplace). Only check item "e" if there has been more than one act of harassment.

9. If the situation is so dangerous that you can't wait for your spouse to be notified of your motion and a hearing to be held, or that your spouse may harm you if he or she finds out you have filed for a personal protection order, check the box in item 6.

10. If you are under age eighteen, and an adult (called a *next friend*) is filing this form on your behalf, check the box in item 7.

11. Sign and date the form on the lines indicated. This is now ready for filing with the clerk. The clerk will fill in additional information and give you copies.

The second page of Form 44 is a Proof of Service, which will be completed by the person who serves your spouse with a copy of this form.

NOTICE OF HEARING ON PETITION FOR PERSONAL PROTECTION ORDER

If you did not request an ex parte order (by checking item 6 in your Petition for Personal Protection Order), you will need to prepare a Notice of Hearing on Petition for Personal Protection Order. Again, it is best to use the clerk's form which has the five required copies. To complete the Notice of Hearing on Petition for Personal Protection Order (Form 46):

1. Complete the top portion according to the instructions in chapter 5.

2. Type your name in the box marked "Petitioner's name," and type your spouse's name in the box marked "Respondent's name."

4. In the box after the word "To," type in your spouse's name and address.

5. In the spaces below item "C," fill in the name of the judge, the date of the hearing, the time of the hearing, and the location of the hearing (the court clerk will give you this information when you file your papers).

6. Date and sign the form on the lines indicated.

The second page of Form 46 is a Proof of Service, which will be completed by the person who serves your spouse with a copy of this form.

PERSONAL PROTECTION ORDER

When you go to the clerk's office, you will need six copies of the Petition for Personal Protection Order (the form available at the clerk's office has the required six copies. To complete the Personal Protection Order (Form 45):

1. Complete the top portion according to the instructions in chapter 5. Check the box for "Ex Parte," if you checked item 6 in your Petition for Personal Protection Order (Form 44).

2. Type in the name, address, and phone number information for you and your spouse in the same manner as you did in your Petition for Personal Protection Order. Again, if you do not want you spouse to have this information, use the address and phone number of a friend or relative.

3. In the item marked D, type your spouse's name, and as much of the other identifying information as you know in the appropriate box.

The judge will complete the rest of Form 45. The second page of Form 45 is a Proof of Service, which will be completed by the person who serves your spouse with a copy of this form once it is signed by the judge.

Keep a copy of any personal protection order issued by the judge. If your spouse does anything you believe violates the order, call the police. Show them the order when they arrive.

KIDNAPPING PREVENTION

If you are worried that your spouse may try to kidnap your children, you should make sure that the day care center, baby-sitter, relative, or whomever you leave the children with at any time, is aware that you are in the process of a divorce and that the children are only to be released to you personally (not to your spouse or to any other relative, friend, etc.).

To prevent your spouse from taking the children out of the United States, you can apply for a passport for each child. Once a passport is issued, the government will not issue another. So get their passport and lock it up in a safe deposit box or other safe place where you are absolutely sure your spouse can't get it. (This won't prevent them from being taken to Canada or Mexico, where passports are not required, but will prevent them from being taken overseas.) You can also file a motion to prevent the removal of the children from the state and to deny passport services. If you are genuinely worried that your spouse may try to take your child out of the country, it would be a good idea for you to consult a lawyer. This is too serious of a matter for you to try to handle yourself just to save some money.

PROTECTING YOUR PROPERTY

If you genuinely fear that your spouse will try to remove money from bank accounts, try to hide important papers showing what property you own, or hide items of property, you may want to take this same action before your spouse can. However, you can make a great deal of trouble for yourself with the judge if you do this to try to get these assets for yourself. So, make a complete list of any property you do take, and be sure to include these items in any financial statement you prepare for the Friend of the Court or for anything else connected with your divorce case. You may need to convince the judge that you only took these items temporarily, in order to preserve them until a Judgment of Divorce is entered. Do not spend any cash you take from a bank account, or sell or give away any items of property. Any cash should be placed in a separate bank account, without your spouse's name on it, and kept separate from any other cash you have. (Of course, you may use funds to pay for necessary living expenses, such as rent, utility bills, food, medical bills, etc.). Any papers, such as deeds, car titles, stock or bond certificates, etc., should be placed in a safe deposit box, without your spouse's name on it. The idea is not to take these things for yourself, but to get them in a safe place so your spouse can't hide them and deny they ever existed.

One other thing you can do to try to protect your property is seek a court order. There are no currently approved SCAO forms, but you can try using the previously approved SCAO forms included in appendix B.

NOTICE OF HEARING
AND MOTION FOR
MUTUAL TEMPORARY
RESTRAINING ORDER
CONSERVING
PROPERTY

To complete the Notice of Hearing and Motion for Mutual Temporary Restraining Order Conserving Property (Form 50):

1. Complete the top portion according to the instructions in chapter 5. Also, check the box for "Interim (ex parte)" if you are asking for a restraining order without prior notice and hearing (see item 6 below for more information on this), or the box for "Temporary" if there will be notice and hearing.

2. Type your name in the box marked "Plaintiff's name." Check the box for "Moving party."

3. Type your spouse's name in the box marked "Defendant's name." Also, if your spouse has an attorney, type in his or her name, address, and telephone number where indicated.

4. Obtain a hearing date from the clerk or the judge's secretary, then fill in the hearing information under the heading "Notice of Hearing."

5. In paragraph 4, type in a brief explanation of what has occurred that makes you believe you need a restraining order.

6. If there is such an emergency that you can't wait for your spouse to be notified and a hearing to be held, check the box for paragraph 5, and type in a brief explanation of the situation justifying an order without notice or hearing (read paragraph 5 for an explanation of what type of situation is required). You will also need to complete the section of this form titled "Attorney/Plaintiff/Defendant Certification," by typing a summary of what you did to try to notify your spouse that you are seeking an order without prior notice and hearing. For example: "I attempted to telephone the other party the night before, and in the morning immediately before filing this motion, but received no answer."

MUTUAL
RESTRAINING
ORDER
CONSERVING
PROPERTY

To complete the Mutual Restraining Order Conserving Property (Form 51):

1. Complete the top portion according to the instructions in chapter 5. Also check the box for "Original," to show that this is the first order and not a modification of an earlier order.

2. Type your name and address in the box marked "Plaintiff's name and address."

3. Type your spouse's name and address in the box marked "Defendant's name and address." If your spouse has an attorney, type in his or her name, address, and telephone number where indicated.

4. Check one of the boxes for either "After hearing" if a hearing is held, "Interim (ex parte)" if the order is being issued without notice and hearing, or "Consent" if your spouse consents (in which case your spouse will need to sign at the bottom of the form).

5. If the order is to be issued without notice, check the box for paragraph 5.

6. Submit this form to the clerk along with your motion (Form 28) if there will not be a hearing. If there will be a hearing, submit this form to the judge at the hearing.

7. If your spouse appears at a hearing, you can give him or her a copy of the order, and have him or her sign the "Acknowledgment of Service" on the second page of the order. Otherwise, you will need to arrange for the sheriff to serve your spouse with a copy, in which case the sheriff will complete the certificate of service on the second page.

TAXES

As you are no doubt aware, the United States' income tax code is complicated and ever-changing. For this reason it is impossible to give detailed legal advice with respect to taxes in a book such as this. Any such information could easily be out of date by the time of publication. Therefore, it is strongly recommended that you consult your accountant, lawyer, or whomever prepares your tax return, about the tax consequences of a divorce. A few general concerns are discussed in this chapter, to give you an idea of some of the tax questions which can arise.

TAXES AND
PROPERTY
DIVISION

You and your spouse may be exchanging title to property as a result of your divorce. Generally, there will not be any tax to pay as the result of such a transfer. However, whomever gets a piece of property will be responsible to pay any tax which may become due upon sale.

The Internal Revenue Service (I.R.S.) has issued numerous rulings about how property is to be treated in divorce situations. You need to be especially careful if you are transferring any tax shelters, or other complicated financial arrangements, in which case you should consult a tax expert.

Be sure to read the following section on alimony, because fancy property settlements are asking for tax problems.

TAXES AND
ALIMONY

Alimony can cause the most tax problems of any aspect of divorce. I.R.S. is always making new rulings on whether an agreement is really alimony, or is really property division. The basic rule is that alimony is treated as income to the person receiving it, and as a deduction for the person paying it. Therefore, in order to manipulate the tax consequences, many couples try to show something as part of the property settlement, instead of as alimony; or the reverse. As I.R.S. becomes aware of these "tax games" it issues rulings on how it will view a certain arrangement. If you are simply talking about the regular, periodic payment of cash, I.R.S. will probably not question that it is alimony. But if you try to call it property settlement, you may run into problems. The important thing is to consult a tax expert if you are considering any unusual or creative property settlement or alimony arrangements.

TAXES AND
CHILD SUPPORT

There are fairly simple tax rules regarding child support:

1. Whomever has custody gets to claim the children on his or her tax return (unless both parents file a special I.R.S. form agreeing to a different arrangement each year).

2. The parent receiving child support does not need to report it as income.

3. The parent paying child support cannot deduct it.

If you are sharing physical custody, the parent with whom the child lives for the most time during the year is entitled to claim the child as a dependent.

The I.R.S. form to reverse this must be filed each year. Therefore, if you and your spouse have agreed that you will get to claim the children (even though you don't have custody), you should get your spouse to sign an open-ended form which you can file each year, so that you don't have to worry about it each year. A phone call to the I.R.S. can help you get answers to questions on this point.

PENSION PLANS

Pension plans, or retirement plans, of you and your spouse are marital assets. They may be very valuable assets. If you and your spouse are young, and have not been working very long, you may not have pension plans worth worrying about. Also, if you have both worked, and have similar pensions plans, it may be best just to include a provision in your settlement agreement that "each party shall keep his or her own pension plan." But if you have been married a long time, and your spouse worked while you stayed home to raise the children, your spouse's pension plan may be worth a lot of money, and may be necessary to see you through retirement.

If you and your spouse cannot agree on how to divide your pension plans, you should see an attorney about obtaining a *Qualified Domestic Relations Order* (or "QDRO," which is commonly pronounced "qwá-drow" by lawyers and judges). This document tells the pension plan manager how to divide payments. The valuation of pension plans, and how they are to be divided, is a complicated matter which you should not attempt.

DEFENDING YOURSELF

If your spouse filed for divorce first, you need to respond in writing within twenty-one days of receiving the Summons and Complaint for Divorce. You can use the Answer and Waiver (Form 13) in appendix C, but this will basically admit what your spouse is asking for in his or her Complaint for Divorce. If you disagree with anything in your spouse's Complaint for Divorce, you will want to file a more complete Answer.

Basically, an Answer has three parts: 1) an admission or denial of the allegations in the Complaint for Divorce, 2) any defenses you may want to raise, and 3) a request for what you want the judge to do. You will need to prepare an Answer in which you admit or deny each of the allegations in the complaint. The best way to admit or deny the allegations in the Complaint for Divorce is to respond to each numbered paragraph in the complaint, such as:

1. The Defendant admits the allegations in paragraphs 1 through 3 of the Complaint.

2. The Defendant denies the allegations in paragraphs 4 through 7 of the Complaint.

If you have any defenses, you will need to state those, such as: "The Plaintiff has not resided in the State of Michigan for at least 180 days," or "The Plaintiff has not resided in this county for more than 10 days." Finally, you will also need to tell the judge what you are asking for, such as that the Complaint for Divorce be dismissed because the residency requirements have not been met, or that a divorce be granted but that you get custody, etc.

Your spouse may get a temporary order for child support or alimony, even without notifying you that he or she has asked for one. If this happens, and you disagree with the temporary order, you can file an Objection to Ex Parte Order and Motion to Rescind or Modify (Form 32). To complete the Objection to Ex Parte Order and Motion to Rescind or Modify (Form 32):

1. Complete the top portion of the form according to the instructions in chapter 5.

2. Type in you and your spouse's name, address, telephone number and social security number in the two boxes.

3. Type in your name in the first, unnumbered paragraph.

4. In paragraph 1, type in the date of the ex parte order.

5. In paragraph 2, check the box or boxes for the matters you wish changed, and type in a brief explanation of why the change should be made.

6. Complete the signature, notice of hearing (obtain a hearing date from the judge's secretary), and certificate of mailing sections of the form. Mail a copy of this form to your spouse.

If successful, you will also need to prepare an Order Modifying Ex Parte Order (Form 33). You will probably either need to hand-write the new order, or type in the information after the hearing and return it to the judge for signature. To complete Order Modifying Ex Parte Order (Form 33):

1. Complete the top of the form the same as you did for items 1 and 2 on Form 34.

2. Fill in the date of the hearing and the name of the judge or referee, if you know it, to the right of the boxes for the names and addresses, etc.

3. In paragraph 1, check the box or boxes for which items are being changed, and fill in the new order.

4. If more space is needed, check the box in paragraph 2 and continue the new order on an additional sheet.

5. In paragraph 3, type in the date the changes take effect.

6. At the end of the hearing, this order will be given to the judge for him or her to sign. You and your spouse may also be asked to sign, and signature spaces are provided.

Appendix A
Michigan Statutes and Court Rules

Michigan Statutes

The following are excerpts from the Michigan Statutes Annotated (and Michigan Compiled Laws Annotated) relating to property distribution, alimony, and child support and custody. References are given to both Michigan Statutes Annotated (MSA) and Michigan Compiled Laws Annotated (MCLA). These are some of the major provisions, but not the only provisions, relating to these subjects. It is strongly recommended that you read Chapter 25, Michigan Statutes Annotated (Chapter 552, Michigan Compiled Laws Annotated) in its entirety before filing for divorce.

MSA §25.86
MCLA §552.6

Complaint for divorce; filing; grounds; answer; judgment

(1) A complaint for divorce may be filed in the circuit court upon the allegation that there has been a breakdown of the marriage relationship to the extent that the objects of matrimony have been destroyed and there remains no reasonable likelihood that the marriage can be preserved. In the complaint the plaintiff shall make no other explanation of the grounds for divorce than by the use of the statutory language.

(2) The defendant, by answer, may either admit the grounds for divorce alleged or deny them without further explanation. An admission by the defendant of the grounds for divorce may be considered by the court but is not binding on the court's determination.

(3) The court shall enter a judgment dissolving the bonds of matrimony if evidence is presented in open court that there has been a breakdown in the marriage relationship to the extent that the objects of matrimony have been destroyed and there remains no reasonable likelihood that the marriage can be preserved.

MSA §25.89
MCLA §552.9

Judgment of divorce; residency requirements, exception

(1) A judgment of divorce shall not be granted by a court in this state in an action for divorce unless the complainant or defendant has resided in this state for 180 days immediately preceding the filing of the complaint and, except as otherwise provided in subsection (2), the complainant or defendant has resided in the county in which the complaint is filed for 10 days immediately preceding the filing of the complaint.

(2)   A person may file a complaint for divorce in any county in the state without meeting the 10-day requirement set forth in subsection (1) if all of the following apply and are set forth in the complaint:

(a)   The defendant was born in, or is a citizen of, a country other than the United States of America.

(b)   The parties to the divorce action have a minor child or children.

(c)   There is information that would allow the court to reasonably conclude that the minor child or children are at risk of being taken out of the United States of America and retained in another country by the defendant.

MSA §25.89
MCLA §552.9

Divorce; domicile of defendant; service of process

(1)   No decree of divorce shall be granted in any case except when 1 of the following facts exists:

(a)   The defendant is domiciled in this state at the time the bill of complaint for divorce is filed.

(b)   The defendant shall have been domiciled in this state when the cause for divorce alleged in the bill or petition arose.

(c)   The defendant shall have been brought in by publication or shall have been personally served with process in this state, or shall have been personally served with a copy of the order for appearance and publication within this state, or elsewhere, or has voluntarily appeared in the action or proceeding. Whenever any such order shall be served outside this state, proof of such service shall be made by the affidavit of the person who shall serve the same, made before a notary public, and when such affidavit shall be made outside this state it shall have attached the certificate of the clerk of a court of record, certifying to the official character of the notary and the genuineness of his or her signature to the jurat of the affidavit.

MSA §25.89(1)
MCLA §552.9a

Divorce; cause occurring out of state, residence

Whenever the cause for divorce charged in the bill or petition has occurred out of this state, no decree of divorce shall be granted unless the complainant or defendant shall have resided in this state 1 year immediately preceding the filing of the bill of complaint for the divorce. Absence from this state for not to exceed 90 days shall not be construed as to interfere with the fulfillment of the 1-year residence requirement provided in the case of causes for divorce occurring without this state.

MSA §25.89(6)
MCLA §552.9f

Divorce; taking of testimony; minor children; perpetuating testimony; nonresident defendant, residence of plaintiff

No proofs or testimony shall be taken in any case for divorce until the expiration of 60 days from the time of filing the bill of complaint, except where the cause for divorce is desertion, or when the testimony is taken conditionally for the purpose of perpetuating such testimony. In every case where there are dependent minor children under the age of 18 years, no proofs or testimony shall be taken in such cases for divorce until the expiration of 6 months from the day the bill of complaint is filed. In cases of unusual hardship or such compelling necessity as shall appeal to the conscience of the court, upon petition and proper showing, it may take testimony at any time after the expiration of 60 days from the time of filing the bill of complaint. Testimony may be taken conditionally at any time for the purpose of perpetuating such testimony. When the defendant in any case for divorce is not domiciled in this state at the time of commencing the suit or shall not have been domiciled herein at the time the cause for divorce arose, before any decree of divorce shall be granted the complainant must prove that the parties have actually lived and cohabitated together as husband and wife within this state, or that the complainant has in good faith resided in this state for 1 year immediately preceding the filing of the bill of complaint for divorce.

MSA §25.93
MCLA §552.13

Alimony; conservation of property; litigation expenses

(1)   In every action brought, either for a divorce or for a separation, the court may require either party to pay alimony for the suitable maintenance of the adverse party, to pay such sums as shall be deemed proper and necessary to conserve any real or personal property owned by the parties or either of them, and to pay any sums necessary to enable the adverse party to carry on or defend the action, during its pendency. It may award costs against either party and award execution for the same, or it may direct such costs to be paid out of any property sequestered, or in the power of the court, or in the hands of a receiver.

(2)   An award of alimony may be terminated by the court as of the date the party receiving alimony remarries unless a contrary agreement is specifically stated in the judgment of divorce. Termination of an award under this subsection shall not affect alimony payments which have accrued prior to that termination.

MSA §25.95
MCLA §552.15

Care, custody and support of minor and post-majority children while action pending; orders; information to friend of the court; support expenses; enforcement; waiver of jurisdiction

(1)   After the filing of a complaint in an action to annul a marriage or for a divorce or separate maintenance, on the motion of either party or the friend of the court, or on the court's own motion, the court may enter such orders concerning the care, custody, and support of the minor children of the parties during the pendency of the action as the court considers proper and necessary. Subject to section [25.96(1), MSA; 16a, MCLA], the court may also order support as provided in this subsection for the parties' children who are not minor children.

(2)   Except as otherwise provided in this section, the court shall order support in an amount determined by application of the child support formula developed by the state friend of the court bureau. The court may enter an order that deviates from the formula if the court determines from the facts of the case that application of the child support formula would be unjust or inappropriate and sets forth in writing or on the record all of the following:

(a)   The support amount determined by application of the child support formula.

(b)   How the support order deviates from the child support formula.

(c)   The value of property or other support awarded in lieu of the payment of child support, if applicable.

(d)   The reasons why application of the child support formula would be unjust or inappropriate in the case.

(3)   Subsection (2) does not prohibit the court from entering a support order that is agreed to by the parties and that deviates from the child support formula, if the requirements of subsection (2) are met.

(4)   Beginning January 1, 1991, each support order entered by the court shall provide that each party shall keep the office of the friend of the court informed of both of the following:

(a)   The name and address of his or her current source of income. As used in this subdivision, "source of income" means that term as defined in section 2 of the support and parenting time enforcement act, Act No. 295 of the Public Acts of 1982, being section [25.164(2) of the Michigan Statutes Annotated; 552.602 of the Michigan Compiled Laws]

(b) Any health care coverage that is available to him or her as a benefit of employment or that is maintained by him or her; the name of the insurance company, nonprofit health care corporation, or health maintenance organization; the policy, certificate, or contract number; and the names and birth dates of the persons for whose benefit he or she maintains health care coverage under the policy, certificate, or contract.

(5) For the purposes of this section, "support" may include payment of the expenses of medical, dental, and other health care, child care expenses, and educational expenses. If a support order is entered, the court shall require that 1 or both parents shall obtain or maintain any health care coverage that is available to them at a reasonable cost, as a benefit of employment, for the benefit of the minor children of the parties and, subject to section [25.96(1), MSA; 552.16a, MCLA], for the benefit of the parties' children who are not minor children. If a parent is self-employed and maintains health care coverage, the court shall require the parent to obtain or maintain dependent coverage for the benefit of the minor children of the parties and, subject to section [25.96(1), MSA; 552.16a, MCLA], for the benefit of the parties' children who are not minor children, if available at a reasonable cost.

(6) Orders concerning the support of children of the parties shall be enforceable as provided in the support and parenting time enforcement act, Act No. 295 of the Public Acts of 1982, being sections [25.164(1) to 25.164(50) of the Michigan Statutes Annotated; 552.601 to 552.650 of the Michigan Compiled Laws].

(7) The court may waive jurisdiction of any minor children under the age of 17 during the pendency of the action to the probate court, to be governed by the laws of this state with respect to dependent and neglected children under the age of 17 years.

MSA §25.96
MCLA §552.16

Care, custody, and support of minor and post-majority children; court orders upon judgment; bond; support formula; information to friend of the court office; enforcement; waiver of jurisdiction

(1) Upon annulling a marriage or entering a judgment of divorce or separate maintenance, the court may enter such orders as it considers just and proper concerning the care, custody, and support of the minor children of the parties. Subject to section [25.96(1),MSA]; [16a, MCLA], the court may also order support as provided in this subsection for the parties' children who are not minor children. The court may require either parent to file a bond with 1 or more sufficient sureties, in a sum to be fixed by the court, guaranteeing payment of the support ordered in the judgment.

(2) Except as otherwise provided in this section, the court shall order support in an amount determined by application of the child support formula developed by the state friend of the court bureau. The court may enter an order that deviates from the formula if the court determines from the facts of the case that application of the child support formula would be unjust or inappropriate and sets forth in writing or on the record all of the following:

(a) The support amount determined by application of the child support formula.
(b) How the support order deviates from the child support formula.
(c) The value of property or other support awarded in lieu of the payment of child support, if applicable.
(d) The reasons why application of the child support formula would be unjust or inappropriate in the case.

(3)   Subsection (2) does not prohibit the court from entering a support order that is agreed to by the parties and that deviates from the child support formula, if the requirements of subsection (2) are met.

(4)   Beginning January 1, 1991, each support order entered by the court shall provide that each party shall keep the office of the friend of the court informed of both of the following:

(a)   The name and address of his or her current source of income. As used in this subdivision, "source of income" means that term as defined in section 2 of the support and parenting time enforcement act, Act No. 295 of the Public Acts of 1982, being section [25.164(2) of the Michigan Statutes Annotated; 552.602 of the Michigan Compiled Laws]

(b)   Any health care coverage that is available to him or her as a benefit of employment or that is maintained by him or her; the name of the insurance company, nonprofit health care corporation, or health maintenance organization; the policy, certificate, or contract number; and the names and birth dates of the persons for whose benefit he or she maintains health care coverage under the policy, certificate, or contract.

(5)   For the purposes of this section, "support" may include payment of the expenses of medical, dental, and other health care, child care expenses, and educational expenses. The judgment shall require that 1 or both parents shall obtain or maintain any health care coverage that is available to them at a reasonable cost, as a benefit of employment, for the benefit of the minor children of the parties and, subject to section [25.96(1), MSA; 552.16a, MCLA], for the benefit of the parties' children who are not minor children. If a parent is self-employed and maintains health care coverage, the court shall require the parent to obtain or maintain dependent coverage for the benefit of the minor children of the parties and, subject to section [25.96(1), MSA; 552.16a, MCLA], for the benefit of the parties' children who are not minor children, if available at a reasonable cost.

(6)   Orders concerning the support of children of the parties are enforceable as provided in the support and parenting time enforcement act…being sections [25.164(1) to 25.164(50), MSA; 552.601 to 552.650, MCLA].

(7)   The court, in the judgment or after entry of the judgment, may waive jurisdiction of any minor children under the age of 17 during the pendency of the action to the probate court, to be governed by the laws of this state with respect to dependent and neglected children under the age of 17 years.

MSA §25.96(1)
MCLA §552.16a

Post-majority child support; full-time students; court orders; validity of prior judgments or orders

(1)   The court may order support for a child pursuant to this chapter to provide support after the child reaches 18 years of age as provided in this section.

(2)   Beginning on the effective date of this section [October 10, 1990], the court may order support for the time a child is regularly attending high school on a full-time basis with a reasonable expectation of completing sufficient credits to graduate high school while residing on a full-time basis with the payee of support or at an institution, but in no case after the child reaches 19 years and 6 months of age. A complaint or motion requesting support as provided in this section may be filed at any time before the child reaches 19 years and 6 months of age.

(3)   A provision contained in a judgment or an order entered under this act before the effective date of this section that provides for the support of a child after the child reaches 18 years of age, without an agreement of the parties as described in subsection

(4), is valid and enforceable to the extent the provision provides support for the child for the time the child is regularly attending high school on a full-time basis with a reasonable expectation completing sufficient credits to graduate from high school while residing on a full-time basis with the payee of support or at an institution, but in no case after the child reaches 19 years and 6 months of age. This subsection shall not require any payment of support for a child after the child reaches 18 years of age for any period between November 8, 1989 and the effective date of this section or reimbursement of support paid between November 8, 1989 and the effective date of this section in those judicial circuits that did not enforce support for a child after the child reached 18 years of age during the period between November 8, 1989 and the effective date of this section.

(4) Notwithstanding subsection (2), a provision contained in a judgment or an order entered under this act before, on, and after the effective date of this section that provides for the support of a child after the child reaches 18 years of age is valid and enforceable if 1 or more of the following apply:

(a) The provision is contained in the judgment or order by agreement of the parties as stated in the judgment or order.

(b) The provision is contained in the judgment or order by agreement of the parties as evidenced by the approval of the substance of the judgment or order by the parties or their attorneys.

(c) The provision is contained in the judgment or order by written agreement signed by the parties.

(d) The provision is contained in the judgment or order by oral agreement of the parties as stated on the record by the parties or their attorneys.

MSA §25.98
MCLA §552.18

Rights to vested or unvested pensions, annuities, or retirement benefits or contributions; inclusions in marital estate; eligible domestic relations orders

(1) Any rights in and to vested pension, annuity, or retirement benefits, or accumulated contributions in any pension, annuity, or retirement system, payable to or on behalf of a party on account of service credit accrued by the party during the marriage shall be considered part of the marital estate subject to award by the court under this chapter.

(2) Any rights or contingent rights in and to unvested pension, annuity, or retirement benefits payable to or on behalf of a party on account of service credit accrued by the party during marriage may be considered part of the marital estate subject to award by the court under this chapter where just and equitable.

(3) Upon motion of a party or upon consent of the parties, an order of the court under this section entered before the effective date of the amendatory act that added this subsection [July 18, 1991] shall be amended to satisfy the requirements of an eligible domestic relations order and to effectuate the intent of the parties or the ruling of the court. As used in this subsection, "eligible domestic relations order" means a domestic relations order that is an eligible domestic relations order under the eligible domestic relations order act.

MSA §25.99
MCLA §552.19

Real and personal estate, restoration to either party

Upon the annulment of a marriage, a divorce from the bonds of matrimony or a judgment of separate maintenance, the court may make a further judgment for restoring to either party the whole, or such parts as it shall deem just and reasonable, of the real and personal estate that shall have come to either party by reason of marriage, or for awarding to either party the value thereof, to be paid by either party in money.

MSA §25.103
MCLA §552.23

Further award of real and personal estate; alimony; public assistance; fees

(1)   Upon the entry of a judgment of divorce or separate maintenance, if the estate and effects awarded to either party are insufficient for the for the suitable support and maintenance of either party and any children of the marriage as are committed to the care and custody of either party, the court may further award to either party the part of the real and personal estate of either party and alimony out of the estate real or personal, to be paid to either party in gross or otherwise as the court considers just and reasonable, after considering the ability of either party to pay and the character and situation of the parties, and all the other circumstances of the case.

(2)   Upon certification by a county department of social services that a complainant or petitioner in a proceeding under this chapter is receiving public assistance either personally or for children of the marriage, payments received by the friend of the court for the support and education of such children or maintenance of the party shall be transmitted to the state department of social services.

(3)   To reimburse the county for the cost of handling alimony or support money payments, the court shall order the payment of a service fee of $2.00 per month, payable semiannually on January 2 and July 2 thereafter, to the friend of the court. The service fee shall be paid by the person ordered to pay the alimony or support money. The service fee shall be computed from the beginning date of the alimony or support order and shall continue while the alimony or support order is operative. The service fee shall be paid 6 months in advance on each due date, except for the first payment, which shall be paid at the same time the alimony or support order is filed, and shall cover the period of time from that month until the next calendar due date. Every order or judgment which provides for the payment of temporary or permanent alimony or support money which requires collection by the friend of the court shall provide for the payment of the service fee. Any such order or judgment for the payment of temporary or permanent alimony or support money, entered before the effective date of this 1983 amendatory act, may be amended by the court, upon its own motion, to provide for the payment of the service fee in the amount provided by this subsection, upon proper notice to the person ordered to pay the alimony or support money. The service fees shall be turned over to the county treasurer and credited to the general fund of the county. If the court appoints the friend of the court custodian, receiver, trustee, or escrow agent of assets owned by the husband and wife, or either of them, the court may fix the amount of the fee for such service, to be turned over to the county treasurer and credited to the general fund of the county. A person who fails or refuses to pay a fee ordered pursuant to this subsection may be held in contempt of court.

MSA §25.105
MCLA §552.27

Alimony or support; lien; foreclosure

If alimony or an allowance for the support and education of the children is awarded to either party, the amount of the alimony or allowance shall constitute a lien upon the real and personal estate of the adverse party as the court by its judgment shall direct. In default of payment of the amount that was awarded, the court may do 1 or more of the following:

(a)   Order the sale of the property against which the lien is adjudged in the same manner and upon like notice as in suits for the foreclosure of mortgage liens.

(b)   Award execution for the collection of the judgment.

(c)   Order the sequestration of the real and personal estate of either party and may appoint a receiver of the real or personal estate, or both, and cause the personal estate and the rents and profits of the real estate to be applied to the payment of the judgment.

(d) Award a division between the husband and wife of the real and personal estate of either party or of the husband and wife by joint ownership or right as the court considers equitable and just.

MSA §25.181
MCLA §552.391

Divorced woman, change of name

The circuit courts of this state, whenever a decree of divorce is granted, may, at the instance of the woman, whether complainant or defendant, decree to restore to her birth name, or the surname she legally bore prior to her marriage to the husband in the divorce action, or allow her to adopt another surname if the change is not sought with any fraudulent or evil intent.

MSA 25.312(6a)
MCLA 722.26a

Joint custody

(1) In custody disputes between parents, the parents shall be advised of joint custody. At the request of either parent, the court shall consider an award of joint custody, and shall state on the record the reasons for granting or denying a request. In other cases joint custody may be considered by the court. The court shall determine whether joint custody is in the best interest of the child by considering the following factors:

(a) The factors enumerated in section [25.312(3), MSA; 722.23, MCLA].

(b) Whether the parents will be able to cooperate and generally agree concerning important decisions affecting the welfare of the child.

(2) If the parents agree on joint custody, the court shall award joint custody unless the court determines on the record, based upon clear and convincing evidence, that joint custody is not in the best interest of the child.

(3) If the court awards joint custody, the court may include in its award a statement regarding when the child shall reside with each parent, or may provide that physical custody be shared by the parents in a manner to assure the child continuing contact with both parents.

(4) During the time a child resides with a parent, that parent shall decide all routine matters concerning the child.

(5) If there is a dispute regarding residency, the court shall state the basis for a residency award on the record or in writing.

(6) Joint custody shall not eliminate the responsibility for child support. Each parent shall be responsible for child support based on the needs of the child and the actual resources of each parent. If a parent would otherwise be unable to maintain adequate housing for the child and the other parent has sufficient resources, the court may order modified support payments for a portion of housing expenses even during a period when the child is not residing in the home of the parent receiving support. An order of joint custody, in and of itself, shall not constitute grounds for modifying a support order.

(7) As used in this section, "joint custody" means an order of the court in which 1 or both of the following is specified:

(a) That the child shall reside alternatively for specific periods with each of the parents.

(b) That the parents shall share decision-making authority as to the important decisions affecting the welfare of the child.

MICHIGAN COURT RULES

The following are portions of the Michigan Court Rules.

Rule 3.206 Pleading

(A) Information in Complaint

(1) In all domestic relations actions, the complaint must state:

    (a) the allegations required by applicable statutes;

    (b) the residence information required by statute;

    (c) the complete names of all parties; and

    (d) the complete names and dates of birth of any minors involved in the action, including all minor children of the parties and all minor children born during the marriage.

(2) In a case that involves a minor, or if child support is requested, the complaint also must state whether any Michigan court has prior continuing jurisdiction of the minor. If so, the complaint must specify the court and the file number.

(3) In a case in which custody of a minor is to be determined, the complaint or an affidavit attached to the complaint also must state the information required by MCL 600.659; MSA 27A.659.

(4) In an action for divorce, separate maintenance, annulment of marriage, or affirmation of marriage, regardless of the contentions of the parties with respect to the existence or validity of the marriage, the complaint also must state:

    (a) the names of the parties before the marriage;

    (b) whether there are any minor children of the parties or minor children born during the marriage;

    (c) whether a party is pregnant;

    (d) the factual grounds for the action, except that in an action for divorce or separate maintenance the grounds must be stated in the statutory language, without further particulars; and

    (e) whether there is property to be divided.

(5) A party who requests spousal support in an action for divorce, separate maintenance, annulment, affirmation of marriage, or spousal support, must allege facts sufficient to show a need for such support and that the other party is able to pay.

(6) A party who requests an order for personal protection or for the protection of property, including but not limited to restraining orders and injunctions against domestic violence, must allege facts sufficient to support the relief requested.

(B) Verified Statement.

(1) In an action involving a minor, or if child support or spousal support is requested, the party seeking relief must attach a verified statement to the copies of the papers served on the other party and provided to the friend of the court, stating:

    (a) the last known telephone number, post office address, residence address, and business address of each party;

    (b) the social security number and occupation of each party;

    (c) the name and address of each party's employer;

    (d) the estimated weekly gross income of each party;

    (e) the driver's license number and physical description of each party, including eye color, hair color, height, weight, race, gender, and identifying marks;

    (f) any other names by which the parties are or have been known;

    (g) the name, age, birth date, social security number, and residence address of each minor involved in the action, as well as of any other minor child of either party;

    (h) the name and address of any person, other than the parties, who may have custody of a minor during the pendency of the action;

(i)   the kind of public assistance, if any, that has been applied for or is being received by either party or on behalf of a minor, and the AFDC and recipient identification numbers; if public assistance has not been requested or received, that fact must be stated; and

(j)   the health care coverage, if any, that is available for each minor child; the name of the policy-holder; the name of the insurance company, health care organization, or health maintenance organization; and the policy, certificate, or contract number.

(2)   The information in the verified statement is confidential, and is not to be released other than to the court, the parties, or the attorneys for the parties, except on court order. For good cause, the addresses of a party and minors may be omitted from the copy of the statement that is served on the other party.

(3)   If any of the information required to be in the verified statement is omitted, the party seeking relief must explain the omission in a sworn affidavit, to be filed with the court.

(C)   Attorney Fees and Expenses.

(1)   A party may, at any time, request that the court order the other party to pay all or part of the attorney fees and expenses related to the action.

(2)   A party who requests attorney fees and expenses must allege facts sufficient to show that the party is unable to bear the expense of the action, and that the other party is able to pay.

Rule 3.207   Ex Parte, Temporary, and Protective Orders

(A)   Scope of Relief. The court may issue ex parte and temporary orders with regard to any matter within its jurisdiction, and may issue protective orders against domestic violence as provided in subrule (D).

(B)   Ex Parte Orders.

(1)   Pending the entry of a temporary order, the court may enter an ex parte order if the court is satisfied by specific facts set forth in a affidavit or verified pleading that irreparable injury, loss, or damage will result from the delay required to effect notice, or that notice itself will precipitate adverse action before an order can be issued.

(2)   The moving party must arrange for the service of true copies of the exparte order on the friend of the court and the other party.

(3)   An exparte order is effective upon entry and enforceable upon service.

(4)   An exparte order remains in effect until modified or superseded by a temporary or final order.

(5)   An exparte order providing for visitation with a minor pursuant to MCL 722.27a; MSA 25.312(7a) must include the following notice:

[see paragraph 12 of Form 26, which contains the required notice.]

(6)   In all other cases, the ex parte order must state that it will automatically become a temporary order if the other party does not file a written objection or motion to modify or rescind the ex parte order and a request for a hearing. The written objection or motion and the request for a hearing must be filed with the clerk of the court, and a true copy provided to the friend of the court and the other party, within 14 days after the order is served.

   (a)   If there is a timely objection or motions and a request for a hearing, the hearing must be held within 21 days after the objection or motion and request are filed.

   (b)   A change that occurs after the hearing may be made retroactive to the date the ex parte order was entered.

(7)   The provisions of MCR 3.310 apply to temporary restraining orders in domestic relations cases.

(C)   Temporary Orders.

(1)   A request for a temporary order may be made at any time during the pendency of the case by filing a verified motion that sets forth facts sufficient to support the relief requested.

(2)   A temporary order may not be issued without a hearing, unless the parties agree otherwise or fail to file a written objection or motion as provided in subrules (B)(5) and (6).

(3) A temporary order may be modified at any time during the pendency of the case, following a hearing and upon a showing of good cause.

(4) A temporary order must state its effective date and whether its provisions may be modified retroactively by a subsequent order.

(5) A temporary order remains in effect until modified or until the entry of the final judgment or order.

(6) A temporary order not yet satisfied is vacated by the entry of the final judgment or order, unless specifically continued or preserved. This does not apply to support arrearages that have been assigned to the state, which are preserved unless specifically waived or reduced by the final judgment or order.

(D) Protective Orders. The court may issue a protective order against domestic violence pursuant to MCL 600.2950; MSA 27A.2950 or MCL 552.14; MSA 25.94 on the basis of violence or threats of violence. The order may not be made mutual unless issued on the basis of violence or threats of violence by both parties.

Rule 3.210   Hearings and Trials

(A) In General.

(1) Proofs or testimony may not be taken in an action for divorce or separate maintenance until the expiration of the time prescribed by the applicable statute, except as otherwise provided by this rule.

(2) In cases of unusual hardship or compelling necessity, the court may, upon motion and proper showing, take testimony and render judgment at any time 60 days after the filing of the complaint.

(3) Testimony may be taken conditionally at any time for the purpose of perpetuating it.

(4) Testimony must be taken in person, except that the court may allow testimony to be taken be telephone or other electronically reliable means, in extraordinary circumstances.

(B) Default Cases.

(1) Default cases are governed by MCR 2.603.

(2) A judgment of divorce, separate maintenance, or annulment may not be entered as a matter of course on the default of the defendant because of failure to appear at the hearing or by consent. Every case must be heard in open court on proofs taken, except as otherwise provided by statute or court rule.

(3) If a party is in default, proofs may not be taken unless the judgment fee has been deposited with the court clerk and the proposed judgment has been given to the court.

(4) If the court determines that the proposed judgment is inappropriate, the party who prepared it must, within 14 days, present a modified judgment in conformity with the court's opinion.

(5) If the court determines not to enter the judgment, the court must direct that the judgment fee be returned to the person who deposited it.

(C) Custody of a Minor.

(1) When the custody of a minor is contested, a hearing on the matter must be held within 56 days
   (a) after the court orders, or
   (b) after the filing of notice that a custody hearing is requested, unless both parties agree to mediation under MCL 552.513; MSA 25.176(13) and mediation is unsuccessful, in which event the hearing must be held within 56 days after the final mediation session.

(2) If a custody action is assigned to a probate judge pursuant to MCL 722.26b; MSA 25.312(6b), a hearing on the matter must be held by the probate judge within 56 days after the case is assigned.

(3) The court must enter a decision within 28 days after the hearing.

(4) The notice required by this subrule may be filed as a separate document, or may be included in another paper filed in the action if the notice is mentioned in the caption.

(5) If a report has been submitted by the friend of the court, the court must give the parties an opportunity to review the report and to file objections before a decision is entered.

(6) The court may extend for good cause the time within which a hearing must be held and a decision rendered under this subrule.

(D) The court must make findings of fact as provided in MCR 2.517, except that

(1) findings of fact and conclusions of law are required on contested postjudgment motions to modify a final judgment or order, and

(2) the court may distribute pension, retirement, and other deferred compensation rights with a qualified domestic relations order, without first making a finding with regard to the value of those rights.

Rule 3.211 Judgments and Orders

(A) Each separate subject in a judgment or order must be set forth in a separate paragraph that is prefaced by an appropriate heading.

(B) A judgment of divorce, separate maintenance, or annulment must include

(1) the insurance and dower provisions required by MCL 552.101; MSA 25.131;

(2) a determination of the rights of the parties in pension, annuity, and retirement benefits, as required by MCL 552.101(4); MSA 25.131(4);

(3) a determination of the property rights of the parties; and

(4) a provision reserving or denying spousal support, if spousal support is not granted; a judgment silent with regard to spousal support reserves it.

(C) A judgment or order awarding custody of a minor must provide that

(1) the domicile or residence of the minor may not be moved from Michigan without the approval of the judge who awarded custody or the judge's successor, and

(2) the person awarded custody must promptly notify the friend of the court in writing when the minor is moved to another address.

(D) A judgment or order awarding child support or spousal support must

(1) provide for income withholding as required by MCL 552.604; MSA 25.164(4), and state the payer's source of income and the source's address, if known;

(2) set forth the parties' residence addresses, and require parties over whom the court has obtained jurisdiction to inform the friend of the court of any subsequent change of address or employment;

(3) provide for the payment of statutory fees, if child support is to be paid through the office of the friend of the court; and

(4) provide that the support be paid through the office of the friend of the court, unless otherwise stated in the judgment or order; if an order is silent as to method of payment, support must be paid through the office of the friend of the court.

(E) A judgment or order awarding child support also must

(1) specify the amount of support both at the time of judgment and as the number of children for whom there is a support obligation decreases;

(2) provide for payment until the child reaches the age of 18, and may provide for payment after the age of 18 as allowed by law;

(3) provide for health care coverage as required by MCL 722.27; MSA 25.312(7) and MCL 722.3; MSA 25.244(3);

(4) provide for the preservation of child support arrearages owing to the state on the date of the entry of the judgment, whether the arrearages arose under a temporary child support order or under a separate judgment entered pursuant to MCL 552.451 et seq.; MSA 25.222(1) et seq., and

(5) contain the following provision regarding nonretroactive support, as required by MCL 552.603(10); MSA 25.164(3)(10):

"Except as otherwise provided in section 3 of the support and visitation enforcement act, Act No. 295 of the Public Acts of 1982, being section 552.603 of the Michigan Compiled Laws, a support order that is part of a judgment or is an order in a domestic relations matter as that term is defined in section 31 of the friend of the court act, Act

No. 294 of the Public Acts of 1982, being section 552.531 of the Michigan Compiled Laws, is a judgment on and after the date each support payment is due, with the full force, effect, and attributes of a judgment of this state, and is not, on and after the date it is due, subject to retroactive modification."

(F) Unless otherwise ordered, all support arrearages owing to the state are preserved upon entry of a final order or judgment. Upon a showing of good cause and notice to the friend of the court, the prosecuting attorney, and other interested parties, the court may waive or reduce such arrearages.

(G) Within 21 days after the court renders an opinion or the settlement agreement is placed on the record, the moving party must submit a judgment, order, or a motion to settle the judgment or order, unless the court has granted an extension.

(H) Friend of the Court Review. For all judgments and orders containing provision identified in subrules (C), (D), (E), and (F), the court may require that the judgment or order be submitted to the friend of the court for review.

(I) Service of Judgment or Order.

(1) When a judgment or order is obtained for temporary or permanent spousal support, child support, or separate maintenance, the prevailing party must immediately deliver one copy to the court clerk. The court clerk must write or stamp "true copy" on the order or judgment and file it with the friend of the court.

(2) The party securing entry of a judgment or order that provides for child support or spousal support must serve a copy on the party ordered to pay the support, as provided in MCR 2.602(D)(1), even if that party is in default.

(3) The record of divorce and annulment required by MCLA 333.2864; MSA 14.15(2864) must be filed at the time of the filing of the judgment.

APPENDIX B
MICHIGAN CHILD SUPPORT GUIDELINES

CHILD SUPPORT GUIDELINES

The information in this appendix is taken from the official child support guidelines. If you would like to read the full text of these guidelines, check with your local law library for a copy of the Michigan Child Support Formula Manual (copies are published by both West Publishing Company and Lawyers Cooperative Publishing). The child support guidelines may also be available at your local office of the Friend of the Court, or by writing to:

Department of Management and Budget
Office Services Division
Publications Section
7461 Crowner Drive
Lansing, MI 48913

Specific requirements for your county, and even for particular judges within your county, may be found in the Michigan Family Law Sourcebook, Volume II, published by the Institute for Continuing Legal Education.

See "Legal Research" in chapter 2 of this book for more sources of information about all aspects of divorce in Michigan. Also, be sure to read chapter 5 of this book for more information about calculating child support.

Other Minor Children Currently in Household

Step 1: Determine the net weekly income of the custodial and the noncustodial parents. (For purposes of an "other children adjustment" only, include the other biological/adoptive child(ren) income, other than from employment, as part of the parents' income. Do not include income of the parties' stepchildren or court ordered child support.)

Step 2: Determine the number of biological/legally adopted children living in the custodial and/or the noncustodial parents' households.

Step 3: Adjust each parent's net income by subtracting the dollar amount of the pre-existing support order (if applicable). Adjust each parent's net income according to the number of biological/legally adopted children in their household by multiplying their net incomes by the appropriate percentage found in Table I.

When parents have other children, the applicable percentages are derived from the average percentages calculated by using Table III. When there is 1 biological/legally adopted child in the custodial or the noncustodial parent's household, multiply net income by .896 (see Table I). The factor of .896 is derived by dividing the average base support percentage for 1 child (20.8%) by 2 and then subtracting that number (10.4) from 100. When there are 2 biological/legally adopted children, multiply by .841, when there are 3 biological/legally adopted children, multiply by .798, when there are 4 biological/legally adopted children, multiply by .773, and when there are 5 biological/legally adopted children, multiply by .752.

Step 4: Apply each parent's income, as determined in Step 3 to the schedule with the correct number of children for whom this modification is being sought. This results in the appropriate amount of support to be paid by the noncustodial parent.

Table I

**Percentages Applied to Net Income
when Parents have Other Children**

1 child	.896
2 children	.841
3 children	.798
4 children	.773
5 or more children	.752

Example:

The noncustodial parent earns $400. The custodial parent, who earns $220 net per week, requests a modification of the support order for the three children. In considering this modification request, the 2 natural children currently living in the noncustodial parent's household should be taken into account.

Step 1: Noncustodial parent earns $400 net per week. Custodial parent earns $220 net per week.

Step 2: There are two biological/legally adopted children living in the noncustodial parent's household.

Step 3: $400 x .841 = $336   is the net income figure used to calculate support for the noncustodial parent.

Step 4: Determine the amount of support for the three children from the prior marriage based on the noncustodial parent's income of $336 and custodial parent's income of $220.

Stepchildren

In general, stepchildren should not be considered when determining the appropriateness of a child support modification for a stepparent. In Michigan, children are the responsibility of their natural/adoptive parents. However, there may be cases in which support is unavailable from **both** natural/adoptive parents **and** stepparents are required to make substantial contributions to their stepchildren's support.

Both of the following conditions **must** be satisfied before stepchildren may be considered:

Condition One:
It may be appropriate to consider stepchildren when their noncustodial parent earns no income and does not have the ability to earn income; and

Condition Two:
It may be appropriate to consider stepchildren when their custodial parent earns no income and does not have the ability to earn income.

After it is established that **both** of these conditions exist, the following method should be used for determining the net incomes of parents who currently have stepchildren living in their households.

Step 1: Determine the net weekly incomes of the parties in the case under review.

Step 2: Determine the number of stepchildren living in the party-stepparent's household for whom the party-stepparent is the sole source of income.

Step 3: Adjust the stepparent's income, according to the number of children in the current household, by multiplying the stepparent's income by the appropriate adjustment percentage from Table II.

The applicable percentages when parents have stepchildren are derived from the average percentages calculated by using Table III. When there is one stepchild in the stepparent's household, multiply by .948 (see Table II). The factor of .948 is derived by dividing the average support percentage for one child (20.8%) by 4 and then subtracting that number (5.2) from 100. When there are 2 stepchildren, multiply by .921, when there are 3 stepchildren, multiply by .899, when there are 4 stepchildren, multiply by .886, when there are 5 stepchildren, multiply by .879.

Step 4: Apply the stepparent's adjusted income, as determined in Step 3, and their former spouse's income to the schedule with the correct number of children for whom this modification is being sought. This results in an appropriate amount of support to be paid by the stepparent.

Table II

Percentages Applied to Net Income when Parents have Stepchildren

1 child	.948
2 children	.921
3 children	.899
4 children	.886
5 or more children	.876

Calculating Child Support Using Table III

Various percentages of net income are used to determine child support in this formula. The percentages are based on the number of children and the level of total net family income. The percentages are displayed in Table III shown below. The total net family income levels against which the percentages are applied are adjusted on an annual basis, using the Consumer Price Index for Metropolitan Detroit, December, 1985 as the base.

Table III

Total Child Support at Various Income Levels

ONE CHILD

Weekly Family Net Income	Percentage Allocated	Basic Support + Marginal Percentage
$ 199	25.5 %	$50.75 + 24.17% over $ 199
$ 320	25.0 %	$80.00 + 17.48% over $ 320
$ 436	23.0 %	$100.28 + 16.68% over $ 436
$ 560	21.6 %	$120.96 + 14.63% over $ 560
$ 727	20.0 %	$145.40 + 13.91% over $ 727
$1,032	18.2 %	$187.82 + 12.37% over $1,032
$1,272	17.1 %	$217.51 + 11.25% over $1,272
$1,600	15.9 %	$254.40 + 10.00% over $1,600

TWO CHILDREN

Weekly Family Net Income	Percentage Allocated	Basic Support + Marginal Percentage
$ 199	39.4 %	$ 78.41 + 36.22% over $ 199
$ 320	38.2 %	$122.24 + 26.17% over $ 320
$ 436	35.0 %	$152.60 + 23.71% over $ 436
$ 560	32.5 %	$182.00 + 22.49% over $ 560
$ 727	30.2 %	$219.55 + 21.74% over $ 727
$1,032	27.7 %	$285.86 + 20.28% over $1,032
$1,272	26.3 %	$334.54 + 17.03% over $1,272
$1,600	24.4 %	$390.40 + 15.00% over $1,600

THREE CHILDREN

Weekly Family Net Income	Percentage Allocated	Basic Support + Marginal Percentage
$ 199	49.4 %	$ 98.31 + 47.28% over $ 199
$ 320	48.6 %	$155.52 + 35.07% over $ 320
$ 436	45.0 %	$196.20 + 30.55% over $ 436
$ 560	41.8 %	$234.08 + 28.74% over $ 560
$ 727	38.8 %	$282.08 + 27.97% over $ 727
$1,032	35.6 %	$367.39 + 23.41% over $1,032
$1,272	33.3 %	$423.58 + 19.64% over $1,272
$1,600	30.5 %	$488.00 + 19.00% over $1,600

FOUR CHILDREN

Weekly Family Net Income	Percentage Allocated	Basic Support + Marginal Percentage
$ 199	55.6 %	$110.64 + 52.69% over $ 199
$ 320	54.5 %	$174.40 + 39.84% over $ 320
$ 436	50.6 %	$220.62 + 34.34% over $ 436
$ 560	47.0 %	$263.20 + 33.07% over $ 560
$ 727	43.9 %	$318.43 + 31.96% over $ 727
$1,032	40.3 %	$415.90 + 24.93% over $1,032
$1,272	37.4 %	$475.73 + 23.25% over $1,272
$1,600	34.5 %	$552.00 + 22.00% over $1,600

FIVE OR MORE CHILDREN

Weekly Family Net Income	Percentage Allocated	Basic Support + Marginal Percentage
$ 199	60.8 %	$120.99 + 57.36% over $ 199
$ 320	59.5 %	$190.40 + 42.59% over $ 320
$ 436	55.0 %	$239.80 + 37.84% over $ 436
$ 560	51.2 %	$286.72 + 37.27% over $ 560
$ 727	48.0 %	$348.96 + 35.82% over $ 727
$1,032	44.4 %	$458.21 + 24.79% over $1,032
$1,272	40.7 %	$517.70 + 24.12% over $1,272
$1,600	37.3 %	$596.80 + 23.00% over $1,600

CHILD SUPPORT FORMULA

The first step in determining each parent's child support obligation is to calculate total net family income per week. If either parent's income is near or below the poverty level, see Section III C. Second, apply the appropriate child support percentage from Table III to the net income determination to calculate the actual child support amount. The third step is to apportion the support amount between both parents based on the ratio of their incomes. The final step in determining child support is to add a health care supplement to the calculated support amount.

Example:

Step 1: Calculate family net weekly income.

Noncustodial parent earns $400 net per week.
Custodial parent earns $200 net per week.

Add the parent's net weekly incomes to determine the total net family income per week:
$400 + $200 = $600

Step 2: Using Table III, calculate the total weekly support amount for the five children in this family.

$255 + (35.2% x 51) = $273 Total Child Support

Step 3: Apportion the child support amount between both parents by dividing each parent's income by the total family income.

Custodial Parent	Noncustodial Parent
$150	$400
$550 = 27.3%	$550 = 72.7%

The custodial parent earns 27.3% and the noncustodial parent earns 72.7% of the total family income. Therefore the custodial parent's contribution is 27.3% and the noncustodial parent must pay 72.7% of the amount calculated in Step 2.

Custodial Contribution	Noncustodial Obligation
$ 273	$ 273
x .273	x .727
$ 75	$ 198

Step 4:   The noncustodial parent must pay $198 per week plus the health care supplement.

$198
+10.5
$208.50

$208.50 is the noncustodial parent's weekly support obligation.

APPENDIX C
FORMS

Be sure to read the section "An Introduction to Legal Forms" in chapter 6 before you begin using the forms in this appendix. Each form in this appendix may be identified by its title, as well as by the form number which is found in the upper, outside corner of the page on which the form begins. Instructions for completing these forms are found throughout this book. The instructions for a particular form may be found by looking for the form by its number under the heading "Forms, instructions" in the index. You will not need to use all of the forms in this appendix.

Do not remove the forms from this appendix. Instead, make photocopies to use for both worksheets and the forms you will actually file with the court. This way, you will still have the blank forms in this appendix to make more copies in the event you make mistakes or need additional copies.

The forms may change, so you may want to check the most recent edition of *Michigan S.C.A.O. Approved Forms* to be sure you are using the most current forms.

Forms listed below which also have a letter-number designation (such as "FOC-34" or "MC-11") are SCAO-approved forms included in volume I of the 1998 edition of *Michigan S.C.A.O. Approved Forms*. The forms in that book are divided into various types of forms: FOC means it is a "Friend of the Court" form, MC means it is a "Michigan Court" form, and CC means it is a "Circuit Court" form. All forms that do not have such a letter-number designation are not current SCAO-approved forms, but are provided here because there is not a current SCAO-approved form for that subject. Some of these forms may have been approved at one time in the past editions of *Michigan S.C.A.O. Approved Forms*, but have since been deleted for unknown reasons. A form that does not currently carry SCAO approval may still be used. The only difference is that an approved form is much less likely to be questioned by the judge or court clerk.

You will notice that certain pages of some of the forms in this appendix are printed upside down. This follows the format of the SCAO-approved forms, and is designed to make the forms more easy to read after they are inserted in the court's file folder. All papers you file with the court clerk will be two-hole punched at the top, and then inserted over the two metal prongs at the top of the clerk's file folder for your case. For example, the Subpoena (Form 13) is a two-sided form. When photocopying this form, you may either copy the first page, then copy the second page upside down on the back, or copy them both right-side-up on two separate pages and staple them together.

TABLE OF FORMS

The following forms is your list of forms:

WHERE TO FIND ADDITIONAL FORMS. This book is designed for the most typical divorce situations. In unusual situations, there are numerous other forms that can be filed for various purposes. The primary source of additional legal forms is your nearest law library. The first place to look is in the most recent edition of *Michigan S.C.A.O. Approved Forms*. Ask the librarian where to find this and other divorce form books. (See the section on chapter 2 on "Legal Research." Two other possible sources of forms are the offices of the Friend of the Court and the Circuit Court Clerk.

PROPERTY INVENTORY

(1) S	(2) DESCRIPTION	(3) ID#	(4) VALUE	(5) BALANCE OWED	(6) EQUITY	(7) OWNER H-W-J	(8) H	(9) W

Form 2

DEBT INVENTORY

(1) S	(2) CREDITOR	(3) ACCOUNT NO.	(4) NOTES	(5) MONTHLY PAYMENT	(6) BALANCE OWED	(7) DATE	(8) OWNER H-W-J	(9) H	(10) W

Approved, SCAO

| | Original - Court | 2nd copy - Defendant |
| | 1st copy - Plaintiff | 3rd copy - Friend of the Court file |

STATE OF MICHIGAN JUDICIAL CIRCUIT COUNTY	CHILD SUPPORT RECOMMENDATION WORKSHEET A	CASE NO.

SOURCES OF INCOME ($/week)	Plaintiff	Defendant	DEDUCTIONS ($/week) Tax Filing Exemption Status:	Plaintiff	Defendant
1. Salaries and Wages (including shift premium and COLA)			23. Federal taxes		
2. Overtime (See instructions on page 4)			24. State taxes		
3. Second Job (See instructions on page 4)			25. Local taxes		
4. Commissions			26. FICA		
5. All bonuses/Profit sharing			27. Alimony /Spousal support		
6. Interest/Dividends			28. Mandatory withholdings		
7. Annuity/Trust fund payments			29. Court ord. health/life insur. (See instructions on page 9)		
8. Pensions/Longevity			30. TOTAL DEDUCTIONS		
9. Deferred Comp./IRA (See instructions on page 5)					
10. Unemployment benefits			31. TOTAL NET INCOME		
11. Strike pay/Sub pay			Have you considered the following adjustments: Pre-existing orders? Second families? Stepchildren?		
12. Sick benefits/Disability pay					
13. Workers' compensation					
14. Social Security benefits			32. ADJUSTED NET INCOME (See Worksheet B)		
15. Veterans Administration benefits					
16. G.I. benefits (Exclude education allotment)			33. COMBINED TOTAL ADJUSTED NET INCOME		
17. Armed Service/National Guard (See instructions on page 2)			34. PLAINTIFF'S SHARE OF TOTAL ADJ. NET INCOME		%
18. Allowance for rent/Rental income (Allowance: if fringe from employer)			35. DEFENDANT'S SHARE OF TOTAL ADJ. NET INCOME		%
19. Alimony/Spousal support					
20. Other					
21. TOTAL GROSS INCOME			36. Social security benefits - Children (See instructions on page 4)		
22. TAXABLE GROSS INCOME					

[E2126]

Approved, SCAO

STATE OF MICHIGAN JUDICIAL CIRCUIT COUNTY	CHILD SUPPORT RECOMMENDATION WORKSHEET B	CASE NO.

A. ADJUSTMENTS TO INCOME WHEN PARENTS HAVE EXISTING SUPPORT ORDERS (See Instructions on page 9)

		PLAINTIFF	DEFENDANT
1.	Each parent's net weekly income. (Worksheet A, item 31)	$ _____	$ _____
2.	Subtract amounts of existing support orders from other cases. (Do not include arrearage payments)	$ _____	$ _____
3.	Adjusted net income after existing support orders.	$ _____	$ _____

B. ADJUSTMENTS TO INCOME WHEN PARENTS HAVE SECOND FAMILIES (See Instructions on page 10)

		PLAINTIFF	DEFENDANT
1.	Each parent's net weekly income or adjusted net weekly income. (Worksheet A, item 31 or item A.3. above)	$ _____	$ _____
2.	Select factor corresponding to number of natural or adopted children living in each parent's household. (Other than the children in this case)		

      1 child: .896
      2 children: .841
      3 children: .798
      4 children: .773
      5 or more children: .752

		PLAINTIFF	DEFENDANT
	(4 children line)	x _____	x _____
3.	Multiply the selected factor by each parent's weekly income amount on line B.1.	$ _____	$ _____

C. ADJUSTMENTS TO INCOME WHEN STEPCHILDREN ARE CONSIDERED (Use this adjustment ONLY when the 2 conditions listed on page 12 are satisfied.)

		PLAINTIFF	DEFENDANT
1.	Each parent's net weekly income or adjusted net weekly income. (Worksheet A, item 31 or A. 3. or B.3. above)	$ _____	$ _____
2.	Select factor corresponding to the number of stepchildren living in each parent's household.		

      1 child: .948
      2 children: .921
      3 children: .899
      4 children: .886
      5 or more children: .876

		PLAINTIFF	DEFENDANT
	(4 children line)	x _____	x _____
3.	Multiply the selected factor by each parent's weekly income amount on line C.1.	$ _____	$ _____

Approved, SCAO

Original - Court
1st copy - Plaintiff

2nd copy - Defendant
3rd copy - Friend of the Court file

STATE OF MICHIGAN JUDICIAL CIRCUIT COUNTY	CHILD SUPPORT RECOMMENDATION WORKSHEET C	CASE NO.

A. CALCULATING CHILD SUPPORT WHEN PARENTS HAVE SPLIT CUSTODY
(See Instructions on page 22)

		PLAINTIFF	DEFENDANT

1. Each parent's adjusted net weekly income. (Worksheet A, item 32) $ _____ $ _____

2. The number of natural or adopted children from this case living in the other parent's household.   _____   _____

3. Each parent's support obligation for the children living in the other parent's household according to the support schedules. $ _____ $ _____

4. Highest support amount from item 3 above: $ _____

   Lowest support amount from item 3 above: - $ _____

5. Amount to be paid by the parent owing the highest support amount: $ _____

B. CALCULATING SUPPORT WHEN PARENTS HAVE JOINT PHYSICAL CUSTODY
(See Instructions on page 24)

Use this formula only when one parent has the child(ren) 128 days or more during the year, and the other parent has the child(ren) 237 days or less during the year.

		PLAINTIFF	DEFENDANT

1. The adjusted net weekly income. (Worksheet A, item 32) $ _____ $ _____

2. For the purposes of this formula:

   A = The number of days the children spend with the plaintiff.   A = _____

   B = The product of A multiplied by itself .   B = _____

   C = The number of days the children spend with the defendant.   C = _____

   D = The product of C multiplied by itself.   D = _____

   E = Plaintiff's normal support obligation determined from the schedule.
   (This is obtained by reading plaintiff's income along the non-custodial axis and the defendant's income along the custodial axis on the appropriate schedule.)   E = $ _____

   F = Defendant's normal support obligation determined from the schedule.
   (This is obtained by reading defendant's income along the non-custodial axis and the plaintiff's income along the custodial axis on the appropriate schedule.)   F = $ _____

3. Insert the above values into the formula to determine weekly support amount and payer.

$$\frac{(B \times F) - (D \times E)}{(B + D)} = \underline{\hspace{6cm}} = \$ \underline{\hspace{2cm}}$$

If formula result is negative, plaintiff is payer.
If formula result is positive, defendant is payer.

PAYER: ☐ Plaintiff ☐ Defendant

Approved, SCAO

Original - Court
1st copy - Plaintiff

2nd copy - Defendant
3rd copy - Friend of the Court file

STATE OF MICHIGAN JUDICIAL CIRCUIT COUNTY	CHILD SUPPORT RECOMMENDATION WORKSHEET D	CASE NO.

CALCULATING CHILD CARE CREDIT AND CHILD CARE APPORTIONMENT
(See Instructions on page 28)

NOTE: IRS Child Care Credit can only be claimed by one parent. For additional information see IRS Form 2441.

1. Parent's weekly child care expense ☐ Plaintiff ☐ Defendant $ _____

2. Multiply by number of weeks of child care.   x _____

3. Yearly child care expense. (Multiply item 1 by item 2) $ _____

4. Child care credit received on last years I.R.S. tax return.
   (If child care credit not declared, see section below) $ _____

5. Total actual yearly child care expense. (Subtract item 4 from item 3). $ _____

6. Divide yearly expense (item 5) by 52.   + _____

7. Weekly child care expense to be divided. $ _____

CALCULATION OF CHILD CARE CREDIT

To calculate child care tax credit, the following chart is used.
   1 Child: $2400 maximum
   2 or more children: $4800 maximum

   a. If yearly child care expense (Item 3 above) is greater than the maximum
      allowable expense (above chart), insert maximum allowable rate. $ _____

      If yearly child care expense (item 3 above) is less than the maximum
      allowable expense (above chart), insert the yearly child care expense.

   b. Multiply by applicable percentage from I.R.S. form 2441 based on gross income $ _____
      from I.R.S. form of parent incurring the child care cost.

   c. Amount of credit allowed by I.R.S. (Insert this value on item 4 above). $ _____

CALCULATING CHILD CARE RECOMMENDATION

8. Transfer Plaintiff's and Defendant's percentage of total adjusted net income
   (Worksheet A - items 34 & 35).

   _____ Plaintiff
   _____ Defendant

9. Multiply the amount in item 7 by plaintiff's/defendant's percentage of
   combined adjusted income from item 8 above.   x _____ %

10. Recommended weekly child care order to be paid by ☐ Plaintiff $ _____
    ☐ Defendant   [E2129]

Approved, SCAO

STATE OF MICHIGAN JUDICIAL DISTRICT JUDICIAL CIRCUIT	SUMMONS AND COMPLAINT	CASE NO.

Court address	Court telephone no.

Plaintiff name(s), address(es), and telephone no(s).	v	Defendant name(s), address(es), and telephone no(s).
Plaintiff attorney, bar no., address, and telephone no.		

NOTICE TO THE DEFENDANT: In the name of the people of the State of Michigan you are notified:

1. You are being sued.

2. YOU HAVE 21 DAYS after receiving this summons to file an answer with the court and serve a copy on the other party or to take other lawful action (28 days if you were served by mail or you were served outside this state).

3. If you do not answer or take other action within the time allowed, judgment may be entered against you for the relief demanded in the complaint.

Issued	This summons expires	Court clerk

*This summons is invalid unless served on or before its expiration date.

☐ There is no other pending or resolved civil action arising out of the same transaction or occurrence as alleged in the complaint.

☐ A civil action between these parties or other parties arising out of the transaction or occurrence alleged in the complaint has

been previously filed in _____ . The docket number and assigned judge are:

Name of court

Docket no.	Judge	Bar no.

The action ☐ remains ☐ is no longer pending.

VENUE	
Plaintiff(s) residence (include city, township, or village)	Defendant(s) residence (include city, township, or village)
Place where action arose or business conducted	

I declare that the complaint information above and attached is true to the best of my information, knowledge, and belief.

Date	Signature of attorney/plaintiff

COMPLAINT IS STATED ON ATTACHED PAGES. EXHIBITS ARE ATTACHED IF REQUIRED BY COURT RULE.

If you require special accommodations to use the court because of disabilities, please contact the court immediately to make arrangements.

MC 01   (6/96) SUMMONS AND COMPLAINT   MCR 2.102(B)(11), MCR 2.104, MCR 2.107, MCR 2.113(C)(2)(a), (b)

PROOF OF SERVICE

TO PROCESS SERVER: You are to serve the summons and complaint not later than 91 days from the date of filing. You must make and file your return with the court clerk. If you are unable to complete service you must return this original and all copies to the court clerk.

CERTIFICATE / AFFIDAVIT OF SERVICE / NON-SERVICE

☐ **OFFICER CERTIFICATE**	**OR**	☐ **AFFIDAVIT OF PROCESS SERVER**
I certify that I am a sheriff, deputy sheriff, bailiff, appointed court officer, or attorney for a party [MCR 2.104(A)(2)], and that: (notary not required)		Being first duly sworn, I state that I am a legally competent adult who is not a party or an officer of a corporate party, and that: (notary required)

☐ I served personally a copy of the summons and complaint,
☐ I served by registered or certified mail (copy of return receipt attached)   a copy of the summons and complaint,

together with _____ on the defendant(s):
          Attachment

Defendant's name	Complete address(es) of service	Day, date, time

☐ After diligent search and inquiry, I have been unable to find and serve the following defendant(s):

_____

I have made the following efforts in attempting to serve process: _____

_____

☐ I have personally attempted to serve the summons and complaint, together with _____
                                                       Attachment

_____ on _____
                                   Name

at _____ and have been unable to complete service because
    Address

the address was incorrect at the time of filing.

Service fee	Miles traveled	Mileage fee	Total fee	Signature
$		$	$	
				Title

Subscribed and sworn to before me on _____ , _____ County, Michigan.
                                    Date

My commission expires: _____ Signature: _____
                      Date   Deputy court clerk/Notary public

ACKNOWLEDGMENT OF SERVICE

I acknowledge that I have received service of the summons and complaint, together with _____
                                                      Attachment

_____ on _____
                                   Day, date, time

_____ on behalf of _____ .

Signature

MCR 2.105

STATE OF MICHIGAN **JUDICIAL CIRCUIT** **COUNTY**	**COMPLAINT FOR DIVORCE** **Page 1 of pages**	**CASE NO.**
Court address		Court telephone no.

Plaintiff's name, address, and telephone no(s).		Defendant's name, address, and telephone no(s).
	V	
Plaintiff's attorney, bar no., address, and telephone no.		Defendant's attorney, bar no., address, and telephone no.

The Plaintiff for his/her Complaint for Divorce against the Defendant, alleges and states:

1.   RESIDENCE: The ❑ Plaintiff ❑ Defendant has been a resident of the State of Michigan for at least 180 days, and of the County of _____ for at least 10 days, prior to filing this action.

2.   PLAINTIFF'S STATISTICAL FACTS:
      A.   Name:_____
      B.   Name prior to marriage, if any:_____
      C.   Current Address:_____
               _____
      D.   Date of Birth:_____
      E.   Social Security Number:_____
      F.   Occupation:_____
      G.   Employer's Name and Address:_____
               _____

3.   DEFENDANT'S STATISTICAL FACTS:
      A.   Name:_____
      B.   Name prior to marriage, if any:_____
      C.   ❑ Current ❑ Last known Address:_____
               _____
      D.   Date of Birth:_____
      E.   Social Security Number:_____
      F.   Occupation:_____
      G.   Employer's Name and Address:_____
               _____

Court address   Court telephone no.

| Plaintiff | | Defendant |

v

4.   MARRIAGE: The parties were married on _____,
at _____.

5.   GROUNDS: There has been a breakdown of the marriage relationship to the extent that the objects of matrimony have been destroyed and there remains no reasonable likelihood that the marriage can be preserved.

6.   CHILDREN:
        ❏ There are no minor or dependent children of the parties.
        ❏ The wife is not pregnant.
        ❏ The wife is pregnant, with an expected delivery date of _____.
        ❏ The parties have the following minor or dependent children:

Name	Address	Birth Date	Age	Sex	Current Custody

        With respect to any minor child(ren) listed above, there is no Michigan court with prior continuing jurisdiction of such minor, except as follows:_____
_____.

7.   PROPERTY:
        ❏ There is no property of the parties to be divided.
        ❏ There is property of the parties to be divided.

8.   SPOUSAL SUPPORT:
       ❏ No spousal support is requested.
       ❏ Spousal support is requested, based upon the following facts:

9.   OTHER:
       ❏ The parties have executed a Marital Settlement Agreement, which is being filed with this Complaint, and the parties request that it be incorporated into the final Judgment of Divorce.

WHEREFORE, the Plaintiff requests this court to grant the following relief:

1.   Grant the parties a divorce from the bonds of marriage.

2.   Divide the property of the parties.

❏ 3.   Award alimony to the Plaintiff.

❏ 4.   Award legal custody of the minor child(ren) of the parties to:
       ❏ Plaintiff
       ❏ Defendant
       ❏ Joint custody
       ❏ Split custody as follows:

Court address   Court telephone no.

| Plaintiff | v | Defendant |

❑ 5.   Award child visitation rights to the noncustodial party as follows:
    ❑ Reasonable visitation
    ❑ Other:

❑ 6.   Award child support to the   ❑ Plaintiff   ❑ Defendant

❑ 7.   Restore the ❑ Plaintiff's ❑ Defendant's
    name to:_____.

❑ 8.   Other:

Dated:_____   _____
                                Signature

                                Name:_____
                                Address:_____

                                _____
                                Telephone No._____

Approved, SCAO

STATE OF MICHIGAN JUDICIAL CIRCUIT COUNTY	FRIEND OF THE COURT CASE QUESTIONNAIRE Page 1	CASE NO.

Friend of the Court address | Telephone no.

Plaintiff name	v	Defendant name

GENERAL INFORMATION

1. Your full name	2. Date of birth	3. Place of birth: City and State

4. Address	City	State	Zip	5. Home telephone

6. Social security number	7. Driver license number	8. Work telephone

9. Sex ☐ M ☐ F	10. Eye color	11. Hair color	12. Height	13. Weight	14. Race	15. Scars, tatoos, etc.

16. Your father's full name	17. Your mother's full maiden name

18. Names of all of your dependent children   Birthdate   Soc. Sec. No.   Address

19. Are you or the other parent in this case pregnant? ☐ Yes ☐ No   If yes, complete a. and b. below.

a. When is the child due?	b. Are the parties in this case the biological parents of the expected child? ☐ Yes ☐ No

INFORMATION REGARDING THE OTHER PARENT IN THIS CASE (If known)

20. Full name	21. Date of birth	22. Place of birth: City and State

23. Address	City	State	Zip	24. Home telephone

25. Social security number	26. Driver license number	27. Work telephone

28. Sex ☐ M ☐ F	29. Eye color	30. Hair color	31. Height	32. Weight	33. Race	34. Scars, tatoos, etc.

35. Father's full name	36. Mother's full maiden name

37. Names of all the other parent's dependent children   Birthdate   Soc. Sec. No.   Address

FOC 39 A (4/87) FRIEND OF THE COURT - CASE QUESTIONNAIRE   (E2131)

STATE OF MICHIGAN JUDICIAL CIRCUIT COUNTY	FRIEND OF THE COURT CASE QUESTIONNAIRE Page 2	CASE NO.

INCOME INFORMATION

38. Your occupation

39. Your employer (If unemployed, name of last employer)

40. Employer's address   City   State   Zip

41. Date hired

42. Gross earnings per pay period (earnings before taxes)
$ ☐ weekly ☐ bi-weekly ☐ bi-monthly ☐ monthly

43. Social security number

44. Hourly pay rate (including shift premium and COLA)

45. Total regular hours worked per pay period

46. Avg. overtime hours for past 12 months

47. Second job

48. Employer

49. Employer's address   City   State   Zip

50. Date hired

51. Gross earnings per pay period (earnings before taxes)
$ ☐ weekly ☐ bi-weekly ☐ bi-monthly ☐ monthly

52. Hourly pay rate

53. Avg. of hours worked per pay period since hire date

54. List MONTHLY income from all other sources, such as:

Commissions	_____	Social Security Benefits	_____
Bonuses	_____	V. A. Benefits	_____
Profit Sharing	_____	Disability Insurance	_____
Interest	_____	G. I. Benefits	_____
Dividends	_____	Nat'l. Guard & Res. Drill Pay	_____
Annuities	_____	Armed Services	_____
Pensions/Longevity	_____	Allowance for Rent	_____
Deferred Compensation/IRA	_____	Rental Income	_____
Trust Funds	_____	Spousal Support/Alimony	_____
Unemployment Benefits	_____	General Assistance	_____
Strike Pay	_____	AFDC	_____
SUB Pay	_____	Supplemental Security Income SSI	_____
Sick Benefits	_____	Other	_____
Workers Compensation	_____		

55. Do you have any other alimony or child support orders? ☐ No ☐ Yes, as payer ☐ Yes, as recipient
If so, complete a. b. and c.

a. Amount of order (do not include arrearages)	b. Type of order/Case No.	c. City, County, and State

56. Do you provide the sole support for stepchildren residing in your home because support is unavailable from <u>both</u> natural/adoptive parents?

☐ No ☐ Yes ☐ If yes, how many stepchildren do you support _____

If yes, state the reason the stepchildren's mother is unable to provide support:

If yes, state the reason the stepchildren's father is unable to provide support:

57. Do any of the children listed on item 18 receive payments from the Social Security Administration? ☐ Yes ☐ No

Child's Name	Amount (monthly)	Type of benefit (check one) SSI	Dependent Benefit	Source of dependent benefit (Mother, Father, Stepparent)

58. Attach your 4 most recent paycheck stubs, or a statement from your employer(s) of wages and deductions, and year-to-date earnings, and a copy of your last federal and state income tax returns, including all schedules. If self-employed, also attach a copy of your 3 most recent business tax returns and/or corporation returns.

STATE OF MICHIGAN JUDICIAL CIRCUIT COUNTY	FRIEND OF THE COURT CASE QUESTIONNAIRE Page 3	CASE NO.

INCOME INFORMATION OF OTHER PARENT IN THIS CASE (If known)

59. Occupation	60. Employer (If unemployed, name of last employer)

61. Employer's address City State Zip	62. Hourly pay rate (including shift premium and COLA)

63. Gross earnings per pay period (earnings before taxes) $ ☐ weekly ☐ bi-weekly ☐ bi-monthly ☐ monthly	64. Avg. overtime hours for past 12 months

HEALTH CARE INFORMATION

65. Medical Insurance company name	Policy number	Beginning date, if known
66. Dental Insurance company name	Policy number	Beginning date, if known
67. Optical Insurance company name	Policy number	Beginning date, if known

68. What dependent coverage is available to you without cost?   ☐ Medical   ☐ Dental   ☐ Optical

69. What dependent coverage is available by payment of an additional premium? (Specify cost per pay period)
☐ Medical $ ☐ Dental $ ☐ Optical $

70. Individuals currently covered by your insurance

Name	Birthdate	Relationship	Medical (√)	Dental (√)	Optical (√)

CHILD CARE INFORMATION

71. Do you have child care expenses for the minor children in this domestic relations case during any time of the year?   ☐ Yes   ☐ No
If yes, complete the following information:

Name of child care provider	Names of children receiving child care
Number of weeks provided during last calendar year	Estimated number of weeks of child care provided in this calendar year
Current weekly child care cost	Amount of child care credit received on last year's federal I.R.S. tax return

72. Check the reason(s) which explain why you need child care and estimate the number of hours child care is received for each.

Reason	Estimated no. of hours per week
☐ Work related	_____
☐ Looking for employment	_____
☐ Enrolled in educational program to improve employment opportunities	_____

73. If your reason for child care is educational related, provide the following information:

Name of educational institution	Total classroom hours per week	Educational goal	Projected graduation date

[E2133]

STATE OF MICHIGAN JUDICIAL CIRCUIT COUNTY	FRIEND OF THE COURT CASE QUESTIONNAIRE Page 4	CASE NO.

INFORMATION FOR LESS THAN FULL TIME EMPLOYMENT

74. If unemployed and not receiving unemployment or worker's compensation benefits, or working part time only, provide the following information:

Name of last full time employer	Address of last full time employer
Position held at last place of full time employment	Last day employed full time
Length of time employed in last full time position	Reason for leaving last full time employment

Gross earnings per pay period at last place of full time employment (earnings before taxes)

$ _____ ☐ weekly   ☐ bi-weekly   ☐ bi-monthly   ☐ monthly

75. Do you have any medical conditions/restrictions that affect your ability to work?   ☐ Yes   ☐ No

If yes, please explain medical condition/restriction:

_____

_____

_____

_____

76. What is your educational background? (Check one)

☐ Less than High School   ☐ High School Graduate
☐ Trade School Graduate   ☐ Associates Degree
☐ Bachelor's Degree   ☐ Graduate Degree

I declare that the information in this questionnaire is true to the best of my information, knowledge, and belief.

_____   _____
Date   Signature

Reminder List:

Have you signed this questionnaire?

Have you attached your 4 most recent paycheck stubs, or a statement from your employer(s) of wages and deductions and year to date earnings?

Have you attached a copy of your last federal and state income tax returns, including all schedules? If self-employed, also attach a copy of your 3 most recent business tax returns and/or corporation returns.

Attach any additional information that may be useful to the Friend of the Court in making a support recommendation.

Retain a copy of this form for your own records. Return the original to the Friend of the Court office.

FOC 39 D (4/87) FRIEND OF THE COURT - CASE QUESTIONNAIRE   [E2134]

STATE OF MICHIGAN
IN THE CIRCUIT COURT FOR THE _____ JUDICIAL CIRCUIT,
COUNTY OF _____

_____, Plaintiff

vs.   File No._____

_____, Defendant

MARITAL SETTLEMENT AGREEMENT

This agreement made this _____ day of _____, _____, by and between _____, Plaintiff, and _____, Defendant.

WHEREAS, an action for divorce is now pending between the parties, and the parties desire to resolve various matters as part of said divorce action, the parties agree to the following:

I. CHILD CUSTODY

❏ There are no children under the age of 18 of the parties or born during the marriage.

❏ The matter of custody must be determined by the court.

❏ Custody of the minor child(ren) of the parties shall be as follows:

F = Father   M = Mother   J = Joint   3rd = Third party (name provided)

CHILD'S NAME	DATE OF BIRTH	LEGAL CUSTODY	PHYSICAL CUSTODY

❏ See attached sheet(s).

II. CHILD SUPPORT

❑ The matter of child support must be determined by the court.

❑ The ❑ Husband ❑ Wife agrees to pay the sum of $_____ per week, through the Friend of the Court, as support and maintenance for the minor child(ren) in the physical custody of the other parent. Payments shall begin on _____. A child shall be included in the calculation of child support until the child is 18, except that inclusion in the calculation shall continue until age 19 $^{1}/_{2}$ if the child is regularly attending high school on a full-time basis, has a reasonable expectation of graduating and is residing full time with one of the parties. Child support shall be adjusted, according to the then existing child support guidelines, upon the occurrence of any of the following events: a child becoming 18 years of age and not attending high school, becoming 19 $^{1}/_{2}$ years of age and regularly attending high school as provided for above, marrying, or becoming self-supporting; the death of a child; or a legal change in custody.

❑ See attached sheet(s).

III. HEALTH CARE INSURANCE AND EXPENSES

1. Health insurance coverage for the minor child(ren) shall be obtained/maintained, as long as such insurance is available to either one of the parties at a reasonable group rate, and shall be initially provided by: ❑ Husband ❑ Wife
2. Health care insurance premiums, if any, shall be paid by:
    ❑ Husband ❑ Wife
    ❑ Divided between the parties according to each party's percentage of their combined income.
3. Health care expenses not covered by insurance shall be paid by:
    ❑ Husband ❑ Wife
    ❑ Divided between the parties according to each party's percentage of their combined income.

❑ See attached sheet(s).

IV. CHILD VISITATION

❑ The matter of child visitation must be determined by the court.

❑ Any parent without physical custody of a child shall have visitation rights with the child as follows

❑ Reasonable visitation.

❑ Specific:

❑ See attached sheet(s).

V. DIVISION OF PROPERTY AND DEBTS

❏ The matter of property and debt division must be determined by the court.

A. Property

❏ There is no property to be divided as the parties have already divided their property and each shall keep what is currently in his or her possession.

❏ The parties shall each keep their own personal clothing and effects, unless otherwise indicated below. All other property shall be divided as follows:

   1. Husband transfers to Wife as her sole and separate property:
     A.
     B.
     C.
     D.
     E.
     F.
     G.
     ❏   Continued on attached sheet(s).

   2. Wife transfers to Husband as his sole and separate property:
     A.
     B.
     C.
     D.
     E.
     F.
     G.
     ❏   Continued on attached sheet(s).

B. Debts

❏ All debts have either been paid, or have already been divided by the parties with each party being responsible for debts in his or her name respectively.

❏ The parties divide responsibility for payment of their debts as follows:

   3. Husband shall pay the following debts and will not at any time hold Wife responsible for them:
     A.
     B.
     C.
     D.
     E.
     F.
     G.
     ❏   Continued on attached sheet(s).

4. Wife shall pay the following debts and will not at any time hold Husband responsible for them:

A.

B.

C.

D.

E.

F.

G.

❏ Continued on attached sheet(s).

VI. ALIMONY

❏ The matter of alimony must be determined by the court.

❏ No alimony shall be awarded to either party.

❏ The ❏ Husband ❏ Wife shall pay alimony to the other party in the lump sum amount of $_____.

❏ The ❏ Husband ❏ Wife shall pay alimony to the other party in the amount of $_____ per week, beginning _____, 19____, to terminate:
   ❏ on _____, 19____, or on the death or remarriage of the payee, whichever occurs first.
   ❏ upon the death or remarriage of the payee.

❏ See attached sheet(s).

VII. OTHER PROVISIONS:

❏ None.   ❏ See attached sheet(s).

DATED:_____   DATED:_____

_____   _____
Husband's signature   Wife's signature

Name_____   Name_____
Address_____   Address_____

_____   _____
Telephone No._____   Telephone No._____

STATE OF MICHIGAN JUDICIAL CIRCUIT COUNTY	JUDGMENT OF DIVORCE Page 1 of pages	CASE NO.

Court address

Plaintiff's name, address, and telephone no(s).		Defendant's name, address, and telephone no(s).
	V	
Plaintiff's attorney, bar no., address, and telephone no.		Defendant's attorney, bar no., address, and telephone no.

❑ After trial   ❑ Default   ❑ Consent

Date of hearing:_____   Judge: _____

                                                                                        Bar no.

IT IS ORDERED:

1. DIVORCE: The parties are divorced.

2. PROPERTY DIVISION: ❑ There is no property to be divided.
                                       ❑ Each party is awarded the property in their possession.
                                       ❑ Property is divided elsewhere in this judgment.

3. MINOR CHILDREN: There   ❑ are   children under 18 of the parties or born during this marriage.
                                   ❑ are not

               (Custody, visitation, support, and/or other required provisions are attached.)

4. NAME CHANGE: Wife's last name is changed to _____.

5. ALIMONY: Alimony is   ❑ not granted for   ❑ wife   ❑ husband
                                   ❑ reserved for   ❑ wife   ❑ husband
                                   ❑ granted elsewhere in this judgment for   ❑ wife   ❑ husband

6. STATUTORY RIGHTS: All interests of the parties in the property of the other, now owned or later acquired, under MCL 700.281 - 700.292, are extinguished, including those known as dower under MCL 558.1 - 558.29.

7. BENEFICIARY RIGHTS: The rights each party has to the proceeds of policies or contracts of life insurance, endowments, or annuities upon the life of the other as a named beneficiary or by assignment during or in anticipation of marriage, are   ❑ extinguished.   ❑ provided for elsewhere in this judgment.

8. PENSION RIGHTS: Any rights of either party in any pension, annuity, or retirement plan benefit of the other, whether vested or unvested, accumulated or contingent, are
                     ❑ extinguished   ❑ provided for elsewhere in this judgment.

9. JOINT REAL ESTATE: All real estate owned by the parties as joint tenants or as tenants by the entireties is   ❑ converted to a tenancy in common.   ❑ provided for elsewhere in this judgment.

10. DOCUMENTATION: Each party shall promptly and properly execute and deliver to the other appropriate documents required to carry out the terms of this judgment. A certified copy of this judgment may be recorded with the register of deeds in any county of this state where property may be located.

11. INTERIM ORDERS: Except as otherwise provided in this judgment, all interim orders and injunctions entered in this action are terminated.

| Plaintiff | V | Defendant |

IT IS FURTHER ORDERED:

SEE DEFINITIONS ON BACK OF FORM

12. **CUSTODY AND SUPPORT:**

The custody of each child shall continue as below until each child is 18, except that child support shall continue until age 191/2 if the child is regularly attending high school on a full-time basis, has a reasonable expectation of completing sufficient credits to graduate from high school, and is residing full-time with the payee of support or at an institution.

CHILD'S NAME	DATE OF BIRTH	LEGAL CUSTODY	PHYSICAL CUSTODY	WEEKLY SUPPORT AMOUNT	CHILD SUPPORT PAYER	HEALTH INSUR. PAYER	HEALTH EXPENSES PAYER

13. **VISITATION:** Any parent without physical custody shall have visitation rights as follows:
  ❏ reasonable.   ❏ specific visitation provided elsewhere in this judgment.

14. **HEALTH CARE INSURANCE:** Coverage for the benefit of the child(ren) shall be maintained, or coverage shall be obtained and maintained if available at a reasonable cost, as a benefit of employment, or as an optional coverage for dependents on a policy already obtained.

15. **SUPPORT PAYMENTS:** Child support amounts shall be paid each week. Payments shall begin:
  ❏ on _____.   ❏ when payer files this judgment or is served with a copy.

16. **OVERDUE AMOUNTS:** Overdue support and service fees of $_____ owing to Michigan and $_____ to recipient are preserved. Payer shall pay   ❏ $_____ immediately.   ❏ $_____ per week.

Except as otherwise provided in section 3 of the support and visitation enforcement act, Act No. 295 of the Public Acts of 1982, being section 552.603 of the Michigan Compiled Laws, a support order that is part of a judgment or is an order in a domestic relations matter as that term is defined in section 31 of the friend of the court act, Act No. 294 of the Public Acts of 1982, being section 552.531 of the Michigan Compiled Laws, is a judgment on and after the date each support payment is due, with the full force, effect, and attributes of a judgment of this state, and is not, on and after the date it is due, subject to retroactive modification.

17. **SERVICE FEES:** If payments are made to the Friend of the Court, payer shall pay statutory service fees (currently $12.00) each January and July while this order is in effect. An initial payment equal to $2.00 per month for each month until the next due date shall be made now.

18. **PAYMENT ROUTING:** Payments of support and overdue support (and service fees, if ordered) shall be made:
  ❏ through the Friend of the Court.   ❏ directly to the person, agency, or court with physical custody.

19. **INCOME WITHHOLDING ORDER:** When income withholding is implemented, the payer's source(s) of income shall withhold from income due the payer and pay to the Friend of the Court amounts sufficient to meet payments ordered for support and service fees and to liquidate overdue support and service fees due at the time this order of income withholding is implemented, as provided by MCL 552.601 et seq. The amount withheld shall not exceed the maximum amount permitted by 15 USC 1673(b), and shall be paid to the Friend of the Court within 3 days after the withholding occurs.

20. **INCOME WITHHOLDING IMPLEMENTATION:** Income withholding shall:
  ❏ continue.   ❏ start on _____ (Consent or after hearing only)
  ❏ start if overdue support reaches an amount greater than 4 weeks of support under the payer's support order.

21. **NOTICE OF CHANGES:** Each party shall immediately notify the Friend of the Court in writing of any changes in their address or employment status.

22. **DOMICILE:** The domicile or residence of the minor child(ren) shall not be changed from the state of Michigan without prior approval of the court.

Plaintiff	v	Defendant

IT IS FURTHER ORDERED:

❑ That the Marital Settlement Agreement filed in this action is hereby approved and incorporated by reference into this Judgment of Divorce, and the parties are ordered to abide by it.

❑ Approved as to form   ❑ Notice and hearing on entry waived   ❑ I stipulate to entry

_____
Plaintiff signature

_____
Defendant signature

_____
Plaintiff attorney signature

_____
Defendant attorney signature

_____
Date

_____
Circuit Court Judge   Bar no.

CERTIFICATE OF MAILING

I certify that on this date copies of this judgment were served upon all parties and/or their attorneys by personal service or ordinary mail to their address of record.

_____
Date

_____
Plaintiff/Defendant/Attorney signature

DEFINITIONS

"LEGAL CUSTODY" includes decision making authority and responsibility for the important decisions affecting the child(ren). If the court orders "joint legal custody," the joint custodians share the decision making authority.

"PHYSICAL CUSTODY" is the right and responsibility of a person to have the child(ren) live with him or her; it included the authority and responsibility to decide all routine matters concerning the child(ren) while the child(ren) reside(s) with that person.

"VISITATION" is a time for a person without physical custody to be with the child(ren), and includes the responsibility to decide routine matters concerning the child(ren) during the visit.

"REASONABLE VISITATION" is to be decided and scheduled by the parties.

"SPECIFIC VISITATION" may be ordered when the parties cannot agree on reasonable visitation, or when they desire to establish an agreed schedule. Specific visitation orders may contain any reasonable terms or conditions designed to facilitate orderly and meaningful exercise of visitation rights, including: specific terms of visitation, division of the responsibility to transport the child(ren), division of the cost of transporting the child(ren), restrictions on the presence of third persons during visitation, requirements that the child(ren) be ready for visitation at a specific time, requirements that the visiting party arrive for visitation and return the child(ren) from visitation at specific times, requirements that visitation occur in the presence of a third person or agency, requirements that a party post a bond to assure compliance with a visitation order, and any other reasonable condition determined to be appropriate in the particular case.

"HEALTH CARE EXPENSES" means those expenses resulting from the provision of human health care.

"HEALTH CARE INSURANCE" means insurance which pays all or part of a person's human health care expenses.

"HEALTH CARE" means the provision of human health care products or services by a person or organization licensed or legally authorized to provide human health care products or services in the place where the products or services are provided, including, but not limited to, those listed in MCL 333.16263(a) to (k) and MCL 333.20106(1), as amended. [This includes the following professionals: chiropractors, dentists, oral surgeons, orthodontists, prosthedontists, periodontists, endodontists, pedodontists, dental hygienists, dental assistants, medical doctors, physician's assistants, registered professional nurses, licensed practical nurses, nurse midwives, nurse anesthetists, nurse practitioners, trained attendants, optometrists, osteopaths, pharmacists, physical therapists, physiotherapists, physical therapy technicians, chiropodists, podiatrists, foot specialists, psychologists, psychological assistants, and psychological examiners. This also includes the following health facilities or agencies (even when located in a correctional institution or a university, college, or other educational institution): ambulances, advanced mobile emergency care services, clinical laboratories, county medical care facilities, freestanding surgical outpatient facilities, health maintenance organizations, homes for the aged, hospitals, and nursing homes.]

"REASONABLE AND NECESSARY EXPENSES" are expenses similar to those expenses normally incurred when providing for a known or provable need.

Plaintiff	v	Defendant

IT IS FURTHER ORDERED:

This page intentionally left blank

Original - Court
1st copy - Applicant
Copies - All appearing parties

Approved, SCAO

STATE OF MICHIGAN JUDICIAL DISTRICT JUDICIAL CIRCUIT	DEFAULT APPLICATION, ENTRY, AFFIDAVIT	CASE NO.

Court address

Court telephone no.

Plaintiff name(s), address(es), and telephone no(s).		Defendant name(s), address(es), and telephone no(s).
	v	
Plaintiff attorney, bar no., address, and telephone no.		Defendant attorney, bar no., address, and telephone no.

Party in default: _____

APPLICATION

In accordance with court rule, I request the clerk to enter the default of the party named above for failure to appear, plead, or otherwise defend as provided by law.

_____   _____
Applicant/Attorney signature   Bar no.

DEFAULT ENTRY

The default of the party named above for failure to appear, plead, or otherwise defend is entered.

_____   _____
Date   Court clerk

The affidavit must be completed by the applicant
before filing the application with the court.

AFFIDAVIT

☐ 1. The claim against the defaulted party is for a sum certain or for a sum which by computation can be made certain, and the plaintiff requests judgment of the amount due from the above party.

The amount due and costs are:

Damages	Interest	Costs	Other*	Total
$	$	$	$	$

*Attach bill of costs

2. The defaulted party is not an infant or incompetent person.

3. The defaulted party ☐ is not in the military service. ☐ is in the military service but there has been notice of the pendency of the action and adequate time and opportunity to appear and defend.

4. The claim ☐ is ☐ is not based on a note or other written evidence. If so, the evidence is attached for filing and for cancellation by the court clerk.

_____
Applicant/Attorney signature

Subscribed and sworn to before me on _____ , _____ County, Michigan.
                                                              Date

My commission expires: _____   Signature: _____
                                          Date   Deputy court clerk/Notary public

MC 07 (6/96) DEFAULT APPLICATION, ENTRY, AFFIDAVIT   MCR 2.603, MCL 32.17; MSA 4.609, 50 USC 520

Form 13

STATE OF MICHIGAN JUDICIAL CIRCUIT COUNTY	ANSWER AND WAIVER	CASE NO.

Court address   Court telephone no.

Plaintiff's name, address, and telephone no(s).		Defendant's name, address, and telephone no(s).
	V	
Plaintiff's attorney, bar no., address, and telephone no.		Defendant's attorney, bar no., address, and telephone no.

The Defendant, _____, answers the Complaint for Divorce as follows:

1. The Defendant hereby acknowledges receipt of a copy of the Complaint for Divorce filed in this action.

2. The allegations of the Complaint for Divorce are true and correct.

3. The residency status of the parties and the grounds for divorce as stated in the Complaint for Divorce are admitted.

4. The Defendant waives notice of the final hearing and agrees that this action may proceed to final hearing.

5. Other:

WHEREFORE, the Defendant requests this Court to:

1. Take jurisdiction over the parties and the marriage, and determine any issues the parties may not agree upon.

2. Enter its Judgment of Divorce.

Dated:_____   _____
                                        Signature of Defendant

                                        Name:_____
                                        Address:_____
                                        _____
                                        Telephone No.:_____

Approved, SCAO

STATE OF MICHIGAN	SUBPOENA	CASE NO.
JUDICIAL DISTRICT **JUDICIAL CIRCUIT** **COUNTY PROBATE**	**Order to Appear**	

Court address   Court telephone no.

Police Report No. (if applicable)

Plaintiff(s)/Petitioner(s)		Defendant(s)/Respondent(s)
☐ People of the State of Michigan ☐ _____	**v**	
☐ Civil ☐ Criminal		Charge
☐ Probate In the matter of _____		

In the Name of the People of the State of Michigan.   TO:

If you require special accommodations to use the court because of disabilities, please contact the court immediately to make arrangements.

YOU ARE ORDERED to appear personally at the time and place stated below:	You may be required to appear from time to time and day to day until you are excused.

1. ☐ The court address above   ☐ Other:

Day	Date	Time
2.		

YOU ARE ALSO ORDERED to:

☐ 3. Testify at trial / examination / hearing.

☐ 4. Produce the following items: _____

_____

_____

☐ 5. Testify as to your assets, and bring with you the items listed in line 4 above.

☐ 6. Testify at deposition.

☐ 7. MCL 600.6119 prohibition against transferring or disposing of property is attached.

☐ 8. Other: _____

☐ 9.

Person requesting subpoena	Telephone no.
Address	
City	State	Zip

NOTE: If you are requesting that an examination of a debtor be heard before a judge, or if you checked item 7, the judge must issue the subpoena. For debtor examinations before the judge, the affidavit of debtor examination on the other side of this form must also be completed.

FAILURE TO OBEY THE COMMANDS OF THE SUBPOENA OR APPEAR AT THE STATED TIME AND PLACE MAY SUBJECT YOU TO PENALTY FOR CONTEMPT OF COURT.

Court use only
☐ Served   ☐ Not served

_____   _____   Bar no. _____
Date   Judge/Clerk/Attorney

MC 11   (6/97)   SUBPOENA, Order to Appear

MCL 600.1455, 600.1701, 600.6110, 600.6119;
MSA 27A.1455, 27A.1701, 27A.6110, 27A.6119, MCR 2.506

TO PROCESS SERVER: You must make and file your return with the court clerk. If you are unable to complete service, you must return this original and all copies to the court clerk.

CERTIFICATE / AFFIDAVIT OF SERVICE / NON-SERVICE

☐ **OFFICER CERTIFICATE**   OR   ☐ **AFFIDAVIT OF PROCESS SERVER**

I certify that I am a sheriff, deputy sheriff, bailiff, appointed court officer, or attorney for a party [MCR 2.104(A)(2)], and that: (notary not required)

Being first duly sworn, I state that I am a legally competent adult who is not a party or an officer of a corporate party, and that: (notary required)

☐ I served a copy of the subpoena, together with _____
Attachment

☐ personally (including required fees, if any)
☐ by registered or certified mail (copy of return receipt attached)   on:

Name(s)	Complete address(es) of service	Day, date, time

☐ After diligent search and inquiry, I have been unable to find and serve the following person(s): _____

I have made the following efforts in attempting to serve process: _____

☐ I have personally attempted to serve the subpoena and required fees, if any, together with _____
Attachment

_____ on _____
Name

at _____ and have been unable to complete service because the address was incorrect at the time of filing.

Service fee	Miles traveled	Mileage fee	Total fee
$		$	$

Signature _____

Title _____

Subscribed and sworn to before me on _____ , _____ County, Michigan.
Date

My commission expires: _____ Signature: _____
Date   Deputy court clerk/Notary public

ACKNOWLEDGMENT OF SERVICE

I acknowledge that I have received service of the subpoena and required fees, if any, together with _____
Attachment

_____ on _____
Day, date, time

_____ on behalf of _____ .
Signature

AFFIDAVIT FOR JUDGMENT DEBTOR EXAMINATION

I request that the court issue a subpoena which orders the party named on this form to be examined under oath before a judge concerning the money or property of:
for the following reasons:

Under penalty of contempt of court, I declare that the above statements are true to the best of my information, knowledge, and belief.

Date _____   Signature _____

MCR 2.105

STATE OF MICHIGAN **JUDICIAL CIRCUIT** **COUNTY**	**NOTICE OF TAKING** **RECORDS DEPOSITION**	**CASE NO.**

Court address   Court telephone no.

Plaintiff's name, address, and telephone no(s).		Defendant's name, address, and telephone no(s).
	V	
Plaintiff's attorney, bar no., address, and telephone no.		Defendant's attorney, bar no., address, and telephone no.

TO:

On _____, _____, at _____ _____ m., _____

_____will take the records deposition of _____

_____.

     There will be no interrogation as this deposition is for copying purposes only. The following documents are requested:_____

_____

_____.

     This notice is given pursuant to MCR 2.306(B).

Dated:_____   _____

NOTICE OF TAKING RECORDS DEPOSITION

Form 16

Approved, SCAO

STATE OF MICHIGAN JUDICIAL CIRCUIT COUNTY	NOTICE OF HEARING	CASE NO.

Court address   FAX no.   Court telephone no.

Plaintiff's name, address, and telephone no.

Attorney:

v

Defendant's name, address, and telephone no.

Attorney:

A hearing will be held on _____ at _____ m.,
                          Date   Time

at _____ before _____
   Location   Bar no.

☐ Judge   ☐ Referee   for the following purpose:

You are required to attend this hearing.

If you require special accommodations to use the court because of a disability, please contact the court immediately to make arrangements. When contacting the court, provide your case number(s).

CERTIFICATE OF MAILING

I certify that on this date I mailed a copy of the notice of hearing by ordinary mail to the parties at the addresses stated above.

_____   _____
Date   Signature

FOC 7 (6/96) **NOTICE OF HEARING**

Approved, SCAO

STATE OF MICHIGAN **JUDICIAL DISTRICT** **JUDICIAL CIRCUIT** **COUNTY PROBATE**	**PROOF OF MAILING**	CASE NO.

Court address   Court telephone no.

Plaintiff(s)		Defendant(s)
	v	

☐ Juvenile   In the matter of _____

☐ Probate   In the matter of _____

On the date below I sent by first class mail a copy of _____

_____

_____ .

to: Names and addresses

I declare that the statements above are true to the best of my information, knowledge, and belief.

_____   _____
Date   Signature

                                                         _____
                                                         Name (type or print)

Form 18

<table>
<tr><td colspan="2" align="center">**RECORD OF**
DIVORCE OR ANNULMENT
MICHIGAN DEPARTMENT OF PUBLIC HEALTH
By authority of MCL 333.28113.</td><td>_____
Court Case Number
_____
County Circuit Court</td></tr>
</table>

_____
State File Number

1. Husband's Name _____   2. Husband's Birthdate _____
   First, Middle, Last   Month, Day, Year

3. Husband's Residence _____
   City, Village or Township   County   State

4. Husband's Birthplace _____   5. Number of this Marriage _____
   State or Foreign Country   First, Second, etc. (Specify)

6. Wife's Name _____   7. Wife's Birthdate _____
   First, Middle, Last   Month, Day, Year

8. Wife's Last Name Before First Married _____

9. Wife's Residence _____
   City, Village or Township   County   State

10. Wife's Birthplace _____   11. Number of this Marriage _____
    State or Foreign Country   First, Second, etc. (Specify)

12. Place of this Marriage _____
    City, Village or Township   County   State or Foreign Country

13. Date of this Marriage _____   14. Date Couple Last Resided   Check if ☐ Not Separated _____
    Month, day, Year   in Same Household   Month, Day, Year

15. Number of Minor Children in Household at Separation Date (Filing Date if Not Separated) Check if None ☐ _____
                                                                                                                          Number

16. Plaintiff ☐ ☐ ☐   17. Plaintiff's Attorney _____
          Husband Wife Other   Name (Type or Print)   Bar Number

18. Attorney's Address _____
    Number and Street   City   State   ZIP Code

19. Judgement of _____   20. Number of Minor Children whose
    Divorce/Annulment (Specify)   Physical Custody was Awarded to: Husband_____ Wife_____ Joint_____ Other_____
                                                                  Number   Number   Number   Number
                                   ☐ No Children

21. Judgement Recorded on _____   22. I certify that this Divorce was granted on _____
    Month. Day, Year   Month, Day, Year

23. Certifying Official _____
    Signature   Title   Date Signed

**Failure to provide the required information is a misdemeanor punishable by imprisonment
of not more than 1 year or a fine of not more than $1,000.00 or both.**

Original - Court
1st copy - Applicant
2nd copy - Opposing party
PROBATE OSM CODE: OSF

Approved, SCAO

		CASE NO.
STATE OF MICHIGAN JUDICIAL DISTRICT JUDICIAL CIRCUIT COUNTY PROBATE	**AFFIDAVIT AND ORDER SUSPENSION OF FEES/COSTS**	

Court address   Court telephone no.

Plaintiff/Petitioner name, address, and telephone no.		Defendant/Respondent name, address, and telephone no.
	v	
Plaintiff's/Petitioner's attorney, bar no., address, and telephone no.		Defendant's/Respondent's attorney, bar no., address, and telephone no.

☐ Probate   In the matter of _____

AFFIDAVIT

1. The attached pleading is to be filed with the court by or on behalf of _____ ,
   Name

   applicant, who is ☐ plaintiff/petitioner.   ☐ defendant/respondent.

2. The applicant is entitled to and asks the court for suspension of fees and costs in the action for the following reason:

   ☐ a. S/he is currently receiving public assistance: $ _____ per _____ Case No.: _____ .

   ☐ b. S/he is unable to pay those fees and costs because of indigency, based on the following facts:

   INCOME: _____
   Employer name and address

   _____   _____   _____   per ☐ week. ☐ month. ☐ two weeks.
   Length of employment   Average gross pay   Average net pay

   ASSETS: State value of car, home, bank deposits, bonds, stocks, etc.

   OBLIGATIONS: Itemize monthly rent, installment payments, mortgage payments, child support, etc.

   REIMBURSEMENT:
3. (in domestic relations cases only) The applicant is entitled to an order requiring his/her spouse to pay attorney fees.

_____
Affiant signature

Subscribed and sworn to before me on _____ , _____County, Michigan.
                                       Date

My commission expires: _____ Signature: _____
                        Date   Deputy clerk/Register/Notary public

(SEE REVERSE SIDE FOR ORDER)

MC 20 (9/95) **AFFIDAVIT AND ORDER, SUSPENSION OF FEES/COSTS**   MCR 2.002

CERTIFICATION OF ATTORNEY

1. I have reviewed the affidavit of indigency, and I certify that its contents are true to the best of my information, knowledge, and belief.

2. I will bring to the court's attention the matter of suspended costs and fees and the availability of funds to pay them before any disposition is entered. I will report at that time any changes in the information contained in the affidavit of indigency or any other information regarding the affiant's financial status or alterations of the fee arrangement.

_____
Date

_____
Attorney signature

_____
Attorney name (type or print)   Bar no.

CERTIFICATION BY PERSON OTHER THAN PARTY

1. I have personal knowledge of the facts appearing in the affidavit.

2. The person in whose behalf the petition is filed is unable to sign it because of

☐ minority: _____   ☐ other disability: _____
Date of birth   Nature of disability

Relationship: _____

_____
Date

_____
Affiant signature

_____
Affiant name (type or print)

_____
Address

_____
City, state, zip   Telephone no.

ORDER

IT IS ORDERED:

☐ 1. Fees and costs in this action required by law or court rule are waived/suspended until further order of the court. Before any final disposition or discontinuance is entered, the moving party shall bring the fee and costs suspension to the attention of the judge for final disposition.

2. Requests for waiver/suspension of transcript costs must be made separately by motion.

☐ 3. The applicant's spouse shall pay the fees and costs required by law or court rule.

☐ 4. This application is denied.

_____
Date

_____
Judge   Bar no.

Approved, SCAO

Original - Court	2nd copy - Defendant/Respondent
1st copy - FOC (if applicable)	3rd copy - Plaintiff/Petitioner

STATE OF MICHIGAN JUDICIAL CIRCUIT PROBATE COURT COUNTY	UNIFORM CHILD CUSTODY JURISDICTION ACT AFFIDAVIT	CASE NO.

Court address

Court telephone no.

CASE NAME:

1. The name and present address of each child (under 18) in this case is:

2. The places where the child(ren) has/have lived within the last 5 years are:

3. The names and present address(es) of custodians with whom the child(ren) has/have lived within the last 5 years are:

4. I do not know of, and have not participated (as a party, witness, or in any other capacity) in any other court decision, order, or proceeding (including divorce, separate maintenance, child neglect, dependency, or guardianship) concerning the custody or visitation of the child(ren), in this state or any other state, **except:** Specify case name and number and court's name and address

5. I do not have information of any pending proceeding (including divorce, separate maintenance, child neglect, dependency, or guardianship) concerning the custody or visitation of the child(ren), in this state or any other state, **except:** Specify case name and number and court's name and address

   That proceeding ☐ is continuing. ☐ has been stayed by the court.
   ☐ Temporary action by this court is necessary to protect the child(ren) because the child(ren) has/have been subjected to or threatened with mistreatment or abuse or is/are otherwise neglected or dependent. Attach explanation

6. I do not know of any person who is not already a party to this proceeding who has physical custody of, or who claims to have custody or visitation rights with, the child(ren), **except:** State name(s) and address(es)

7. The child(ren)'s "home state" is _____ . See back for definition of "home state"

I acknowledge a continuing duty to advise this court of any custody or visitation proceeding (including divorce, separate maintenance, child neglect or dependency) concerning the child(ren) in this state or any other state about which information is obtained during this proceeding.

_____   _____   _____
Signature of affiant   Name of affiant   Address of affiant

Subscribed and sworn to before me on _____, in _____County, Michigan.
                                                              Date

My commission expires: _____   Signature: _____
                                                                                              Notary Public

MC 416 (11/86) **UNIFORM CHILD CUSTODY JURISDICTION ACT AFFIDAVIT** MCL 600.651 et seq.; MSA 27A.651 et seq.

"Home state" means the state in which the child(ren) immediately preceding the time involved lived with his or her parents, a parent, or a person acting as a parent, for at least 6 consecutive months, and in the case of a child less than 6 months old the state in which the child lived from birth with any of the persons mentioned. Periods of temporary absence of the named persons are counted as part of the month or other period.

Approved, SCAO

STATE OF MICHIGAN JUDICIAL CIRCUIT COUNTY	VERIFIED STATEMENT	CASE NO.

1. Mother's last name	First name	Middle name	2. Any other names by which mother is or has been known

3. Date of birth	4. Social security number	5. Driver license number and state

6. Mailing address and residence address (if different)

7. Eye color	8. Hair color	9. Height	10. Weight	11. Race	12. Scars, tattoos, etc.

13. Home telephone no.	14. Work telephone no.	15. Maiden name	16. Occupation

17. Business/Employer's name and address	18. Gross weekly income

19. Has wife applied for or does she receive public assistance? If yes, please specify kind. ☐ Yes ☐ No	20. AFDC and recipient identification numbers

21. Father's last name	First name	Middle name	22. Any other names by which father is or has been known

23. Date of birth	24. Social security number	25. Driver license number and state

26. Mailing address and residence address (if different)

27. Eye color	28. Hair color	29. Height	30. Weight	31. Race	32. Scars, tattoos, etc.

33. Home telephone no.	34. Work telephone no.	35. Occupation

36. Business/Employer's name and address	37. Gross weekly income

38. Has husband applied for or does he receive public assistance? If yes, please specify kind. ☐ Yes ☐ No	39. AFDC and recipient identification numbers

40. a. Name of Minor Child Involved in Case	b. Birth Date	c. Age	d. Soc. Sec. No.	e. Residential Address

41. a. Name of Other Minor Child of Either Party	b. Birth Date	c. Age	d. Soc. Sec. No.	e. Residential Address

42. Health care coverage available for each minor child

a. Name of Minor Child	b. Name of Policy Holder	c. Name of Insurance Co./HMO	d. Policy/Certificate/Contract No.

43. Names and addresses of person(s) other than parties, if any, who may have custody of child(ren) during pendency of this case

• If any of the public assistance information above changes before your judgment is entered, you are required to give the Friend of the Court written notice of the change.

I declare that the statements above are true to the best of my information, knowledge, and belief.

_____
Date

_____
Signature

FOC 23 (5/93) **VERIFIED STATEMENT**

MCR 3.206(B)

Approved, SCAO

STATE OF MICHIGAN JUDICIAL DISTRICT JUDICIAL CIRCUIT	MOTION AND VERIFICATION FOR ALTERNATE SERVICE	CASE NO.

Court address

Court telephone no.

Plaintiff name(s), address(es), and telephone number(s)

v

Defendant name(s), address(es), and telephone number(s)

1. Service of process upon _____ cannot reasonably be made as otherwise provided in MCR 2.105, as shown in the following verification of process server.

2. Defendant's last known home and business addresses are:

Home address	City	State	Zip

Business address	City	State	Zip

a. I believe the ☐ home ☐ business address shown above is current.

b. I do not know defendant's current ☐ home ☐ business address. I have made the following efforts to ascertain the current address: _____

_____

_____

3. I request the court order service by alternate means.

I declare that the statements above are true to the best of my information, knowledge and belief.

Date	Attorney signature

Address	Attorney name (type or print)	Bar no.

City, state, zip	Telephone no.

VERIFICATION OF PROCESS SERVER

1. I have tried to serve process on this defendant as described: State date, place, and what occurred on each occasion

I declare that the statements above are true to the best of my information, knowledge and belief.

Date	Signature

Process Server (type or print)

MC 303 (6/86)   **MOTION AND VERIFICATION FOR ALTERNATE SERVICE**   MCR 2.105

Approved, SCAO

STATE OF MICHIGAN JUDICIAL DISTRICT JUDICIAL CIRCUIT	ORDER FOR ALTERNATE SERVICE	CASE NO.

Court address _____ Court telephone no.

Plaintiff name(s), address(es), and telephone no.(s)		Defendant name(s), address(es), and telephone no.(s)
	v	
Plaintiff's attorney, bar no., address, and telephone no.		

THE COURT FINDS:

1. Service of process upon defendant _____

cannot reasonably be made as provided in MCR 2.105, and service of process may be made in a manner which is reasonably

calculated to give defendant actual notice of the proceedings and an opportunity to be heard.

IT IS ORDERED:

2. Service of the summons and complaint and a copy of this order may be made by the following method(s):

a. ☐ First class mail to _____

b. ☐ Tacking or firmly affixing to the door at _____

c. ☐ Delivering at _____

to a member of defendant's household who is of suitable age and discretion to receive process, with instructions to deliver

it promptly to defendant.

d. ☐ Other: _____

_____

3. For each method used, proof of service must be filed promptly with the court.

Date _____ Judge _____ Bar no. _____

MC 304 (8/88) ORDER FOR ALTERNATE SERVICE MCR 2.103, MCR 2.105

I served a copy of the summons and complaint and a copy of the order for alternate service upon

by: _____

☐ 1. First class mail to _____ , on _____
Date

☐ 2. Tacking or firmly affixing to the door at _____ , on _____
Date

☐ 3. Delivering at _____ , on _____
Date

to a member of defendant's household who is of suitable age and discretion to receive process, with instructions to deliver it promptly to defendant.

☐ 4. Other: _____ , on _____
Date

_____   _____
Date   Signature

                                                   _____
                                                   Title

Subscribed and sworn to before me on _____ , _____ County, Michigan.
Date

My commission expires: _____   Signature: _____   Deputy court clerk/Notary public
Date

Approved, SCAO

STATE OF MICHIGAN JUDICIAL DISTRICT JUDICIAL CIRCUIT	ORDER FOR SERVICE BY PUBLICATION/POSTING AND NOTICE OF ACTION	CASE NO.

Court address   Court telephone no.

Plaintiff name(s) and address(es)		Defendant name(s) and address(es)
	v	

Plaintiff's attorney, bar no., address, and telephone no.

TO: _____

IT IS ORDERED:

1. You are being sued by plaintiff in this court to _____

_____ . You must file your answer or take other action

permitted by law in this court at the court address above on or before _____ . If you fail to do

Date

so, a default judgment may be entered against you for the relief demanded in the complaint filed in this case.

2. A copy of this order shall be published once each week in _____

Name of publication
    ☐ three consecutive weeks,

for ☐ _____ , and proof of publication shall be filed in this court.

3. _____ shall post a copy of this order in the courthouse, and

Name

at _____ and

Location

at _____

Location

    ☐ three continuous weeks,

for ☐ _____ , and shall file proof of posting in this court.

4. A copy of this order shall be sent to _____ at the last known address

Name

by registered mail, return receipt requested, before the   ☐ date of the last publication,
☐ last week of posting,   and the affidavit of mailing shall be

filed with this court.

_____   _____

Date   Judge   Bar no.

MC 307 (8/88) ORDER FOR SERVICE BY PUBLICATION/POSTING AND NOTICE OF ACTION   MCR 2.106

AFFIDAVIT OF MAILING

As ordered, on _____ I mailed a copy of the attached summons and
Date

complaint and this order to _____
Name

at _____ .
Address

The mailing receipt and return receipt are attached at right.

_____   _____
Date   Affiant signature

Subscribed and sworn to before me on _____ , _____ County, Michigan.
Date

My commission expires: _____   Signature: _____   Court clerk/Notary public
Date

[Box: Attach mailing receipt and return receipt here]

AFFIDAVIT OF POSTING

I have posted this order in a conspicuous place in the _____ courthouse and the

following places as ordered by this court: _____

_____

_____

It has been posted for ☐3 continuous weeks   ☐ _____ continuous weeks   as ordered by this court.

_____   _____
Date   Affiant signature

Subscribed and sworn to before me on _____ , _____ County, Michigan.
Date

My commission expires: _____   Signature: _____   Court clerk/Notary public
Date

AFFIDAVIT OF PUBLISHING

Name of   ☐ publisher   ☐ agent of publisher
Name

_____ | _____
Name of newspaper | County where published

This newspaper is a qualified newspaper. The attached copy was published in this
newspaper for at least 3 consecutive weeks on these dates: _____

_____

_____   _____
Date   Affiant signature

Subscribed and sworn to before me on _____ , _____ County, Michigan.
Date

My commission expires: _____   Signature: _____   Court clerk/Notary public
Date

[Box: Attach copy of publication here]

STATE OF MICHIGAN JUDICIAL CIRCUIT COUNTY	REQUEST FOR CERTIFICATE OF MILITARY SERVICE STATUS	CASE NO.

Court address   Court telephone no.

Plaintiff's name, address, and telephone no(s).	**V**	Defendant's name

TO: U.S. Coast Guard Commander, GPIM-2, Locators
2100 2nd St., S.W.
Washington, DC 20593

AFMPC/RMIQL, Attn: Air Force Locator
Randolph AFB, TX 78150-6001

Department of Navy, Bureau of Navy Personnel
2 Navy Annex
Washington, DC 20370-5000

CMC MMSB-10, HQ USMC, Bldg. 2008
Quantico, VA 22134-5002

Surgeon General, U.S. Public Health Service
Div. of Comm., Off. Personnel
5600 Fishers Lane
Rockville, MD 20857

Army World Wide Locator
U.S. Army Enlisted Records Center
Fort Benjamin Harrison, IN 46249-5601

Commander, U.S. Army Personnel Center, Officer Locator Branch
Attn: Locators
200 Stovall Street, Alexandria, VA 22332

RE: _____   _____
                  [Party]   [Soc. Sec. #]

    This case involves a divorce. It is imperative that a determination be made whether the above-named individual, who has an interest in these proceedings, is presently in the military service of the United States, and the date of induction and discharge, if any. This information is necessary to comply with §601 of the Soldier's and Sailor's Civil Relief Act of 1940, as amended. A self-addressed, stamped envelope is enclosed for your reply.

DATED:_____   _____

                                        Signature

                                        Name_____
                                        Address_____

                                        Telephone No._____

REQUEST FOR CERTIFICATE OF MILITARY SERVICE STATUS

STATE OF MICHIGAN JUDICIAL CIRCUIT COUNTY	STIPULATION TO WITHDRAW ANSWER ORDER	CASE NO.

Court address   Court telephone no.

Plaintiff's name, address, and telephone no(s).		Defendant's name, address, and telephone no(s).
	V	
Plaintiff's attorney, bar no., address, and telephone no.		Defendant's attorney, bar no., address, and telephone no.

IT IS STIPULATED by the parties that the Defendant's Answer be withdrawn and that the Plaintiff may proceed as in an uncontested matter.

Dated:_____   Dated:_____

_____   _____
Plaintiff   Defendant

_____   _____
Plaintiff's Attorney   Defendant's Attorney

ORDER

UPON READING and filing of the above Stipulation, with the Court being fully advised in the premises,

IT IS ORDERED that the Defendant's Answer be withdrawn and that Plaintiff proceeds as if this were an uncontested matter.

DATED this _____ day of _____, _____.

_____
Circuit Judge

Approved, SCAO

Original - Court
1st copy - Other Party
2nd copy - Moving Party

3rd copy - Friend of the Court
4th copy - Proof of Service
5th copy - Proof of Service

STATE OF MICHIGAN JUDICIAL CIRCUIT COUNTY	MOTION REGARDING SUPPORT	**Ⓐ** CASE NO.

Court address

Court telephone no.

Ⓑ Plaintiff's name, address, and telephone no.   ☐ moving party

v

Defendant's name, address, and telephone no.   ☐ moving party

Third party name, address, and telephone no.   ☐ moving party

Ⓒ 1. ☐ a. On _____ a judgment
Date
or order was entered regarding support.
☐ b. There is currently no order regarding support.

Ⓓ ☐ 2. The ☐ plaintiff ☐ defendant   is ordered to pay support of $ _____ each _____ .
week, month, etc.

Ⓔ ☐ 3. The ☐ plaintiff ☐ defendant   is ordered to pay child care of $ _____ each _____ .
week, month, etc.

Ⓕ ☐ 4. The ☐ plaintiff ☐ defendant   is ordered to pay health care of $ _____ each _____ .
week, month, etc.

Ⓖ ☐ 5. Conditions regarding support have changed as follows:
Use a separate sheet to explain in detail what has happened and attach. Include all necessary facts.

Ⓗ ☐ 6. _____ and I have agreed to support as follows:
Name
Use a separate sheet to explain in detail what you have agreed on and attach. Include all necessary facts.

Ⓘ 7. **I ask the court to order that support be** paid as follows: ☐ See 6. above for details.
Use a separate sheet to explain in detail what you want the court to order and attach.

I declare that the above statements are true to the best of my information, knowledge, and belief.

Ⓙ _____
Date

_____
Moving party's signature

NOTICE OF HEARING

A hearing will be held on this motion before _____
Name of judge or referee

Ⓚ on _____ at _____ at _____ .
Date   Time   Place

NOTE: If you are the person receiving this motion, you may file a response. Contact the friend of the court office and request form FOC 51.

CERTIFICATE OF MAILING

I certify that on this date I mailed a copy of this motion and notice of hearing on the other party(ies) by ordinary mail at the above address(es).

Ⓛ _____
Date

_____
Moving party's signature

FOC 50 (12/96) **MOTION REGARDING SUPPORT**   MCL 552.14; MSA 25.94, MCR 2.119; MCR 3.213

Form 28

| Original - Court
1st copy - Moving Party
2nd copy - Responding Party | 3rd copy - Friend of the Court
4th copy - Proof of Service
5th copy - Proof of Service |

| STATE OF MICHIGAN
_____ JUDICIAL CIRCUIT
_____ COUNTY | RESPONSE TO
MOTION REGARDING SUPPORT | (A) | CASE NO. |

Court address _____ **Court telephone no.** _____

(B) Plaintiff's name, address, and telephone no. ☐ moving party

v

Defendant's name, address, and telephone no. ☐ moving party

Third party name, address, and telephone no. ☐ moving party

(C) 1. ☐ a. On _____ a judgment
    Date
or order was entered regarding support.
☐ b. There is currently no order regarding support.

(D) ☐ 2. The ☐ plaintiff ☐ defendant is ordered to pay support of $ _____ each _____ .
week, month, etc.

(E) ☐ 3. The ☐ plaintiff ☐ defendant is ordered to pay child care of $ _____ each _____ .
week, month, etc.

(F) ☐ 4. The ☐ plaintiff ☐ defendant is ordered to pay health care of $ _____ each _____ .
week, month, etc.

(G) ☐ 5. I ☐ agree ☐ do not agree that conditions regarding support have changed as stated in the motion.
Explain in detail what you do not agree with and why. Include all necessary facts. Use a separate sheet of paper if needed.

(H) ☐ 6. I agreed with the other party to start/change support:
☐ a. exactly as stated in the motion.
☐ b. but not as stated in the motion.
If b. is checked, explain in detail what you did agree on. Include all necessary facts. Use a separate sheet of paper if needed.

(I) 7. ☐ a. I agree with what is being asked for in the motion.
☐ b. I do not agree with what is being asked for in the motion and ask the court to order that support be paid as follows:
If you do not agree with the request in the motion, explain in detail why and what you want the court to order. Use a separate sheet of paper if needed.

I declare that the above statements are true to the best of my information, knowledge, and belief.

(J) _____
Date

_____
Responding party's signature

CERTIFICATE OF MAILING

I certify that on this date I mailed a copy of this response on the other party(ies) by ordinary mail at the above address(es).

(K) _____
Date

_____
Responding party's signature

FOC 51 (12/96) **RESPONSE TO MOTION REGARDING SUPPORT**   MCL 552.14; MSA 25.94, MCR 2.119

Form 29

Approved, SCAO

Original - Court
1st copy - Other Party
2nd copy - Moving Party

3rd copy - Friend of the Court
4th copy - Proof of Service
5th copy - Proof of Service

| STATE OF MICHIGAN JUDICIAL CIRCUIT COUNTY | ORDER REGARDING SUPPORT Page 1 | Ⓐ CASE NO. |

Court address

FAX no.   Court telephone no.

Ⓑ Plaintiff's name, address, and telephone no.

v

Defendant's name, address, and telephone no.

Third party's name, address, and telephone no.

Ⓒ Date: _____

Judge: _____

Ⓓ 1. This order is entered ☐ after hearing. ☐ on consent of the parties. ☐ on stipulation of the parties.

THE COURT FINDS:

Ⓔ ☐ 2. A motion requesting support or a change to support was filed.

Ⓕ ☐ 3. A response to the motion was filed.

Ⓖ ☐ 4. A material change of circumstances exists which warrants a change in the support order.

Ⓗ ☐ 5. Applying the Child Support Formula would be unjust or inappropriate because: _____

_____

IT IS ORDERED:

Ⓘ ☐ 6. The motion regarding support is dismissed.

Ⓙ ☐ 7. Starting _____ Date ☐ Plaintiff ☐ Defendant shall pay _____ weekly, monthly, etc. through the
Office of the Friend of the Court the amount of child support for the total number of children being supported as follows.
Support shall continue until each child reaches the age of 18 or graduates from high school, whichever is later, but no
longer than the age 19 1/2. Each child over 18 must be attending school on a full-time basis with a reasonable expectation
of graduating. This amount ☐ follows ☐ does not follow the Child Support Formula.

Number of Children Supported				
5 or more	4	3	2	1

Ⓚ ☐ 8. ☐ Plaintiff ☐ Defendant shall pay through the Office of the Friend of the Court child care expenses as follows:

Ⓛ ☐ 9. Overdue support is preserved and shall be paid as follows:

Ⓜ ☐ 10. The payer shall receive a credit of _____ % of the child support obligation each time after the child(ren) spend
6 or more consecutive overnight periods with the payer in accordance with the payer's parenting time rights.

11. Income withholding shall continue or be implemented immediately upon entry of this order.

Continued on page 2.

FOC 52 (12/96) **ORDER REGARDING SUPPORT, Page 1** MCL 552.14; MSA 25.94, MCL 552.517b(3); MSA 25.176(17b)(3), MCR 2.119

STATE OF MICHIGAN JUDICIAL CIRCUIT COUNTY	ORDER REGARDING SUPPORT Page 2	(A)	CASE NO.

Court address

FAX no.   Court telephone no.

(B) Plaintiff's name

Third party's name

v   Defendant's name

IT IS FURTHER ORDERED:

(N) ☐ 12. Each party shall maintain or obtain health coverage for the benefit of the child(ren) if available at a reasonable cost, as a benefit of employment, or as an optional coverage for dependents on a policy already obtained.

(O) ☐ 13. ☐ Plaintiff shall pay _____% ☐ Defendant shall pay _____% of the reasonable and necessary health care expenses of the child(ren) not covered by health care insurance. Overdue health care expenses of $_____ are preserved and are to be paid as follows:

14. The payer of support shall pay to the Office of the Friend of the Court a service fee of $2.00 per month, payable semi-annually on January 2 and July 2 of each year. In addition, every person required to make payments of support or maintenance through the Office of the Friend of the Court shall pay $1.25 per month for every month or portion of a month that support maintenance is required to be paid to cover the cost of services provided by the Office of the Friend of the Court which are not reimbursed under title IV-D.

15. Each party shall notify the friend of the court in writing of any change in their mailing and residence address no later than 21 days of the change, of any change in the name and address of current source of income, and whether he/she holds a driver's or occupational license. Each party shall also keep the friend of the court informed of any health care coverage available to them; the name of the insurance company, health care organization, or health maintenance organization; the policy, certificate, or contract number; and the names and birth dates of the persons who are covered. A surcharge will be added to support payments that are past due.

16. Except as otherwise provided in Section 3 of the Support and Parenting Time Enforcement Act, Act No. 295 of the Public Acts of 1982, being Section 552.603 of the Michigan Compiled Laws, a support order that is part of a judgment or is an order in a domestic relations matter as that term is defined in Section 31 of the Friend of the Court Act, Act No. 294 of the Public Acts of 1982, being Section 552.531 of the Michigan Compiled Laws, is a judgment on and after the date each support payment is due, with the full force, effect, and attributes of a judgment of this state, and is not, on and after the date it is due, subject to retroactive modification. A surcharge of 8% annually will be added to support payments that are past due as of January 1 and July 1 of each year as provided in MCL 552.603a.

17. Except as changed in this order, any prior order remains in effect.

(P) _____   _____
Plaintiff's signature (consent/stipulation)   Defendant's signature (consent/stipulation)

_____
Third party's signature (consent/stipulation)

(Q) Approved as to form: _____
           Friend of the court signature (only if required)

_____
Date

_____
Circuit court judge

PROOF OF SERVICE

I certify that on this date I served copies of this order on the other party(ies) by ordinary mail at the above address(es).

(R) _____
Date

_____
Signature

Approved, SCAO

Original - Court
1st copy - Other Party
2nd copy - Moving Party

3rd copy - Friend of the Court
4th copy - Proof of Service
5th copy - Proof of Service

STATE OF MICHIGAN JUDICIAL CIRCUIT COUNTY	NOTICE OF HEARING TO ENTER ORDER	**Ⓐ** CASE NO.

Court address

Court telephone no.

Ⓑ Plaintiff's name ☐ moving party

v

Defendant's name ☐ moving party

Third party's name ☐ moving party

Ⓒ 1. On _____ a hearing was held on a motion regarding _____
   Date   Type of order

and a decision was made.

2. The attached proposed order states what the judge or referee said at the hearing.

Ⓓ 3. This is your notice that a hearing will be held before _____ on
   Name of judge or referee

_____ at _____ at _____
Date   Time   Place

to have the proposed order signed. If you don't think that the order accurately states what was ordered in court, attend

the scheduled hearing.

4. Parties may be represented by their attorneys in this matter.

Ⓔ _____   _____
   Date   Signature of moving party

CERTIFICATE OF MAILING

I certify that on this date I mailed a copy of this notice of hearing and proposed order on the other party(ies) by ordinary mail at the above address(es).

Ⓕ _____   _____
   Date   Signature of moving party

Approved, SCAO

| | Original - Court
1st copy - Other Party
2nd copy - Moving Party | 3rd copy - Friend of the Court
4th copy - Proof of Service
5th copy - Proof of Service |

| STATE OF MICHIGAN
JUDICIAL CIRCUIT
COUNTY | NOTICE TO ENTER ORDER
WITHOUT HEARING | **Ⓐ** CASE NO. |

Court address _____   Court telephone no.

Ⓑ

| Plaintiff's name | ☐ moving party | | Defendant's name | ☐ moving party |
| | | **v** | | |

| Third party's name | ☐ moving party |

Ⓒ 1. On _____ a hearing was held on a motion regarding _____
Date   Type of order

and a decision was made.

2. The attached proposed order states what the judge or referee said at the hearing.

3. This is your notice that the proposed order will be given to the judge to sign. If you don't think that the order accurately states what was ordered in court, you must file your written objections with the court within 7 days of the date this notice was mailed. A form to use for filing objections is available at the friend of the court office. Contact the friend of the court and ask for form FOC 78.

4. If you do not file written objections to the proposed order within 7 days of the date of this notice, the judge may sign the proposed order without a hearing. If the judge decides that a hearing is needed, you will be notified of the hearing date.

5. If you file written objections to the proposed order, a hearing will be scheduled. You will be notified of the hearing date.

6. Parties may be represented by their attorneys in this matter.

Ⓓ _____   _____
Date   Signature of moving party

CERTIFICATE OF MAILING

I certify that on this date I mailed a copy of this notice proposed order on the other party(ies) by ordinary mail at the above address(es).

Ⓔ _____   _____
Date   Signature of moving party

FOC 54 (12/96) **NOTICE TO ENTER ORDER WITHOUT HEARING**   MCR 2.602(B)

| | | Original - Court | 2nd copy - Defendant |
| | | 1st copy - Plaintiff | 3rd copy - Friend of the Court |

STATE OF MICHIGAN JUDICIAL CIRCUIT COUNTY	OBJECTION TO EX PARTE ORDER AND MOTION TO RESCIND OR MODIFY	CASE NO.

Court address   Court telephone no.

Plaintiff's name, address, telephone no., and social security no.

Please print or type information.

v

Defendant's name, address, telephone no., and social security no.

OBJECTION AND MOTION

I, _____ , state:
Name of party filing motion

1. I have been served with an ex parte order in this case dated _____ .

2. I object to the ☐ custody ☐ visitation ☐ support provisions of that order because:

I request that a hearing be held to rescind or modify the ex parte order.

I declare that the statements above are true to the best of my information, knowledge, and belief.

_____
Date

_____
Signature of party filing motion

NOTICE OF HEARING

See instructions for details on getting a hearing date, time, and location.

A hearing will be held on this motion before _____ on
Name of judge or referee

_____ at _____ at _____ .
Date   Time   Place or location

CERTIFICATE OF MAILING

See instructions to make sure this motion gets mailed on time.

I certify that on this date I mailed a copy of this motion and notice of hearing to the other party and their attorney, if any, at the address stated above.

_____
Date

_____
Signature

MCL 722.27a(9),(10); MSA 25.312(7a)(9),(10)

FOC 61 (8/89) **OBJECTION TO EX PARTE ORDER AND MOTION TO RESCIND OR MODIFY**

Form 33

		Original - Court 1st copy - Plaintiff	2nd copy - Defendant 3rd copy - Friend of the Court

STATE OF MICHIGAN JUDICIAL CIRCUIT COUNTY	ORDER MODIFYING EX PARTE ORDER	CASE NO.

Court address   Court telephone no.

```
┌─────────────────────────────────────────────────┐
│ Plaintiff's name, address, telephone no., and    │
│ social security no.                              │
│                                                  │
│                                                  │
│                                                  │
└─────────────────────────────────────────────────┘
```

Please print or type information.

v

```
┌─────────────────────────────────────────────────┐
│ Defendant's name, address, telephone no., and    │
│ social security no.                              │
│                                                  │
│                                                  │
│                                                  │
└─────────────────────────────────────────────────┘
```

On _____ ,
      Date of hearing

_____
Circuit court judge/Referee

found that the ex parte order should be modified.

IT IS ORDERED:

1. ☐ Custody   ☐ Visitation   ☐ Support   is changed to:

☐   2. Other (see attached)

3.   The changes made in this order shall start on _____ .
                                                              Date

4.   Except as changed in this order, all other provisions of the ex parte order shall remain in effect until further order of the court.

_____
Plaintiff's signature (approved as to form and content)

_____
Defendant's signature (approved as to form and content)

_____
Date

_____
Circuit court judge   Bar no.

FOC 62 (8/89) **ORDER MODIFYING EX PARTE ORDER**   MCL 722.27a(10); MSA 25.312(7a)(10)

Original - Court
2nd copy - Friend of the Court
3rd copy - Plaintiff
4th copy - Defendant

Approved, SCAO

STATE OF MICHIGAN JUDICIAL CIRCUIT COUNTY	AGREEMENT SUSPENDING IMMEDIATE INCOME WITHHOLDING	CASE NO.

Friend of the Court address

Court telephone no.

Plaintiff's name, address, and social security no.

v

Defendant's name, address, and social security no.

NOTE: MCL 552.604(3); MSA 25.164(4)(3) requires that all new and modified support orders after December 31, 1990 include a provision for immediate income withholding and that income withholding take effect immediately unless the parties enter into a written agreement that the income withholding order shall not take effect immediately.

We understand that by law an order of income withholding in a support order shall take effect immediately. However, we agree to the following:

1. The order of income withholding shall not take effect immediately.

2. An alternative payment arrangement shall be made as follows:

3. Both the payer and the recipient of support shall keep the friend of the court informed of the following:
    a. the name and address of his/her current source of income;
    b. any health care coverage that is available to him/her as a benefit of employment or that is maintained by him/her; the name of the insurance company, health care organization, or health maintenance organization; the policy, certificate or contract number; and the name(s) and birth date(s) of the person(s) for whose benefit s/he maintains health care coverage under the policy, certificate, or contract; and
    c. his/her current residence and mailing address.

4. We further understand that proceedings to implement income withholding shall commence if the payer of support falls one month behind in his/her support payments.

5. We recognize that the court may order withholding of income to take effect immediately for cause or at the request of the payer.

_____
Date

_____
Date

_____
Plaintiff's signature

_____
Defendant's signature

FOC 63 (3/93) **AGREEMENT SUSPENDING IMMEDIATE INCOME WITHHOLDING**   MCL 552.604; MSA 25.164(4)

Form 35

Approved, SCAO

STATE OF MICHIGAN **JUDICIAL CIRCUIT** COUNTY	ORDER SUSPENDING IMMEDIATE INCOME WITHHOLDING	**CASE NO.**

Friend of the Court address   **Court telephone no.**

Plaintiff's name, address, and social security no.

v

Defendant's name, address, and social security no.

1. Date of hearing: _____ Judge: _____
2. **THE COURT FINDS:**   Bar no.
   ☐ There is good cause for the order of income withholding not to take effect immediately as follows:
   a. It is in the best interest of the child for immediate income withholding not to take effect for the following stated reasons:

   b. Proof of timely payment of previously ordered support has been provided.
   c. Both the payer and the recipient of support will notify the friend of the court in writing of any change in:
      1) the name and address of his/her current source of income;
      2) any health care coverage that is available to him/her as a benefit of employment or that is maintained by him/her, the name of the insurance company, health care organization, or health maintenance organization; the policy, certificate, or contract number; and the names and birth dates of the persons for whose benefit s/he maintains health care coverage under the policy, certificate, or contract; and
      3) his/her current residence and mailing address within 21 days of the change.

   ☐ The parties have entered into a written agreement that has been reviewed and entered in the record as follows:
   a. The order of income withholding shall not take effect immediately.
   b. An alternative payment arrangement has been agreed upon (attached).
   c. Both the payer and the recipient of support will notify the friend of the court in writing of any change in:
      1) the name and address of his/her current source of income;
      2) any health care coverage that is available to him/her as a benefit of employment or that is maintained by him/her, the name of the insurance company, health care organization, or health maintenance organization; the policy, certificate, or contract number; and the names and birth dates of the persons for whose benefit s/he maintains health care coverage under the policy, certificate, or contract; and
      3) his/her current residence and mailing address within 21 days of the change.

IT IS ORDERED:
3. Income withholding shall not take effect immediately.
4. Income withholding shall take effect if the fixed amount of arrearage is reached, as specified in law.

_____   _____
Date   Judge

FOC 64 (6/94) **ORDER SUSPENDING IMMEDIATE INCOME WITHHOLDING**   MCL 552.511; MSA 25.176(11),
                                                                          MCL 552.604; MSA 25.164(4) .
                                                                          MCL 552.607; MSA 25.164(7)

Form 36

Original - Court
1st copy - Other Party
2nd copy - Moving Party

3rd copy - Friend of the Court
4th copy - Proof of Service
5th copy - Proof of Service

STATE OF MICHIGAN JUDICIAL CIRCUIT COUNTY	MOTION REGARDING PARENTING TIME	(A) CASE NO.

Court address

Court telephone no.

(B) Plaintiff's name, address, and telephone no. ☐ moving party

v

Defendant's name, address, and telephone no. ☐ moving party

Third party name, address, and telephone no. ☐ moving party

(C) 1. ☐ a. On _____ a judgment
Date
or order was entered regarding parenting time.
☐ b. There is currently no order regarding parenting time.

(D) ☐ 2. _____ has disobeyed the parenting time order as follows:
Name

☐ a. he/she has denied me parenting time with the child(ren) as follows:
☐ b. he/she has not had parenting time with the child(ren) as follows:
☐ c. he/she has made changes in parenting time without court order as follows:
☐ d. he/she has not followed the specific conditions of parenting time as follows:
Use a separate sheet to explain in detail what has happened and attach. Include all necessary facts.

(E) ☐ 3. _____ and I have agreed to parenting time as follows:
Name
Use a separate sheet to explain in detail what you have agreed on and attach. Include all necessary facts.

(F) 4. It is in the best interests of the child(ren) to ☐ establish parenting time ☐ change parenting time because:
Use a separate sheet to explain why it is in the best interests of the child(ren) and attach.

(G) 5. **I ask the court to order that parenting time be** ☐ established ☐ changed ☐ made up as follows:
Use a separate sheet to explain in detail what you want the court to order and attach.

I declare that the above statements are true to the best of my information, knowledge, and belief.

(H) _____
Date

_____
Moving party's signature

NOTICE OF HEARING

(I) A hearing will be held on this motion before _____
Name of judge or referee

on _____ at _____ at _____ .
Date   Time   Place

NOTE: If you are the person receiving this motion, you may file a response. Contact the friend of the court office and request form FOC 66.

CERTIFICATE OF MAILING

I certify that on this date I mailed a copy of this motion and notice of hearing on the other party(ies) by ordinary mail at the above address(es).

(J) _____
Date

_____
Moving party's signature

FOC 65 (12/96) MOTION REGARDING PARENTING TIME

MCL 552.14; MSA 25.94, MCR 2.119

Form 37

Original - Court 1st copy - Moving Party 2nd copy - Responding Party	3rd copy - Friend of the Court 4th copy - Proof of Service 5th copy - Proof of Service	

STATE OF MICHIGAN JUDICIAL CIRCUIT COUNTY	RESPONSE TO MOTION REGARDING PARENTING TIME	(A) CASE NO.

Court address _____ Court telephone no.

(B)

Plaintiff's name, address, and telephone no. ☐moving party

v

Defendant's name, address, and telephone no. ☐ moving party

Third party name, address, and telephone no. ☐moving party

(C) 1. ☐ a. On _____ a judgment
        _____Date_____
        or order was entered regarding parenting time.
   ☐ b. There is currently no order regarding parenting time.

(D) ☐2. I ☐ have ☐ have not   disobeyed the parenting time order as stated in the motion.
        Explain in detail what you do not agree with in item 2. of the motion and why. Include all necessary facts. Use a separate sheet of paper if needed.

(E) ☐3. ☐a. I agreed with the other party to start or make changes in parenting time as stated in the motion.
        ☐b. I agreed with the other party to start or make changes in parenting time. They were not what was stated in the motion.
        ☐c. I did not agree with the other party to start or make changes in parenting time.
        If b. is checked, explain in detail what you did agree on. Include all necessary facts. Use a separate sheet of paper if needed.

(F) 4. I ☐agree   ☐ do not agree   that it is in the best interests of the child(ren) to ☐establish ☐change
        parenting time as stated in the motion.
        If you do not agree with the motion, explain why it is in the best interests of the child(ren). Use a separate sheet of paper if needed.

(G) 5. **I ask the court to order that parenting time** ☐be ☐not be ☐established ☐changed ☐made up
        as stated in the motion.
        If you do not agree with the request in the motion, explain in detail what you want the court to order. Use a separate sheet of paper if needed.

I declare that the above statements are true to the best of my information, knowledge, and belief.

(H) _____   _____
    Date   Responding party's signature

CERTIFICATE OF MAILING

I certify that on this date I mailed a copy of this response on the other party(ies) by ordinary mail at the above address(es).

(I) _____   _____
    Date   Responding party's signature

FOC 66   (12/96)   **RESPONSE TO MOTION REGARDING PARENTING TIME**   MCL 552.14; MSA 25.94, MCR 2.119

Approved, SCAO

Original - Court
1st copy - Other Party
2nd copy - Moving Party

3rd copy - Friend of the Court
4th copy - Proof of Service
5th copy - Proof of Service

STATE OF MICHIGAN
JUDICIAL CIRCUIT
COUNTY

ORDER REGARDING PARENTING TIME

(A) **CASE NO.**

Court address

Court telephone no.

(B) Plaintiff's name, address, and telephone no.

v

Defendant's name, address, and telephone no.

Third party's name, address, and telephone no.

(C) Date: _____

Judge: _____

(D) 1. This order is entered ☐ after hearing. ☐ on consent of the parties. ☐ on stipulation of the parties.

THE COURT FINDS:

(E) ☐2. A motion requesting parenting time/change to parenting time was filed.

(F) ☐3. A response to the motion was filed.

(G) ☐4. It ☐ is ☐ is not in the best interests of the child(ren) to ☐ establish ☐ change parenting time.

(H) ☐5. It is in the best interests of the child(ren) to dismiss the motion.

IT IS ORDERED:

(I) ☐6. The motion is dismissed. Parenting time is unchanged and the existing order remains in effect.

(J) ☐7. Parenting time is ☐ established ☐ changed ☐ to be made up as follows:
Explain in detail what the court has ordered.

8. Except as changed in this order, the prior order (if one) remains in effect.

(K) _____
Plaintiff's signature (consent/stipulation)

_____
Defendant's signature (consent/stipulation)

_____
Third party's signature (consent/stipulation)

(L) Approved as to form:_____
Friend of the court signature (only if required)

_____
Date

_____
Circuit court judge

PROOF OF SERVICE

(M) I certify that on this date I mailed a copy of this order on the other party(ies) by ordinary mail at the above address(es).

_____
Date

_____
Signature

FOC 67 (12/96) **ORDER REGARDING PARENTING TIME**

MCL 552.14; MSA 25.94, MCR 2.119

Approved, SCAO

Original - Court
1st copy - Moving Party
2nd copy - Objecting Party

3rd copy - Friend of the Court
4th copy - Proof of Service
5th copy - Proof of Service

STATE OF MICHIGAN JUDICIAL CIRCUIT COUNTY	OBJECTION TO REFEREE'S RECOMMENDED ORDER	(A) CASE NO.

Court address   Court telephone no.

(B)

Plaintiff's name, address, and telephone no. ☐ Moving party		Defendant's name, address, and telephone no. ☐ Moving party
	v	
Third party's name, address, and telephone no. ☐ Moving party		

I object to the entry of the referee's recommended order dated **(C)** _____ and request a de novo hearing by the court. My objection is based on the following reason(s):

(D)

I declare that the statements above are true to the best of my information, knowledge, and belief.

(E) Date _____   Signature of objecting party _____

Name (type or print) _____

NOTICE OF HEARING

(F) A hearing will be held on this objection before Hon. _____
Name of judge

on _____ at _____ at _____ .
Date   Time   Place

CERTIFICATE OF MAILING

I certify that on this date I mailed a copy of this objection and notice of hearing on the other party(ies) by ordinary mail at the above address(es).

(G) Date _____   Signature of objecting party _____

FOC 68 (12/96) **OBJECTION TO REFEREE'S RECOMMENDED ORDER**   MCR 3.215(E)

Approved, SCAO

Original - Court
1st copy - Moving Party
2nd copy - Objecting Party

3rd copy - Friend of the Court
4th copy - Proof of Service
5th copy - Proof of Service

STATE OF MICHIGAN JUDICIAL CIRCUIT COUNTY	OBJECTION TO PROPOSED ORDER	(A) CASE NO.

Court address

Court telephone no.

(B)

Plaintiff's name, address, and telephone no.	☐ Moving party

v

Defendant's name, address, and telephone no.	☐ Moving party

Third party's name, address, and telephone no.	☐ Moving party

I received a notice to enter a proposed order without a hearing dated (C) _____
I object to the entry of the proposed order and request a hearing by the court. My objection is based on the following reason(s):

(D)

I declare that the statements above are true to the best of my information, knowledge, and belief.

(E) _____
Date

_____
Signature of objecting party

_____
Name (type or print)

CERTIFICATE OF MAILING

I certify that on this date I mailed a copy of this objection on the other party(ies) by ordinary mail at the above address(es).

(F) _____
Date

_____
Signature of objecting party

FOC 78 (12/96) **OBJECTION TO PROPOSED ORDER**

MCR 2.602(B)

	Original - Court	3rd copy - Friend of the Court
	1st copy - Other Party	4th copy - Proof of Service
	2nd copy - Moving Party	5th copy - Proof of Service

STATE OF MICHIGAN JUDICIAL CIRCUIT COUNTY	MOTION REGARDING CUSTODY	(A) CASE NO.

Court address   Court telephone no.

(B) Plaintiff's name, address, and telephone no.   ☐ moving party   v   Defendant's name, address, and telephone no.   ☐ moving party

Third party name, address, and telephone no.   ☐ moving party

(C) 1. ☐ a. On _____ a judgment
Date
or order was entered regarding custody.
☐ b. There is currently no order regarding custody.

(D) ☐ 2. The ☐ plaintiff ☐ defendant ☐ third party   was ordered to have custody of the following child(ren):

(E) 3. The following child(ren) have been living with _____ at
Name(s)

_____ since _____ .
Complete address   Date

(F) 4. Circumstances have changed as follows that require custody or a change in custody:
Use a separate sheet to explain in detail what has happened and attach. Include all necessary facts.

(G) 5. Proper cause exists as follows that require custody or a change in custody: Use a separate sheet to explain in detail which factors
of the Child Custody Act for determining best interests of the child(ren) are affected by the circumstances in 4. above. Include all necessary facts.

(H) ☐ 6. _____ and I agree to custody, support, and parenting time as follows:
Name
Use a separate sheet to explain in detail what you have agreed on and attach. Include all necessary facts.

(I) 7. **I ask the court to order that custody, parenting time, and support be** as follows:
Use a separate sheet to explain in detail what you want the court to order and attach.

I declare that the above statements are true to the best of my information, knowledge, and belief.

(J) _____   _____
Date   Moving party's signature

NOTICE OF HEARING

A hearing will be held on this motion before _____
Name of judge or referee

(K) on _____ at _____ at _____ .
Date   Time   Place

NOTE: If you are the person receiving this motion, you may file a response. Contact the friend of the court office and request form FOC 88.

CERTIFICATE OF MAILING

I certify that on this date I mailed a copy of this motion and notice of hearing on the other party(ies) by ordinary mail at the above address(es).

(L) _____   _____
Date   Moving party's signature

FOC 87 (12/96) **MOTION REGARDING CUSTODY**   MCL 722.21 et seq.; MSA 25.312(1) et seq., MCR 2.119, MCR 3.213

Approved, SCAO

Original - Court
1st copy - Moving Party
2nd copy - Responding Party

3rd copy - Friend of the Court
4th copy - Proof of Service
5th copy - Proof of Service

STATE OF MICHIGAN JUDICIAL CIRCUIT COUNTY	RESPONSE TO MOTION REGARDING CUSTODY	**(A)** CASE NO.

Court address

Court telephone no.

(B) Plaintiff's name, address, and telephone no. ☐ moving party

v

Defendant's name, address, and telephone no. ☐ moving party

Third party name, address, and telephone no. ☐ moving party

(C) 1. ☐ a. On _____ a judgment
Date
or order was entered regarding custody.
☐ b. There is currently no order regarding custody.

(D) ☐ 2. The ☐ plaintiff ☐ defendant ☐ third party was ordered to have custody of the following child(ren):

(E) 3. The following child(ren) have been living with _____ at
Name(s)
_____ since _____ .
Complete address   Date

(F) 4. I ☐ agree ☐ do not agree that circumstances have changed as stated in the motion.
Explain in detail what you do not agree with and why. Include all necessary facts. Use a separate sheet of paper if needed.

(G) 5. I ☐ agree ☐ do not agree that proper cause exists as stated in the motion.
Explain in detail what you do not agree with and why. Include all necessary facts. Use a separate sheet of paper if needed.

(H) ☐ 6. I agreed with the other party to custody, parenting time, and support:
☐ a. exactly as stated in the motion.
☐ b. but not as stated in the motion.
If b. is checked, explain in detail what you did agree on. Include all necessary facts. Use a separate sheet of paper if needed.

(I) 7. ☐ a. I agree with what is being asked for in the motion.
☐ b. I do not agree with what is being asked for in the motion and ask the court to order custody, parenting time, and
support as follows: If b. is checked, explain in detail why and what you want the court to order. Use a separate sheet of paper if needed.

I declare that the above statements are true to the best of my information, knowledge, and belief.

(J) _____   _____
Date   Responding party's signature

CERTIFICATE OF MAILING

I certify that on this date I mailed a copy of this response on the other party by ordinary mail at the above address.

(K) _____   _____
Date   Responding party's signature

FOC 88 (12/96) **RESPONSE TO MOTION REGARDING CUSTODY**   MCL 722.21 et seq.; MSA 25.312(1) et seq., MCR 2.119

Form 43

Original - Court
1st copy - Other Party
2nd copy - Moving Party

3rd copy - Friend of the Court
4th copy - Proof of Service
5th copy - Proof of Service

STATE OF MICHIGAN JUDICIAL CIRCUIT COUNTY	ORDER REGARDING CUSTODY, PARENTING TIME, AND SUPPORT Page 1	Ⓐ	CASE NO.

Court address   Court telephone no.

Ⓑ Plaintiff's name, address, and telephone no.

v

Defendant's name, address, and telephone no.

Third party's name, address, and telephone no.

Ⓒ

Date: _____

Judge: _____

Ⓓ 1. This order is entered ☐ after hearing. ☐ on consent of the parties. ☐ on stipulation of the parties.

THE COURT FINDS:

Ⓔ ☐ 2. A motion requesting custody, parenting time, and support or a change to custody, parenting time, and support was filed.

Ⓕ ☐ 3. A response to the motion was filed.

Ⓖ ☐ 4. A change of circumstances ☐ does ☐ does not exist which warrants a custody order or change in custody.

Ⓗ ☐ 5. Proper cause ☐ does ☐ does not exist which warrants a custody order or a change in custody.

Ⓘ ☐ 6. It ☐ is ☐ is not in the best interests of the child(ren) to ☐ establish ☐ change parenting time.

Ⓙ ☐ 7. A material change of circumstances exists which warrants a change in the support order.

Ⓚ ☐ 8. It is in the best interests of the child(ren) to dismiss the motion.

IT IS ORDERED:

Ⓛ ☐ 9. The motion regarding custody, parenting time, and support is dismissed. The prior order remains in effect.

Ⓜ ☐ 10. Custody is granted as follows:

Name(s) of child(ren):_____

☐ Joint legal to   ☐ plaintiff   ☐ defendant   ☐ third party

☐ Joint physical to   ☐ plaintiff   ☐ defendant   ☐ third party

☐ Sole legal to   ☐ plaintiff   ☐ defendant   ☐ third party

☐ Sole physical to   ☐ plaintiff   ☐ defendant   ☐ third party

Continued on page 2.

FOC 89 (12/96) **ORDER REGARDING CUSTODY, PARENTING TIME, AND SUPPORT**

MCL 552.14; MSA 25.94, MCL 552.517b(3); MSA 25.176(17b)(3), MCL 722.21 et seq.; MSA 25.312(1) et seq.; MCR 2.119

STATE OF MICHIGAN JUDICIAL CIRCUIT COUNTY	ORDER REGARDING CUSTODY, PARENTING TIME, AND SUPPORT Page 2	Ⓐ CASE NO.

Court address   Court telephone no.

Ⓑ Plaintiff's name   v   Defendant's name

Third party's name

IT IS FURTHER ORDERED:

Ⓝ 11. Parenting time is ☐ established ☐ changed as follows:
Explain in detail what the court has ordered.

Ⓞ 12. Starting _____ ☐ Plaintiff ☐ Defendant shall pay _____ through the
Date   weekly, monthly, etc.

Office of the Friend of the Court the amount of child support for the total number of children being supported as follows. Support shall continue until each child reaches the age of 18 or graduates from high school, whichever is later, but no longer than the age 19 1/2. Each child over 18 must be attending school on a full-time basis with a reasonable expectation of graduating. This amount ☐ follows ☐ does not follow the Child Support Formula.

Number of Children Supported				
5 or more	4	3	2	1

Ⓟ ☐ 13. ☐ Plaintiff ☐ Defendant shall pay through the Office of the Friend of the Court child care expenses as follows:

Ⓠ ☐ 14. Overdue support is preserved and shall be paid as follows:

Ⓡ ☐ 15. The payer shall receive a credit of _____% of the child support obligation each time after the child(ren) spend 6 or more consecutive overnight periods with the payer in accordance with the payer's parenting time rights.

16. Income withholding shall continue or be implemented immediately upon entry of this order.

Ⓢ ☐ 17. Each party shall maintain or obtain health coverage for the benefit of the child(ren) if available at a reasonable cost, as a benefit of employment, or as an optional coverage for dependents on a policy already obtained.

Ⓣ ☐ 18. ☐ Plaintiff shall pay _____% ☐ Defendant shall pay _____% of the reasonable and necessary health care expenses of the child(ren) not covered by health care insurance. Overdue health care expenses of $_____ are preserved and are to be paid as follows:

19. The payer of support shall pay to the Office of the Friend of the Court a service fee of $2.00 per month, payable semi-annually on January 2 and July 2 of each year. In addition, every person required to make payments of support or maintenance through the Office of the Friend of the Court shall pay $1.25 per month for every month or portion of a month that support maintenance is required to be paid to cover the cost of services provided by the Office of the Friend of the Court which are not reimbursed under title IV-D.

Continued on page 3.

STATE OF MICHIGAN JUDICIAL CIRCUIT COUNTY	ORDER REGARDING CUSTODY, PARENTING TIME, AND SUPPORT Page 3	(A) CASE NO.

Court address

Court telephone no.

(B) Plaintiff's name	v	Defendant's name

Third party's name

IT IS FURTHER ORDERED:

20. Each party shall notify the friend of the court in writing of any change in their mailing and residence address no later than 21 days of the change, of any change in the name and address of current source of income, and whether he/she holds a driver's or occupational license. Each party shall also keep the friend of the court informed of any health care coverage available to them; the name of the insurance company, health care organization, or health maintenance organization; the policy, certificate, or contract number; and the names and birth dates of the persons who are covered. A surcharge will be added to support payments that are past due.

21. Except as otherwise provided in Section 3 of the Support and Parenting Time Enforcement Act, Act No. 295 of the Public Acts of 1982, being Section 552.603 of the Michigan Compiled Laws, a support order that is part of a judgment or is an order in a domestic relations matter as that term is defined in Section 31 of the Friend of the Court Act, Act No. 294 of the Public Acts of 1982, being Section 552.531 of the Michigan Compiled Laws, is a judgment on and after the date each support payment is due, with the full force, effect, and attributes of a judgment of this state, and is not, on and after the date it is due, subject to retroactive modification. A surcharge of 8% annually will be added to support payments that are past due as of January 1 and July 1 of each year as provided in MCL 552.603a.

22. Except as changed above, any prior order remains in effect.

(U) _____
Plaintiff's signature (consent/stipulation)

_____
Defendant's signature (consent/stipulation)

_____
Third party's signature (consent/stipulation)

(V) Approved as to form: _____
Friend of the court signature (only if required)

_____
Date

_____
Circuit court judge

PROOF OF SERVICE

(W) I certify that on this date I mailed a copy of this order on the other party(ies) by ordinary mail at the above address(es).

_____
Date

_____
Signature

Original - Court
1st copy - Judge/Assignment clerk (green)
2nd copy - Respondent (blue)

3rd copy - Petitioner (pink)
4th copy - Return (yellow)

Approved, SCAO

STATE OF MICHIGAN JUDICIAL CIRCUIT COUNTY	PETITION FOR PERSONAL PROTECTION ORDER (DOMESTIC RELATIONSHIP)	CASE NO.

Court address   Court telephone no.

(A) Petitioner's name   ☐ under 18 years old   Respondent's name, address, and telephone no.   ☐ under 18 years old

Address and telephone no. where court can reach petitioner   v

(B) 1. The petitioner and respondent: ☐ are husband and wife.   ☐ were husband and wife.   ☐ have a child in common.
☐ have or had a dating relationship.   ☐ reside or resided in the same household.

(C) 2. ☐ The respondent is required to carry a firearm in the course of his/her employment.   ☐ Unkown.

(D) 3. a. There ☐ are ☐ are not   other pending actions in this or any other court regarding the parties.

Case number	Name of court and county	Name of judge

b. There ☐ are ☐ are not   orders/judgments entered by this or any other court, regarding the parties.

Case number	Name of court and county	Name of judge

(E) 4. I need a personal protection order because: Explain what has happened (attach additional sheets)

(F) 5. I ask the court to grant a personal protection order prohibiting the respondent from:
☐ a. entering onto the property where I live. I state that either I have a property interest in the premises, I am married to to the respondent, or the respondent has no property interest in the premises.

☐ b. entering onto the property at _____ .
                                address

☐ c. assaulting, attacking, beating, molesting, or wounding _____ .
                                              name(s)

☐ d. removing the minor children from the petitioner who has **court ordered** custody, except as allowed by a custody or parenting time order as long as removal of the children does not violate other conditions of the personal protection order.

☐ e. stalking as defined under MCL 750.411h and MCL 750.411i which includes but is not limited to:
     ☐ following me or appearing within my sight.
     ☐ appearing at my workplace or residence.
     ☐ approaching or confronting me in a public place or on private property.
     ☐ entering onto or remaining on property owned, leased, or occupied by me.
     ☐ contacting me by telephone.
     ☐ sending mail or other communications to me.
     ☐ placing an object on or delivering an object to property owned, leased, or occupied by me.

☐ f. interfering with efforts to remove my children/ personal property from premises solely owned/leased by the respondent.

☐ g. threatening to kill or physically injure _____ .
                                        name(s)

☐ h. interfering with me at my place of employment or engaging in conduct that impairs my employment relationship.
☐ i. purchasing or possessing a firearm.
☐ j. other: _____

(G) 6. I make this petition under authority of MCL 600.2950/MCL 600.2950a and ask the court to grant a personal protection order.
☐ I request an ex parte order because immediate and irreparable injury, loss, or damage will occur between now and a hearing or because notice itself will cause irreparable injury, loss, or damage before the order can be entered.

(Ч) ☐ 7. I have a next friend petitioning for me. I certify that the next friend is not disqualified by statute and is an adult.

I declare that the statements above are true to the best of my information, knowledge, and belief.

(I) _____
Date

                                      Petitioner's signature
                                MCL 600.2950; MSA 27A.2950, MCL 600.2950a; MSA 27A.2950a, MCR 3.703

CC 375 (8/97) **PETITION FOR PERSONAL PROTECTION ORDER (Domestic Relationship)**

PROOF OF SERVICE	**Petition for Personal Protection Order** Case No.

TO PROCESS SERVER: You must serve the copies of the petition for personal protection order and file proof of service with the court clerk. If you are unable to complete service, you must return this original and all copies to the court clerk.

CERTIFICATE / AFFIDAVIT OF SERVICE / NON-SERVICE

☐ **OFFICER CERTIFICATE**	**OR**	☐ **AFFIDAVIT OF PROCESS SERVER**
I certify that I am a sheriff, deputy sheriff, bailiff, appointed court officer, or attorney for a party [MCR 2.104(A)(2)], and that: (notary not required)		Being first duly sworn, I state that I am a legally competent adult who is **not** a party or an officer of a corporate party, and that: (notary required)

☐ I served a copy of the petition for personal protection order by:
☐ personal service ☐ registered mail, delivery restricted to the respondent (return receipt attached)
on:

Respondent's name	Complete address of service	Day, date, time

☐ After diligent search and inquiry, I have been unable to find and serve the respondent. I have made the following efforts in

attempting to serve process: _____

_____

☐ I have personally attempted to serve a copy of the petition for personal protection order on

Name _____

at _____
Address

and have been unable to complete service because the address was incorrect at the time of filing.

Service fee	Miles traveled	Mileage fee	Total fee
$		$	$

Signature _____

Title _____

Subscribed and sworn to before me on _____, _____ County, Michigan.
Date

My commission expires: _____ Signature: _____
Date   Deputy court clerk/Notary public

ACKNOWLEDGMENT OF SERVICE

I acknowledge that I have received a copy of the petition for personal protection order on _____.
Day, date, time

_____
Signature of respondent

MCR 2.105(A)

Approved, SCAO

Original - Court
1st copy - Law enforcement agency (file) (green)
2nd copy - Respondent (blue)

3rd copy - Petitioner (pink)
4th copy - Return (yellow)
5th copy - Return (goldenrod)

STATE OF MICHIGAN JUDICIAL CIRCUIT COUNTY	(A)	PERSONAL PROTECTION ORDER ☐ EX PARTE (DOMESTIC RELATIONSHIP)	(B)	CASE NO.

Court address

Court telephone no.

ORI
MI-

(C)

Petitioner's name

Address and telephone no. where court can reach petitioner

v

Respondent's name, address, and telephone no.

(D)

Full name of respondent (type or print) *

Social security no. (if known) | Driver's license number (if known)

Height	Weight	Race *		Sex *	Date of birth or Age*	Hair color	Eye color	Other identifying information

*these items must be filled in for the police/sheriff to enter on LEIN; the other items are not required but are helpful

Date: _____ Judge: _____   Bar no.

1. This order is entered ☐ without a hearing. ☐ after hearing.

THE COURT FINDS:

☐ 2. A petition requested respondent be prohibited from entry onto the premises, and either the parties are married, petitioner has property interest in the premises, or respondent does not have a property interest in the premises.

☐ 3. Petitioner requested an ex parte order which should be entered without notice because irreparable injury, loss, or damage will result from the delay required to give notice or notice itself will precipitate adverse action before the order can be issued.

IT IS ORDERED:

4. _____ is prohibited from:

　☐ a. entering onto property where petitioner lives.

　☐ b. entering onto property at _____ .

　☐ c. assaulting, attacking, beating, molesting, or wounding _____ .

　☐ d. removing minor children from petitioner who has **court ordered** custody, except as allowed by custody or parenting time order provided removal of the children does not violate other conditions of this order. Existing custody order dated _____ . Existing parenting time order dated _____ .

　☐ e. stalking as defined under MCL 750.411h and MCL 750.411i which includes but is not limited to:

　　☐ following or appearing within sight of the petitioner.

　　☐ appearing at workplace/residence of the petitioner.

　　☐ approaching or confronting the petitioner in a public place or on private property.

　　☐ entering onto or remaining on property owned, leased, or occupied by the petitioner.

　　☐ sending mail/other communications to the petitioner.

　　☐ contacting the petitioner by telephone.

　　☐ placing an object on or delivering an object to property owned, leased, or occupied by the petitioner.

　☐ f. interfering with petitioner's efforts to remove his/her children or personal property from premises solely owned or leased by respondent.

　☐ g. threatening to kill or physically injure _____ .

　☐ h. interfering with petitioner at his/her place of employment or engaging in conduct that impairs his/her employment relationship or environment.

　☐ i. purchasing or possessing a firearm.

　☐ j. other: _____ .

5. Violation of this order subjects respondent to immediate arrest and to the civil and criminal contempt powers of the court. If found guilty, respondent shall be imprisoned for not more than 93 days and may be fined not more than $500.00.

6. **This order is effective when signed, enforceable immediately, and remains in effect until** _____ . This order is enforceable anywhere in the United States by any law enforcement agency under the Full Faith and Credit provisions of the Violence Against Women's Act.

7. The court clerk shall file this order with _____ who shall enter it in the LEIN system. Name of law enforcement agency

8. Respondent may file a motion to modify or rescind this order. Forms and instructions are available from the clerk of the court.

9. Other:

Date and time issued _____   Judge _____   MCL 600.2950; MSA 27A.2950, MCR 3.705, MCR 3.706

CC 376 (8/97) **PERSONAL PROTECTION ORDER (Domestic Relationship)**

Personal Protection Order	PROOF OF SERVICE	Case No.

TO PROCESS SERVER: You must serve the personal protection order and file proof of service with the court clerk. If you are unable to complete service, you must return this original and all copies to the court clerk.

CERTIFICATE / AFFIDAVIT OF SERVICE / NON-SERVICE

☐ **OFFICER CERTIFICATE**	OR	☐ **AFFIDAVIT OF PROCESS SERVER**
I certify that I am a sheriff, deputy sheriff, bailiff, appointed court officer, or attorney for a party [MCR 2.104(A)(2)], and that: (notary not required)		Being first duly sworn, I state that I am a legally competent adult who is not a party or an officer of a corporate party, and that: (notary required)

☐ I served a copy of the personal protection order by:

☐ personal service   ☐ registered mail, delivery restricted to the respondent (return receipt attached)

on:

Name of respondent	Complete address of service	Day, date, time

Law enforcement agency	Complete address of service	Day, date, time

☐ After diligent search and inquiry, I have been unable to find and serve the respondent. I have made the following efforts in attempting to serve to serve process:

_____

☐ I have personally attempted to serve a copy of the personal protection order

on _____
Name

at _____
Address

and have been unable to complete service because the address was incorrect at the time of filing.

Service fee $	Miles traveled	Mileage fee $	Total fee $

_____ Signature

_____ Title

Subscribed and sworn to before me on _____ , _____ County, Michigan.
Date

My commission expires: _____   Signature: _____
Date   Deputy court clerk/Notary public

ACKNOWLEDGMENT OF SERVICE

I acknowledge that I have received a copy of the personal protection order on _____ .
Day, date, time

_____
Signature of respondent

MCR 2.105(A)

Approved, SCAO

STATE OF MICHIGAN JUDICIAL CIRCUIT COUNTY	NOTICE OF HEARING ON PETITION FOR PERSONAL PROTECTION ORDER	CASE NO.

Court address _____ Court telephone no.

Ⓐ Petitioner's name _____ v Respondent's name _____

Ⓑ TO: _____

Ⓒ **You are notified that the petitioner has requested a personal protection order be issued against you. A hearing has been scheduled to decide whether to issue the personal protection order for:**

Judge: _____

Date: _____

Time: _____

Location: _____

If you require special accommodations to use the court because of disabilities, please contact the court immediately to make arrangements.

If you do not attend this hearing, a personal protection order can still be entered against you.

Ⓓ Date _____   Signature _____

TO THE PETITIONER: You should serve this notice no later than 5 days before the date of the hearing stated above so that the respondent receives notice at least 1 day before the hearing. See other side for proof of service.

CC 381   (8/97)   **NOTICE OF HEARING ON PETITION FOR PERSONAL PROTECTION ORDER**   MCR 3.705(A)(5), (B)

TO PROCESS SERVER: You must serve the copies of the notice of hearing on petition for personal protection order and file proof of service with the court clerk. If you are unable to complete service, you must return this original and all copies to the court clerk.

CERTIFICATE / AFFIDAVIT OF SERVICE / NON-SERVICE

☐ **OFFICER CERTIFICATE**	OR	☐ **AFFIDAVIT OF PROCESS SERVER**
I certify that I am a sheriff, deputy sheriff, bailiff, appointed court officer, or attorney for a party [MCR 2.104(A)(2)], and that: (notary not required)		Being first duly sworn, I state that I am a legally competent adult who is **not** a party or an officer of a corporate party, and that: (notary required)

☐ I served a copy of the notice of hearing on petition for personal protection order by:
　☐ personal service　☐ registered mail, delivery restricted to the respondent (return receipt attached)
　on:

Respondent's name	Complete address of service	Day, date, time

☐ After diligent search and inquiry, I have been unable to find and serve the respondent. I have made the following efforts in

attempting to serve process: _____

_____

☐ I have personally attempted to serve a copy of the notice of hearing on petition for personal protection order on

_____
Name

at _____
　Address

and have been unable to complete service because the address was incorrect at the time of filing.

Service fee	Miles traveled	Mileage fee	Total fee	Signature
$		$	$	
				Title

Subscribed and sworn to before me on _____ , _____ County, Michigan.
　　　　　　　　　　　　　　　　　　　　Date

My commission expires: _____ Signature: _____
　　　　　　　　　　　　Date　　　　　　　　　　　　　　　Deputy court clerk/Notary public

ACKNOWLEDGMENT OF SERVICE

I acknowledge that I have received a copy of the notice of hearing on petition for personal protection order on

_____
Day, date, time

_____
Signature of respondent

STATE OF MICHIGAN JUDICIAL CIRCUIT COUNTY	MOTION REGARDING SPOUSAL SUPPORT	CASE NO.

Court address _____   Court telephone no. _____

Plaintiff's name, address, and telephone no. ❑ moving party		Defendant's name, address, and telephone no ❑ moving party
	V	

Third party name, address, and telephone no. ❑ moving party

1. ❑ a. On _____ a judgment or order
      Date
      was entered regarding spousal support.
   ❑ b. There is currently no order regarding spousal support.

❑ 2. The ❑ plaintiff ❑ defendant is ordered to pay spousal support of $_____ each _____.
      week, month, etc.

❑ 3. The ❑ plaintiff ❑ defendant is ordered to pay the following for the other party in addition to spousal support:

❑ 4. Conditions regarding spousal support have changed as follows:
      Use a separate sheet to explain in detail what has happened and attach. Include all necessary facts.

❑ 5. _____ and I have agreed to spousal support as follows:
      Use a separate sheet to explain in detail what you have agreed on and attach. Include all necessary facts.

6. **I ask the court to order that spousal support be** paid as follows: ❑ See 5. above for details.
      Use a separate sheet to explain in detail what you want the court to order and attach.

I declare that the above statements are true to the best of my information, knowledge, and belief.

_____   _____
Date   Moving party's signature

NOTICE OF HEARING

A hearing will be hel on this motion before _____
                                              Name of judge or referee
on _____ at _____ at _____.
   Date   Time   Place
NOTE: If you are the person receiving this motion, you may file a response.

CERTIFICATE OF MAILING

I certify that on this date I mailed a copy of this motion and notice of hearing to the other party(ies) by ordinary mail at the above address(es).

_____   _____
Date   Moving party's signature

MOTION REGARDING SPOUSAL SUPPORT

Form 48

Original - Court
1st copy - Moving Party
2nd copy - Responding Party

3rd copy - Friend of the Court
4th copy - Proof of Service
5th copy - Proof of Service

STATE OF MICHIGAN JUDICIAL CIRCUIT COUNTY	RESPONSE TO MOTION REGARDING SPOUSAL SUPPORT	CASE NO.

Court address   Court telephone no.

Plaintiff's name, address, and telephone no. ❑ moving party		Defendant's name, address, and telephone no ❑ moving party
	V	

Third party name, address, and telephone no. ❑ moving party

1. ❑ a. On _____ a judgment or order
        Date
        was entered regarding spousal support.
   ❑ b. There is currently no order regarding spousal support.

❑ 2. The ❑ plaintiff ❑ defendant is ordered to pay spousal support of $_____ each _____.
                                                                                    week, month, etc.

❑ 3. The ❑ plaintiff ❑ defendant is ordered to pay the following for the other party in addition to spousal support:

❑ 4. I agree do not agree that conditions regarding spousal support have changed as stated in the motion.
     Explain in detail what you do not agree with and why. Include all necessary facts. Use a separatre sheet of paper if needed.

❑ 5. I agreed with the other party to start/change spousal support:
     ❑   a. exactly as stated in the motion.
     ❑   b. but not as stated in the motion.
     If b. is checked, explain in detail what you do agreed on. Include all necessary facts. Use a separatre sheet of paper if needed.

❑ 6. ❑   a. I agree with what is being asked for in the motion.
     ❑   b. I do not agree with what is being asked for in the motion and ask the court to order that spousal
           support be   ❑ denied   ❑ paid as follows:
     If you do not agree with the request in the motion, explain in detail why and what you want the court to order. Include all necessary facts. Use a separatre sheet of paper if needed.

I declare that the above statements are true to the best of my information, knowledge, and belief.

_____   _____
Date   Responding party's signature

CERTIFICATE OF MAILING

I certify that on this date I mailed a copy of this response to the other party(ies) by ordinary mail at the above address(es).

_____   _____
Date   Responding party's signature

RESPONSE TO MOTION REGARDING SPOUSAL SUPPORT

STATE OF MICHIGAN JUDICIAL CIRCUIT COUNTY	ORDER REGARDING SPOUSAL SUPPORT Page 1	CASE NO.

Court address   Court telephone no.

Plaintiff's name, address, and telephone no.		Defendant's name, address, and telephone no
	V	
Third party name, address, and telephone no.		

Date: _____

Judge: _____

1. This order is entered ❑ after hearing. ❑ on consent of the parties. ❑ on stipulation of the parties.

THE COURT FINDS:

❑ 2. A motion requesting spousal support or a change to spousal support was filed.

❑ 3. A response to the motion was filed.

❑ 4. A material change of circumstances exists which warrants a change in the spousal support order.

IT IS ORDERED:

❑ 5. The motion regarding spousal support is dismissed.

❑ 6. Starting _____ ❑ Plaintiff ❑ Defendant shall pay spousal support in
          Date
      the amount of $_____ each _____.
          amount   week, month, etc.

❑ 7. Overdue spousal support is preserved and shall be paid as follows:

❑ 8. Said spousal support shall be paid to the: ❑ Plaintiff ❑ Defendant
                                                   ❑ Office of the Friend of the Court

9. Income withholding shall continue or be implemented upon entry of this order.

10. Except as changed in this order, any prior order remains in effect.

ORDER REGARDING SPOUSAL SUPPORT, Page 1

STATE OF MICHIGAN JUDICIAL CIRCUIT COUNTY	ORDER REGARDING SPOUSAL SUPPORT Page 2	CASE NO.

Court address | Court telephone no.

Plaintiff's name	V	Defendant's name

Third party name

IT IS FURTHER ORDERED:

11. The payer of support shall pay to the Office of the Friend of the Court a service fee of $2.00 per month, payable semi-annually on January 2 and July 2 of each year. In addition, every person required to make payments of support or maintenance through the Office of the Friend of the Court shall pay $1.25 per month for every month or portion of a month that support maintenance is required to be paid to cover the cost of services provided by the Office of the Friend of the Court which are not reimbursed under title IV-D.

12. Each party shall notify the Friend of the Court in writing of any change in their mailing and residence address no later than 21 days of the change, of any change in the name and address of current source of income, and whether he/she holds a driver's or occupational license. Each party shall also keep the Friend of the Court informed of any health care coverage available to them; the name of the insurance company, health care organization, or health maintenance organization; the policy, certificate, or contract number; and the name and birth dates of the persons who are covered. A surcharge will be added to support payments that are past due.

13. Except as otherwise provided in Section 3 of the Support and Parenting Time Enforcement Act, Act No. 295 of the Public Acts of 1982, being Sectino 552.603 of the Michigan Compiled Laws, a support order that is part of ajudgment or is an order in a domestic relations matter as that term is defined in Section 31 of the Friend of the Court Act, Act No. 294 of the Public Acts of 1982, being Section 552.531 of the Michigan Compiled Laws, is a judgment on and after the date each support payment is due, with the full force, effect, and attributes of a judgment of this state, and is not, on and after the date it is due, subject to retroactive modification. A surcharge of 8% annually will be added to support payments that are past due as fo January 1 and July 1 of each year as provided in MCL 552.603a.

_____
Plaintiff's signature (consent/stipulation)

_____
Defendant's signature (consent/stipulation)

_____
Third party's signature (consent/stipulation)

Approved as to form: _____
                      Friend of the court signature (only if requried)

_____
Date

_____
Circuit court judge

PROOF OF SERVICE

I certify that on this date I served copies of this order on the other party(ies) by ordinary mail at the above address(es).

_____
Date

_____
Moving party's signature

STATE OF MICHIGAN JUDICIAL CIRCUIT COUNTY	NOTICE OF HEARING AND MOTION FOR MUTUAL TEMPORARY RESTRAINING ORDER CONSERVING PROPERTY ❑ Interim (ex parte) ❑ Temporary	CASE NO.

Court address

Plaintiff's name, address, and telephone no. ❑ Moving party		Defendant's name, address, and telephone no. ❑ Moving party
	V	
Plaintiff's attorney, bar no., address, and telephone no.		Defendant's attorney, bar no., address, and telephone no.

NOTICE OF HEARING

This matter has been placed on the motion calendar for:

Judge	Date	Time

Hearing location
☐ Court address above, room   ☐

MOTION

1.   The parties are husband and wife and an action for annulment, divorce, or separate maintenance is pending.

2.   The parties own property and unwarranted loss of property rights and interests will occur unless a restraining order is entered.

3.   Subject to the provisions of the revised judicature act, the court should assert jurisdiction over all property of either party, wherever located and regardless of when, where, how, by whom or from whom acquired.

4.   A restraining order is needed because the following events have occurred or have been threatened: Specify

5.   A temporary restraining order should be granted without notice to the other party. Immediate and irreparable injury, loss, or damage will occur during the delay required to give notice (or from the risk that notice itself will cause the loss) before an order can be entered, because: Specify   (COMPLETE CERTIFICATION BELOW)

I declare that the statements above are true to the best of my information, knowledge, and belief.

_____   _____
Date   Plaintiff/Defendant signature

_____   _____   _____
Date   Plaintiff/Defendant attorney signature   Bar no.

ATTORNEY/PLAINTIFF/DEFENDANT CERTIFICATION

The following efforts have been made to give notice to the other party (or his/her attorney) that a restraining order would be requested outside the formal notice and hearing procedure:

_____   _____
Date   Attorney/Plaintiff/Defendant signature

This page intentionally left blank.

Original - Court   2nd copy - Plaintiff
1st copy - Defendant   3rd copy - Friend of the Court
                            4th copy - Return

STATE OF MICHIGAN JUDICIAL CIRCUIT COUNTY	MUTUAL TEMPORARY RESTRAINING ORDER CONSERVING PROPERTY ☐ Original ☐ Modified	CASE NO.

Court address   Court telephone no.

Plaintiff's name, address, and telephone no(s).		Defendant's name, address, and telephone no(s).
	V	
Plaintiff's attorney, bar no., address, and telephone no.		Defendant's attorney, bar no., address, and telephone no.

☐ After hearing   ☐ Interim (ex parte)   ☐ Consent

Date:_____   Judge:_____

                                                      Bar no.

THE COURT FINDS:

1. An action for annulment, divorce, or separate maintenance is pending.

2. A mutual temporary restraining order conserving property has been requested.

3. Misconduct has occurred or has been threatened regarding property rights.

4. This order protects the property rights of the parties.

☐ 5. This order should be entered without notice to the other party to protect property rights and interests which would otherwise be harmed during the delay required to give notice.

6. Subject to the provisions of the revised adjudicature act, all property of either party, wherever situated and regardless of when, where, how, by whom or from whom acquired, is subject to the jurisdiction of the court. "Property" includes an interest, present or future, legal or equitable, vested or contingent, tangible or intangible, in real, personal, or mixed property.

IT IS ORDERED:

7. The parties and their officers, agents, servants, employees, and attorneys (and those persons in active concert or participation with them) are PROHIBITED from selling, assigning, transferring, encumbering, concealing, or otherwise disposing of any property of the parties whether titled in the names of either or both parties.

8. This order does not prevent the parties from providing for the necessities of life or from engaging in transactions necessary in the ordinary course of business. However, the parties shall notify each other before taking any extraordinary actions.

9. VIOLATION OF THIS ORDER SUBJECTS YOU TO THE CONTEMPT POWERS OF THE COURT.

10. No bond is required because no property rights are being determined, the parties are husband and wife, and this order is to preserve the status quo.

11. This order is effective on all persons at the time they receive actual notice of it. This order continues in effect until it is dissolved, the case dismissed, or a judgment is entered.

☐ Approved as to form   ☐ Notice and hearing on entry waived   ☐ I stipulate to entry

_____   _____
Plaintiff signature   Defendant signature

_____   _____   _____   _____
Plaintiff attorney signature   Bar no.   Defendant attorney signature   Bar no.

_____   _____
Date and time   Circuit Court Judge

MUTUAL TEMPORARY
RESTRAINING ORDER
CONSERVING PROPERTY
Case No.

CERTIFICATE / AFFIDAVIT OF SERVICE / NON-SERVICE

OFFICER CERTIFICATE	OR	AFFIDAVIT OF PROCESS SERVER
I certify that I am a sheriff, deputy sheriff, bailiff, appointed court officer, or attorney for a party [MCR 2.140(A)(2)], and that: (notary not required)		Being first duly sworn, I state that I am a legally competent adult who is not a party or an officer of a corporate party, and that: (notary required)

☐ I served personally a copy of the restraining order.

☐ I served by registered or certified mail (copy of return receipt attached) a copy of the restraining order.

together with _____ , on:
Attachment

Name(s)	Complete address(es) of service	Day, date, time

☐ After diligent search and inquiry, I have been unable to find and serve the following person(s): _____

I have made the following efforts in attempting to serve process: _____

☐ I have personally attempted to serve the restraining order, together with _____
Attachment
on _____
Name
at _____ and have been unable to com-
Address
plete service because the address was incorrect at the time of filing.

Service fee $	Miles traveled	Mileage fee $	Total fee $

_____
Signature

_____
Title

Subscribed and sworn to before me on _____ , _____ County, Michigan.
Date

My commission expires: _____ Signature: _____ _____
Date   Deputy court clerk/Notary public

ACKNOWLEDGMENT OF SERVICE

I acknowledge that I have received service of the restraining order, together with _____
Attachment
on _____
Day, date, time

_____ on behalf of _____
Signature

INDEX

R

real estate, 42

Record of Divorce or Annulment, 74, 85, 90, 99, 242

records deposition, *See* Notice of Taking Records Deposition.

Request for Certificate of Military Service Status, 90, 96, 253

research, legal, 22

residency requirements, 20, 183

response, 132, 135

Response to Motion Regarding Custody, 133, 135, 138, 271

Response to Motion Regarding Parenting Time, 133, 151, 266

Response to Motion Regarding Spousal Support, 133, 156, 282

Response to Motion Regarding Support, 133, 145, 256

retirement benefits, *See* pensions.

rules of court, 191

rules of evidence, 15

S

Saginaw County, 24

self-employment tax, 53

separate maintenance, 8

separate property, *See* nonmarital property.

separation, legal, 8

separation, trial, 13

service,

    personal, 64

    publication, 125-30

settlement agreements, *See* Marital Settlement Agreement.

setting a court hearing, 67, 113

sheriff, 64

social security benefits, 51

social security payments, 53

split custody, 55

spousal support, *See* alimony.

spouse abuse, 37, 109, 170

State Court Administrative Office, 59

statutes, 5, 20, 22, 183-90

stocks and bonds, 42

Stipulation to Withdraw Answer, 97, 254

Subpoena, 104, 237

Summons, 64, 90, 91, 102, 215

T

table of forms, 206

taxes, 53, 178

temporary support and custody, 131, 192

trial separation, 13

U

uncontested divorce, 57, 58, 89-99

unemployment benefits, 50

Uniform Child Custody Jurisdiction Act Affidavit, 74, 78, 90, 94, 102, 245

union dues, 53

V

vehicles, 42

Verified Statement, 74, 76, 90, 94, 102, 191, 247

visitation, child, *See* child visitation.

W

Washtenaw County, 24

Wayne County, 24

West's Michigan Digest, 23

withdrawal of answer, 97

witnesses, 118-22

workers' compensation, 51

Your #1 Source for Real World Legal Information...

SPHINX® PUBLISHING
A Division of Sourcebooks, Inc.®

- Written by lawyers
- Simple English explanation of the law
- Forms and instructions included

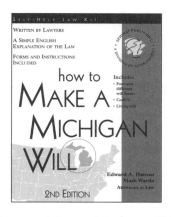

HOW TO WRITE YOUR OWN PREMARITAL AGREEMENT, 2ND ED.

With a divorce rate of over 50 percent, it is wise to consider drafting your own premarital agreement. With this book you can also cancel or modify an existing premarital agreement. Includes inheritance and divorce laws, with forms and instructions.

192 pages; $19.95;
ISBN 1-57071-344-8

HOW TO START A BUSINESS IN MICHIGAN, 2ND ED.

Provides essential legal information on matters crucial to business success, such as: licensing, name registration, taxes, workers' compensation and advertising rules. Includes state and federal forms and information. Don't start a business in Michigan without it!

224 pages; $16.95;
ISBN 1-57071-407-X

HOW TO MAKE A MICHIGAN WILL, 2ND ED.

This book explains how you can make your own simple will. It covers joint ownership of property, guardianship of your children and their property, different ways to distribute your property, living wills, and anatomical gifts.

112 pages; $12.95;
ISBN 1-57248-077-7

See the following order form for books written specifically for California, Florida, Georgia, Illinois, Massachusetts, Michigan, Minnesota, New York, North Carolina, Pennsylvania, and Texas! *Coming soon—Ohio and New Jersey!*

What our customers say about our books:

"It couldn't be more clear for the lay person." —R.D.

"I want you to know I really appreciate your book. It has saved me a lot of time and money." —L.T.

"Your real estate contracts book has saved me nearly $12,000.00 in closing costs over the past year." —A.B.

"...many of the legal questions that I have had over the years were answered clearly and concisely through your plain English interpretation of the law." —C.E.H.

"If there weren't people out there like you I'd be lost. You have the best books of this type out there." —S.B.

"...your forms and directions are easy to follow." —C.V.M.

SPHINX® PUBLISHING'S NATIONAL TITLES
Valid in All 50 States

LEGAL SURVIVAL IN BUSINESS

How to Form Your Own Corporation (2E)	$19.95
How to Form Your Own Partnership	$19.95
How to Register Your Own Copyright (2E)	$19.95
How to Register Your Own Trademark (2E)	$19.95
Most Valuable Business Legal Forms You'll Ever Need (2E)	$19.95
Most Valuable Corporate Forms You'll Ever Need (2E)	$24.95
Software Law (with diskette)	$29.95

LEGAL SURVIVAL IN COURT

Crime Victim's Guide to Justice	$19.95
Debtors' Rights (3E)	$12.95
Defend Yourself against Criminal Charges	$19.95
Grandparents' Rights	$19.95
Help Your Lawyer Win Your Case	$12.95
Jurors' Rights (2E)	$9.95
Legal Malpractice and Other Claims against Your Lawyer	$18.95
Legal Research Made Easy (2E)	$14.95
Simple Ways to Protect Yourself from Lawsuits	$24.95
Victims' Rights	$12.95
Winning Your Personal Injury Claim	$19.95

LEGAL SURVIVAL IN REAL ESTATE

How to Buy a Condominium or Townhome	$16.95
How to Negotiate Real Estate Contracts (3E)	$16.95
How to Negotiate Real Estate Leases (3E)	$16.95
Successful Real Estate Brokerage Management	$19.95

LEGAL SURVIVAL IN PERSONAL AFFAIRS

How to File Your Own Bankruptcy (4E)	$19.95
How to File Your Own Divorce (3E)	$19.95
How to Make Your Own Will	$12.95
How to Write Your Own Living Will	$9.95
How to Write Your Own Premarital Agreement (2E)	$19.95
How to Win Your Unemployment Compensation Claim	$19.95
Living Trusts and Simple Ways to Avoid Probate (2E)	$19.95
Most Valuable Personal Legal Forms You'll Ever Need	$14.95
Neighbor vs. Neighbor	$12.95
The Power of Attorney Handbook (3E)	$19.95
Simple Ways to Protect Yourself from Lawsuits	$24.95
Social Security Benefits Handbook (2E)	$14.95
Unmarried Parents' Rights	$19.95
U.S.A. Immigration Guide (3E)	$19.95
Guia de Inmigracion a Estados Unidos	$19.95

Legal Survival Guides are directly available from Sourcebooks, Inc., or from your local bookstores.

For credit card orders call 1–800–43–BRIGHT, write P.O. Box 372, Naperville, IL 60566,
or fax 630-961-2168

SPHINX® PUBLISHING ORDER FORM

<table>
<tr><td colspan="2">BILL TO:</td><td colspan="2">SHIP TO:</td></tr>
<tr><td colspan="2"></td><td colspan="2"></td></tr>
<tr><td colspan="2"></td><td colspan="2"></td></tr>
<tr><td>Phone #</td><td>Terms</td><td>F.O.B. Chicago, IL</td><td>Ship Date</td></tr>
</table>

Charge my: ☐ VISA   ☐ MasterCard   ☐ American Express

☐ **Money Order or Personal Check**

Credit Card Number

Expiration Date

Qty	ISBN	Title	Retail	Ext.
		SPHINX PUBLISHING NATIONAL TITLES		
___	1-57071-166-6	Crime Victim's Guide to Justice	$19.95	___
___	1-57071-342-1	Debtors' Rights (3E)	$12.95	___
___	1-57071-162-3	Defend Yourself against Criminal Charges	$19.95	___
___	1-57248-001-7	Grandparents' Rights	$19.95	___
___	0-913825-99-9	Guia de Inmigracion a Estados Unidos	$19.95	___
___	1-57248-021-1	Help Your Lawyer Win Your Case	$12.95	___
___	1-57071-164-X	How to Buy a Condominium or Townhome	$16.95	___
___	1-57071-223-9	How to File Your Own Bankruptcy (4E)	$19.95	___
___	1-57071-224-7	How to File Your Own Divorce (3E)	$19.95	___
___	1-57071-227-1	How to Form Your Own Corporation (2E)	$19.95	___
___	1-57071-343-X	How to Form Your Own Partnership	$19.95	___
___	1-57071-228-X	How to Make Your Own Will	$12.95	___
___	1-57071-331-6	How to Negotiate Real Estate Contracts (3E)	$16.95	___
___	1-57071-332-4	How to Negotiate Real Estate Leases (3E)	$16.95	___
___	1-57071-225-5	How to Register Your Own Copyright (2E)	$19.95	___
___	1-57071-226-3	How to Register Your Own Trademark (2E)	$19.95	___
___	1-57071-349-9	How to Win Your Unemployment Compensation Claim	$19.95	___
___	1-57071-167-4	How to Write Your Own Living Will	$9.95	___
___	1-57071-344-8	How to Write Your Own Premarital Agreement (2E)	$19.95	___
___	1-57071-333-2	Jurors' Rights (2E)	$9.95	___
___	1-57248-032-7	Legal Malpractice and Other Claims against...	$18.95	___
___	1-57071-400-2	Legal Research Made Easy (2E)	$14.95	___
___	1-57071-336-7	Living Trusts and Simple Ways to Avoid Probate (2E)	$19.95	___
___	1-57071-345-6	Most Valuable Bus. Legal Forms You'll Ever Need (2E)	$19.95	___
___	1-57071-346-4	Most Valuable Corporate Forms You'll Ever Need (2E)	$24.95	___
___	1-57071-347-2	Most Valuable Personal Legal Forms You'll Ever Need	$14.95	___

Qty	ISBN	Title	Retail	Ext.
___	0-913825-41-7	Neighbor vs. Neighbor	$12.95	___
___	1-57071-348-0	The Power of Attorney Handbook (3E)	$19.95	___
___	1-57248-020-3	Simple Ways to Protect Yourself from Lawsuits	$24.95	___
___	1-57071-337-5	Social Security Benefits Handbook (2E)	$14.95	___
___	1-57071-163-1	Software Law (w/diskette)	$29.95	___
___	0-913825-86-7	Successful Real Estate Brokerage Mgmt.	$19.95	___
___	1-57071-399-5	Unmarried Parents' Rights	$19.95	___
___	1-57071-354-5	U.S.A. Immigration Guide (3E)	$19.95	___
___	0-913825-82-4	Victims' Rights	$12.95	___
___	1-57071-165-8	Winning Your Personal Injury Claim	$19.95	___
		CALIFORNIA TITLES		
___	1-57071-360-X	CA Power of Attorney Handbook	$12.95	___
___	1-57071-355-3	How to File for Divorce in CA	$19.95	___
___	1-57071-356-1	How to Make a CA Will	$12.95	___
___	1-57071-408-8	How to Probate an Estate in CA	$19.95	___
___	1-57071-357-X	How to Start a Business in CA	$16.95	___
___	1-57071-358-8	How to Win in Small Claims Court in CA	$14.95	___
___	1-57071-359-6	Landlords' Rights and Duties in CA	$19.95	___
		FLORIDA TITLES		
___	1-57071-363-4	Florida Power of Attorney Handbook (2E)	$12.95	___
___	1-57071-403-7	How to File for Divorce in FL (5E)	$21.95	___
___	1-57071-401-0	How to Form a Partnership in FL	$19.95	___
___	1-57248-004-1	How to Form a Nonprofit Corp. in FL (3E)	$19.95	___
___	1-57071-380-4	How to Form a Corporation in FL (4E)	$19.95	___
___	1-57071-361-8	How to Make a FL Will (5E)	$12.95	___

___ *Form Continued on Following Page*   **SUBTOTAL** ___

SPHINX® PUBLISHING ORDER FORM

Qty	ISBN	Title	Retail	Ext.
		FLORIDA TITLES (CONT'D)		
_____	1-57248-056-4	How to Modify Your FL Divorce Judgement (3E)	$22.95	_____
_____	1-57071-364-2	How to Probate an Estate in FL (3E)	$24.95	_____
_____	1-57248-005-X	How to Start a Business in FL (4E)	$16.95	_____
_____	1-57071-362-6	How to Win in Small Claims Court in FL (6E)	$14.95	_____
_____	1-57071-335-9	Landlords' Rights and Duties in FL (7E)	$19.95	_____
_____	1-57071-334-0	Land Trusts in FL (5E)	$24.95	_____
_____	0-913825-73-5	Women's Legal Rights in FL	$19.95	_____
		GEORGIA TITLES		
_____	1-57071-387-1	How to File for Divorce in GA (3E)	$19.95	_____
_____	1-57248-075-0	How to Make a GA Will (3E)	$12.95	_____
_____	1-57248-076-9	How to Start a Business in Georgia (3E)	$16.95	_____
		ILLINOIS TITLES		
_____	1-57071-405-3	How to File for Divorce in IL (2E)	$19.95	_____
_____	1-57071-415-0	How to Make an IL Will (2E)	$12.95	_____
_____	1-57071-416-9	How to Start a Business in IL (2E)	$16.95	_____
		MASSACHUSETTS TITLES		
_____	1-57071-329-4	How to File for Divorce in MA (2E)	$19.95	_____
_____	1-57248-050-5	How to Make a MA Will	$9.95	_____
_____	1-57248-053-X	How to Probate an Estate in MA	$19.95	_____
_____	1-57248-054-8	How to Start a Business in MA	$16.95	_____
_____	1-57248-055-6	Landlords' Rights and Duties in MA	$19.95	_____
		MICHIGAN TITLES		
_____	1-57071-409-6	How to File for Divorce in MI (2E)	$19.95	_____
_____	1-57248-077-7	How to Make a MI Will (2E)	$12.95	_____
_____	1-57071-407-X	How to Start a Business in MI (2E)	$16.95	_____
		MINNESOTA TITLES		
_____	1-57248-039-4	How to File for Divorce in MN	$19.95	_____
_____	1-57248-040-8	How to Form a Simple Corporation in MN	$19.95	_____
_____	1-57248-037-8	How to Make a MN Will	$9.95	_____
_____	1-57248-038-6	How to Start a Business in MN	$16.95	_____

Qty	ISBN	Title	Retail	Ext.
		NEW YORK TITLES		
_____	1-57071-184-4	How to File for Divorce in NY	$19.95	_____
_____	1-57071-183-6	How to Make a NY Will	$12.95	_____
_____	1-57071-185-2	How to Start a Business in NY	$16.95	_____
_____	1-57071-187-9	How to Win in Small Claims Court in NY	$14.95	_____
_____	1-57071-186-0	Landlords' Rights and Duties in NY	$19.95	_____
_____	1-57071-188-7	New York Power of Attorney Handbook	$19.95	_____
		NORTH CAROLINA TITLES		
_____	1-57071-326-X	How to File for Divorce in NC (2E)	$19.95	_____
_____	1-57071-327-8	How to Make a NC Will (2E)	$12.95	_____
_____	0-913825-93-X	How to Start a Business in NC	$16.95	_____
		PENNSYLVANIA TITLES		
_____	1-57071-177-1	How to File for Divorce in PA	$19.95	_____
_____	1-57071-176-3	How to Make a PA Will	$12.95	_____
_____	1-57071-178-X	How to Start a Business in PA	$16.95	_____
_____	1-57071-179-8	Landlords' Rights and Duties in PA	$19.95	_____
		TEXAS TITLES		
_____	1-57071-330-8	How to File for Divorce in TX (2E)	$19.95	_____
_____	1-57248-009-2	How to Form a Simple Corporation in TX	$19.95	_____
_____	1-57071-417-7	How to Make a TX Will (2E)	$12.95	_____
_____	1-57071-418-5	How to Probate an Estate in TX (2E)	$19.95	_____
_____	1-57071-365-0	How to Start a Business in TX (2E)	$16.95	_____
_____	1-57248-012-2	How to Win in Small Claims Court in TX	$14.95	_____
_____	1-57248-011-4	Landlords' Rights and Duties in TX	$19.95	_____

SUBTOTAL THIS PAGE _____

SUBTOTAL PREVIOUS PAGE _____

Illinois residents add 6.75% sales tax
Florida residents add 6% state sales tax plus applicable discretionary surtax _____

Shipping— $4.00 for 1st book, $1.00 each additional _____

TOTAL _____